Privatisation and Financial Collapse in the Nuclear Industry

This is the story of the British experiment in privatising the nuclear power industry and its subsequent financial collapse. It tells how the UK's pioneering role in nuclear power was followed by poor technology choices, a badly flawed restructuring of the electricity industry and the end of government support for nuclear power. Privatisation led to a soaring share price, but then a financial crisis in which only emergency government loans avoided bankruptcy and the threat of power cuts. Simon Taylor has combined interviews with former executives, regulators and analysts with his own unique insight into the nuclear industry to provide an incisive analysis of the origins of the crisis and the financial and corporate strategies used by British Energy plc.

Taylor's two main arguments are that the stock market was a major factor in the company's collapse by misunderstanding its finances, over-valuing the shares and giving wrong signals to management, and that the government policy of trying to put all responsibility for nuclear liabilities in the hands of the private sector was neither credible nor realistic. The book concludes that failure was not inevitable but resulted from a mixture of internal and external causes that casts doubt on the policy of combining a wholly nuclear generator with liberalised power markets.

This book will be of great interest to students engaged with the history of nuclear power in the UK, privatisation, regulation and financial and corporate strategy, as well as experts, policy makers and strategists in the field.

Simon Taylor spent 14 years working in the investment banking industry before returning to academia in 2005. He currently teaches economics and corporate finance at the Judge Business School, Cambridge.

Routledge studies in business organizations and networks

Privatisation and Financial Collapse in the Nuclear Industry

The origins and causes of the British Energy crisis of 2002

Simon Taylor

Routledge
Taylor & Francis Group

LONDON AND NEW YORK

First published 2007
by Routledge
2 Park Square, Milton Park, Abingdon, Oxon OX14 4RN

Simultaneously published in the USA and Canada
by Routledge
711 Third Avenue, New York, NY 10017

Routledge is an imprint of the Taylor & Francis Group, an informa business

First issued in paperback 2012

© 2007 Simon Taylor

Typeset in Times by Wearset Ltd, Boldon, Tyne and Wear

British Library Cataloguing in Publication Data
A catalogue record for this book is available from the British Library

Library of Congress Cataloging in Publication Data
Taylor, Simon, 1961 Dec. 19–
Privatisation and financial collapse in the nuclear industry : the origins and causes of the British energy crisis of 2002 / Simon Taylor.
p. cm.
Includes bibliographical references and index.
1. Nuclear industry–Great Britain. 2. Energy policy–Great Britain.
3. Privatization–Great Britain. I. Title.
HD9698.G72T39 2007
333.792'430941090511–dc22

2006103324

ISBN13: 978-0-415-54200-5 (pbk)
ISBN13: 978-0-415-43175-0 (hbk)
ISBN13: 978-0-203-94627-5 (ebk)

Contents

Figures

Tables

Preface

My involvement with the company British Energy began when I joined BZW's equity research department in early 1996. My main task was to help Daniel Martin and the rest of the BZW nuclear team with the tough but interesting job of helping to float the company British Energy on the stock exchange. The company was duly sold to investors in July 1996. When Daniel left BZW in 1997 I took over primary coverage of the company. I continued to cover it when I moved to Salomon Brothers (later Salomon Smith Barney) in 1998 until I stopped being an equity analyst in early 2000.

My reasons for writing this book were a mixture of curiosity, personal responsibility and hope that it would be of interest to others. I advised many clients to buy British Energy shares at privatisation and for two years afterwards, though as the shares rose from 1998 my recommendation shifted to "neutral" then "sell" (a rare recommendation in the late 1990s). I wanted to find out why the company had got into trouble and whether the policy of privatisation was mistaken. I also hoped that the story of British Energy would have wider value, chiefly to those concerned with the dismal history of nuclear power in the UK. And as nuclear power became a topic of policy debate I wanted also to make sure that the lessons from British Energy were identified.

I have used three types of resource. First, I have re-visited the historical literature and key sources on government policy, because the roots of British Energy's problems lie in decisions taken decades before privatisation and in the failure to sell nuclear power the first time round in 1989–1990. Second, I have examined the company's financial statements and those of its key competitors. Third, I have interviewed many of the key decision makers, analysts and interested parties. Most of these interviews were held off the record, so that managers and advisors could speak freely. This increased frankness at the expense of attribution.

I have used multiple sources to establish the key events and decisions, on occasions confirmed by sight of board minutes and other private documents. These sources were shown privately and remain private. Only one of the crucial parts of the story depends on these private documents or accounts, namely the previously secret history of British Energy's near merger with Southern Electric in 1997. Those events were described in detail independently by several different parties to the discussions.

Many people have helped me with the research for this book, either by being interviewed or by helping with access to people and data. I am very grateful to all of the following people and to others who chose to remain anonymous: Robert Armour, Norman Askew, John Baker, Terry Brookshaw, Alistair Buchanan, Andy Clements, David Gilchrist, Richard Gillingwater, Richard Green, Bob Hawley, Paul Heward, Robin Jeffrey, George Jenkins, Mike Kirwan, Mike Langley, Stephen Littlechild, Mike Low, Ian Marchant, Daniel Martin, David Newbery, Tom Reid, Roger Siddle, Ed Wallis, Peter Warry, Tony White and Roger Witcomb.

In particular I want to thank Bob Hawley for lending me his detailed personal archive and Becky Allen for reading the whole manuscript. I'm also grateful for helpful comments on parts of the book which were given as seminars at the London School of Economics and at the Cambridge Endowment for Research in Finance. Lastly I want to thank the staff of the University Library, Judge Business School library, Betty and Gordon Moore Library and Rayleigh Library in Cambridge, and of the British Library of Political and Economic Science in London.

1 Introduction

On 5 September 2002 the board of British Energy plc, Britain's largest electricity generator and the owner of eight nuclear power stations, announced the company had run out of cash and faced insolvency. Although the company had bank credit lines available, the company's lawyers advised the directors that they might be breaking the law if they borrowed more money, if they believed the company faced no early prospect of recovery. The company's credit rating was on the brink of junk status so it would have to post collateral – cash to cover the risk of non-delivery – to continue selling its power. Without cash it couldn't trade. Unless it got hundreds of millions of pounds of immediate aid British Energy might have to shut down its power stations.

The England and Wales national electricity grid is designed to cope with the sudden loss of both nuclear power stations at Sizewell in Suffolk, roughly 2,000 MW of capacity. But even a controlled shutdown of the rest of British Energy's English power stations – another 6,000 MW – would cause a catastrophic loss of power and widespread blackouts. Scotland gets about a third of its power from nuclear energy. Without it, large parts of the Scottish economy would have been closed down. Faced with this crisis the British government over-rode its instinctive desire to let troubled private companies fail and provided £450 million of emergency lending to keep British Energy operating. The government had another reason to keep the company afloat; the company had £14 billion of long term nuclear liabilities, which would fall to the taxpayer if the company went under.

Over the winter of 2002–2003, the company's finances were restructured, the creditors were persuaded – some would say forced – to accept conversion of their claims into new equity in the company. In 2005 a new British Energy was re-floated on the stock exchange where it traded profitably at power prices triple the level of 2002, with about a third of the cashflow surplus going to the government. The power stations stayed open, the power carried on flowing and most customers never knew what happened. But the affair was a fiasco. Shareholders lost the vast majority of their investment. The restructuring costs ran into hundreds of millions of pounds. The government was forced to take on liabilities it thought it had privatised in 1996. And after a brief, golden period when it seemed that British Energy had restored the battered name of nuclear power in Britain, the industry's reputation sank to another low.

This book is the story of the causes of the financial crisis of British nuclear power. Unlike the bankruptcy in 2001/2002 of US companies Enron and World-com, there is no suggestion of wrongdoing at British Energy. The company's collapse is a tale of relentless market forces, missed opportunities and a failure to manage risk. The company's managers transformed the performance of the British nuclear power stations but failed to cope with the commercial risks of the deregulated power market. They were encouraged in this failure by an investor community which took a disastrously short term view of the company's finances and overvalued the shares. But the management also had to deal with assets and obligations, the origins of which lay in government decisions taken in the 1950s and 1960s. The British Energy failure was the latest act in the long running drama – some might say farce – of British nuclear power.

Nuclear power is an industry with very long time scales. The roots of British Energy's problems lie in the path of British nuclear development after the Second World War, compounded by the wrong choice of reactor type in the 1960s and 1970s. The British designed power stations were unusual, expensive and unreliable. On top of this was the burden of treating the waste fuel. Britain's long standing commitment to "reprocessing" of fuel – long since abandoned by the US and many other nuclear power countries – saddled British Energy with costly and inflexible contracts that contributed to its financial problems.

The main external cause of the crisis was the collapse in wholesale power prices that started in 1999 and reached its worst point in 2002. Although com-modity prices are volatile and hard to forecast, the British electricity price fall should have been expected. It resulted from the assertion of market forces after a long period of restricted competition. The absurdly uncompetitive structure of the electricity generation market in the early 1990s arose, ironically, from the failed attempt by the Conservative government to privatise nuclear power in 1990. It took a decade for the privatisation-led industry distortions to allow competition to flourish, taking British Energy down with it. The company was obviously at risk of lower power prices – the privatisation prospectus made this explicit. In doing so little to prepare for the risk of lower prices, the company showed a serious lack of commercial judgement.

The company's UK corporate strategy – to vertically integrate – was sensible but wasn't achieved. In particular the board failed to close on a particular merger that would probably have saved the company. The fault for this lies entirely with the directors. But even this failure wasn't decisive. What practically guaranteed that the company would not survive the power price fall was its return of £432 million of cash to shareholders in May 1999. This disastrous decision was taken under enormous pressure from investors, who were following the City mantra that "cash-rich" companies must return that cash to shareholders for fear that otherwise the managers will squander it on ill-conceived and vainglorious schemes. What the investors failed to realise was that the cash wasn't "surplus"; it was essential ballast for the coming storm. A stronger and more self confident company board would have resisted the City pressures. Once the money had gone, there was little that the management could do to avoid the rocks.

In telling the story of a corporate collapse this book tries to show the many dimensions of failure and success. No single thing entirely explains the company's collapse, although the financial policy was the most unhelpful. All managers of enterprises must deal with internal and external pressures, the constant development of what in politics Harold Macmillan famously called "events". Enterprises that prosper are lauded and their chief executives regarded as geniuses who possess the critical factor for success. But corporate successes and failures are complex and contingent. British Energy's story – and the story of its predecessor companies – shows the interaction between technology, politics, regulation, industrial policy, corporate strategy, financial strategy and leadership. In this author's view, the crisis of 2002 was avoidable and the government was right to privatise the company in 1996.

The book is structured as follows. Part I tells the often depressing story of British civil nuclear power from the 1940s to the end of the 1980s. Britain's leading role in nuclear physics and its post-war ambition to remain a "great power" led to the development of the British atomic bomb. The bomb project, combined with economic pressures and shortages of key materials such as enriched uranium and heavy water, led the UK to back gas-cooled nuclear reactors, which would prove a technological dead end. Rather than accept in the 1960s that gas-cooled reactors had no future – as the similarly placed French did – British governments doubled their bet on gas-cooling. Successive Labour and Conservative governments committed the country to another 20 years of extremely costly choices that brought neither exports nor cheap power. As Britain lost out in the international nuclear power market, the government tried to compensate by grabbing a share of the nuclear fuel reprocessing business. This led to the setting up of British Nuclear Fuels (BNFL) and its costly infrastructure at Windscale (later named Sellafield). Part of that cost was borne by the nuclear power stations, locked into expensive and inflexible contracts that made nuclear's already high fixed cost base even higher.

Part II covers the period when nuclear power was put onto a commercial basis for the first time, although still in the public sector. It explains the abortive plan to privatise nuclear power as part of the broader electricity sell off of 1989–1990. The plan failed because of the contradiction between commercially liberalised private ownership of the companies on the one hand and the hopelessly uneconomic cost of nuclear power on the other. In trying to square this circle the Thatcher government privatised a distorted duopoly generation industry that stifled electricity competition for a decade. The electricity regulator, seeking to bring competition into the industry, encouraged a huge wave of new gas power station construction which eventually led to over capacity and the power price collapse that sank British Energy.

The shock of being excluded from electricity privatisation led the newly created Nuclear Electric (in England and Wales) and Scottish Nuclear companies to focus for the first time on making the British nuclear stations work properly. In the most economically successful phase of British nuclear history, these companies saw a dramatic improvement in costs and productivity to the point where the British nuclear stations briefly led the world. Despite political misgivings the Major government decided to privatise the combined companies in the form of a single, Scottish-based holding company, British Energy.

Part III starts with the controversial privatisation of British Energy in 1996. Mired in Anglo-Scottish politics, bitter disputes over the company's liabilities and technical failures, the sale was initially seen as a flop – shareholders made immediate losses. But remarkably the company gradually became a stock market darling and trebled its value, despite instability in the boardroom and repeated failures of corporate strategy. In early 1999, with the shares trading at £7.33 (compared with £2.03 at privatisation), the board decided to pay £432 million to investors. Together with dividends and acquisitions of other assets, the company paid out around £1 billion in one year, severely weakening its previously rock solid balance sheet. Almost immediately the long feared fall in electricity prices began. In 2000 the company started a secret correspondence with the government to request help but failed to convey the seriousness of its situation. Government ministers, reluctant to rescue a company that was still paying dividends to its shareholders, suspected the board of crying wolf. In September 2002, with all options for staving off bankruptcy exhausted, the company suspended its shares and announced it had run out of money.

Part IV then analyses the key causes of the company's downfall: the company's financial strategy; its corporate strategy; the collapse in power prices; the burden of fuel reprocessing contracts with BNFL; and the role of the British reactor design. These causes intersected to cause the crisis of 2002. But no one cause in isolation destroyed the shareholders' money. The biggest external factor was the power price fall of 1999–2002. The biggest unforced error was the payback of shareholder cash in 1999. The stockmarket played an important and unhelpful role. But a different corporate strategy, more attention to the commercial side of electricity markets and greater reliability of the power stations might have been enough to get the company through the trough of 2002–2003.

For the greatest tragedy of the story – for the shareholders, the taxpayers and the employees who all lost out – was the fact that only two years after that dismal September announcement, the price of electricity was back in profitable territory. At the time of writing (December 2006) British power prices are some *four times* their level when the company faced insolvency.

Part V concludes by pulling together the causes of British Energy's failure. The UK's history of civil nuclear power is contrasted with that of the US, Germany and especially France, to gauge how far Britain made unique mistakes and what could reasonably have been done differently. The French comparison is instructive because the two countries had similar starting positions after the Second World War, but their policies diverged sharply in the late 1960s. France is now the world's leading nuclear nation and dominates the growing nuclear export business. Indeed, if Britain ever does build new nuclear power stations they will probably be built by the French. It is hard to imagine a more dismaying end to the dreams of the British nuclear pioneers of the 1950s.

There is something tragic about British Energy's failure – but does it matter? Aside from the devastating financial cost – to investors, employees and the taxpayer – there is another, more damaging legacy. In this author's view British Energy's failure meant that the financial markets' frail confidence in the commercial viability of nuclear power was wrecked. And this happened just when the long term need for new investment in nuclear power was beginning to look vital.

How will new nuclear capacity be financed and built? It has been government policy since the early 1980s that the state will not finance nuclear power stations. The Labour government reaffirmed this view in its 2006 energy review. The private sector must come up with the money. So the collapse of British Energy came at a very bad time. Just when the private sector was getting comfortable with private management and ownership of nuclear power stations the company failed. Shareholders lost virtually all of their investment. And the credibility of nuclear power as an investment disappeared like the invisible radiation that the stations so carefully restrict their emissions of.

Private financial markets can handle the unusual risks of nuclear power generation. Each of the risks – commodity pricing risk, decommissioning risk and regulatory risk – has counterparts in other industries such as metals, petrochemicals and pharmaceuticals and the financial markets have learnt to deal with all of them. The only risk that cannot be insured against – a major nuclear accident – is covered by the state through long standing international treaties.

Other countries have privatised nuclear power companies but only the UK combined private ownership with a deregulated power market and full company responsibility for fuel reprocessing. The collapse of British Energy does not mean that private capital will never flow into nuclear investment. But the task is now going to be harder than it needed to be. This book explains how that collapse happened.

Part I
The years of optimism (1945–1989)

2 Influence of the bomb

Calder Hall and the Magnoxes (1945–1960)

Introduction

To understand the state of the British nuclear power industry when it was privatised in 1996 we must go back to the Second World War. Britain was a leader in research into atomic physics. This scientific expertise, combined with the country's continuing great power aspirations, was to affect the path of atomic development for decades to come. British nuclear power development departed from what became the mainstream of reactor design, at great cost and great damage to public confidence in nuclear power in the UK. This chapter tells the story of why the UK went down a technological cul-de-sac, which was to leave the future British Energy with seven non-standard and problematic British designed power stations.

The British atomic bomb programme

The British policy of creating an independent atomic bomb was to be the main influence on atomic development through the late 1940s and early 1950s. Key decisions were dominated by the military need for plutonium. In October 1945 the Chiefs of Staff urged the government to develop an independent nuclear deterrent, rather than wait for international talks on the possible control of nuclear weapons. Of the two bombs dropped on Japan, the plutonium bomb had proved much more efficient than the uranium one. British scientists who had worked on the Manhattan Project also strongly supported the development of a plutonium weapon. It would also be cheaper to manufacture plutonium in a reactor using natural uranium than to create enriched uranium for a bomb. Enriching uranium (increasing the proportion of the fissile isotope U-235) was a major industrial process that would be costly and take several years. So the government approved the design and construction of a reactor to produce plutonium, even though the formal decision to make atomic bombs was not taken until January 1947. It was recognised that the heat inevitably generated from the reaction might be used for generating electricity but this was very much a secondary consideration (Gowing, 1974a pp. 164–166).

In October 1945 the British Parliament was told of the decision to set up an atomic consultative council under John Cockroft (who had led the wartime

Canadian heavy water project at Chalk River, near Montreal). At this stage the UK was still enjoying cooperation with the US nuclear authorities in line with a secret personal memorandum signed between Churchill and Roosevelt in Hyde Park, New York in 1944. Two new organisations were set up at the beginning of January 1946. The Atomic Energy Research Establishment was created under Cockroft at Harwell near Oxford. And a new industrial facility was set up at Risley in Lancashire in January 1946 to build the reactors that would create plutonium for the military, headed by Christopher Hinton.

Hinton, previously a chemical engineer at ICI before the war, had two tasks: first, to build a plant for uranium production from ore at Springfields, near Blackpool; and second, to build a reactor based on the US plutonium generating ones at Hanford, Washington. This was a water-cooled and graphite-moderated reactor. The military wanted a Hanford-style reactor because they knew it would definitely work and opposed the alternative of an air-cooled reactor. But water-cooled reactors were known to be inherently dangerous because, in the event of a loss of coolant, the remaining water could boil and cause an explosion that might blast fission products over a large area. Siting such a reactor in the highly populated United Kingdom was very difficult. The only feasible site was seen as Aisaig in north-western Scotland, which was remote and expensive to service. On top of this General Groves, the head of the Manhattan Project, advised against a Hanford-style approach on safety grounds when he met Lord Portal, the new Controller of Atomic Energy in the Ministry of Supply, in the US in May 1946. But the UK's lack of facilities to make heavy water ruled out copying the NRX Canadian reactor.

In 1946 a directive by President Truman and the McMahon Act shut out the UK from US atomic research. The US halted supplies of uranium oxide to ICI for production of metallic uranium. Water-cooled graphite reactors were prohibited on safety grounds; heavy water-moderated reactors of the Canadian type were ruled out by the enormous cost and delay in manufacturing heavy water. So the only option was to use natural uranium and air cooling, which therefore became the design for the Windscale "piles".

In January 1947 Cabinet committee Gen 163 formally took the decision to build a British nuclear bomb (Hennessy, 2002 p. 49). In May 1947 this led to the decision to build two reactors ("piles") at Sellafield in Cumbria, on the site of a wartime TNT factory. The site was subsequently renamed Windscale to avoid confusion with the Springfields uranium facility nearby. (It was renamed back to Sellafield in 1981, on public relations grounds). The first reactor went critical in October 1950; the second in June 1951. The programme of plutonium production came to fruition when the UK exploded its first atomic bomb at the Monte Bello islands off Australia in 3 October 1952.

The Windscale reactors generated about 45 kg of plutonium a year, rising to 60 kg after 1954, enough for about ten bombs. But as the Cold War became more intense with the conflict in Korea, the Chiefs of Staff in 1952 raised their need sharply. The military wanted at least 200 bombs, which it calculated was the minimum to deter the USSR by destroying 59 cities (Simpson, 1986 p. 65).

The original Windscale piles lacked enough capacity and were only expected to last five years in any case, so an additional plutonium source was needed.

Sir Christopher Hinton, who had been knighted for his work in building the Windscale plutonium piles, argued for a new, more efficient reactor that could generate electricity as well as plutonium, the natural uranium design known as PIPPA (pile for production of plutonium and power). This choice was adopted largely by default. The successful Canadian heavy water-moderated reactor was still ruled out because there were still no reliable supplies of heavy water. An enriched uranium reactor could use ordinary (light) water as a moderator, but there would be no supply of enriched uranium for some years, pending the construction of a new enrichment factory in Cheshire. The military need for plutonium was ultimately decisive in selecting the PIPPA design for what became Calder Hall, built next to the existing piles at Windscale. Winston Churchill, Prime Minister again from October 1951, had hoped that he could renew close cooperation with the Americans on nuclear matters and there was hope of a deal in which the US would supply atomic bombs directly. When Churchill failed to get this result after a meeting with President Eisenhower in January 1953, he finally sanctioned the building of Calder Hall (Simpson, 1986 p. 88).

The electricity industry had practically no involvement in these early decisions on nuclear power even though it was the main prospective customer for nuclear power stations. The British electricity industry, nationalised in 1948, was run by the BEA (British Electricity Authority), whose chairman was Lord Citrine. The BEA been expecting to play a role in nuclear power from the early 1950s, and in its 1954 annual report had looked forward to a time when nuclear stations would be a central part of their operations. Citrine revealed in his memoirs that he attended a meeting in 1953 armed with authority from his board to contribute £3 million to the cost of Calder Hall, which would produce electricity for the grid. When he realised that the military's needs meant the station would go ahead anyway, he kept quiet (Citrine, 1967 p. 302, cited in Williams, 1980).

British atomic activities were handed over to the newly created UK Atomic Energy Authority (UKAEA) on 19 July 1954. The creation of the UKAEA marked the birth of a powerful new actor on the British political scene. Chaired by Sir Edwin Plowden, a former Chief Planning Officer at the Treasury and Chairman of the Economic Planning Board since 1947, the UKAEA had an unusual degree of independence from central government and a large annual budget of £53m which was received by a direct "vote", meaning that it was treated as if it were another department of government. This independence had been recommended by Churchill's scientific advisor and the Minister responsible for atomic energy policy in the 1951–1955 government, Lord Cherwell. Cherwell believed that the atomic programme had been held back by civil service constraints and a different and more flexible organization was needed (Arnold, 1992 p. 19). The board included Sir Christopher Hinton, Sir John Cockroft and Sir William Penney (who became known as the "nuclear knights") in charge of the Industrial, Research and Weapons groups respectively. Plowden's political skills gave the UKAEA great influence in Whitehall. It had no representation from the electricity industry until 1965, despite the fact that its main decisions would concern nuclear electricity generation.

Fuel worries and the first programme

The context of these nuclear decisions was a sense of national urgency about future energy supplies. Harsh winters in the early 1950s had underlined the country's dependence on coal. In 1951 Britain had even been forced to import a small amount of coal (1.2 million tons out of a total annual use of 223 million). It was therefore of some concern when the National Coal Board announced that it couldn't meet the electricity industry's forecast needs for coal over the next decade. In 1954, the Conservative government, mindful of the political threat of an even stronger coal industry, was keen that the electricity industry should adapt some of its stations to run on oil, even though oil was far more expensive.

With coal scarce and oil expensive, the third way in fuel was nuclear power. Its confidence growing as the research reactors went critical and the construction of Calder Hall kept on schedule, the UKAEA argued in 1954 for a new nuclear power programme of 1,700 MW by 1965, based on a scaled-up version of the Calder Hall reactor, even though it wasn't actually running yet. Although the Treasury was concerned at the cost of these new stations, the need for energy security, encouraged by the UKAEA's enthusiasm for the new technology, proved decisive. A government working party under Burke Trend recommended the UKAEA's nuclear programme be adopted. Once again, the committee excluded any representation from the electricity industry, the intended customer for these stations (Hannah, 1982 ch.14). It therefore overestimated the cost of non-nuclear generation, which was falling as new, more efficient coal power stations were coming available.

Nobody doubted that nuclear power would cost more than coal power but the UKAEA argued that the gap would be narrowed by the "plutonium credit"; the value of the plutonium produced by the Magnoxes could be deducted from the cost of producing the electricity. On some accounts, plutonium was valued at several hundred times the price of gold (Gowing, 1974b p. 292), but at this stage the only buyer was the military. As the chairman of the Central Electricity Authority Lord Citrine put it, "The value that can be attached to plutonium is somewhat arbitrary." Citrine argued that if a free market for plutonium had existed it would set a price equivalent to the fissionable content of uranium; only one part in 140 of natural uranium was the fissionable U-235 so plutonium was worth some 140 times the price of natural uranium (Citrine, 1956). But future use of plutonium as a fuel was purely conjectural at this point. Use of the credit in justifying a 20 year nuclear investment was therefore somewhat optimistic.

The electricity industry was divided up geographically in 1955 and the England and Wales part of the industry was now led by the CEA (Central Electricity Authority). The CEA was concerned at the prospect of being forced to buy nuclear power stations that it wasn't sure it needed and regarded the new nuclear programme as "a bold step" (CEA, 1957 para. 56, cited in Williams

1980). But it felt obliged to fall in with government policy. With the National Coal Board formally announcing that it couldn't produce enough coal to meet the CEA's own forecast needs, it was hard to argue. The CEA did at least win the right to construct and operate the stations themselves.

In February 1955 the Government publicly announced a programme to build 1,500–2,000 MW of nuclear power stations in a White Paper. The paper asserted confidently that "Nuclear energy is the energy of the future" (British Government, 1955 para. 1). It also argued that the cost of nuclear electricity would be about 0.5p/kWh (amounts have been converted into new pence), "about the same as the probable future cost of electricity generated by new coal-fired power stations", though it conceded that without the plutonium credit it would cost substantially more (British Government, 1955 para.19). Geoffrey Lloyd, Minister of Fuel and Power, told the press: "Here is new scope for our traditional genius ... for mixing a small proportion of imported materials with a large proportion of skill, ingenuity and inventiveness. . . . Our nuclear pioneers have now given us a second chance – to lead another industrial revolution in the second half of the twentieth century" (Lloyd, 1955, cited in Hannah 1982). Calder Hall, the first prototype station, still wasn't finished. But the government was concerned about coal supply (because of a shortage of labour) and was also looking forward to "the time when a valuable export trade can be built up" (British Government, 1955 para. 41).

The CEA found that all the key decisions on the new power stations had already been taken. The UKAEA had decided they would be gas-cooled reactors on the Calder Hall model, using fuel encased in the same magnesium alloy cans, which gave the name Magnox for the whole reactor series. The UKAEA had also set out the construction and design arrangements. Sir Claude Gibb, of the major engineering company C. A. Parsons, recommended that the complexity and breadth of skills needed for building nuclear power stations would too much for any one firm. The UKAEA took his advice and encouraged the formation of four consortia of companies, each based around a combination of a boiler maker, a turbo alternator manufacturer and a civil engineering contractor. Allowing the consortia a degree of independence in the design of each station was to lead to a seriously inefficient lack of standardisation across the stations, a theme that was to recur even more expensively with the next generation of British reactors, the AGRs.

Calder Hall was opened officially on 17 October 1956, by the Queen. At 65 MW of electrical energy for each of the first two reactors, Calder Hall was "the first station anywhere in the world to produce electricity from atomic energy on a full industrial scale" in the carefully chosen words of Rab Butler, the member of the government who spoke at the ceremony (*The Times*, 1956b). The US had produced 100 kW of electricity from a nuclear reactor in 1952 at Arco, Idaho. The USSR had produced 5 MW of power from a reactor in Obninsk in June 1954. So Calder Hall was truly original only in its scale.

But it was seen as a great British achievement. *The Times* ran a special supplement on the day of the opening in which Sir Edwin Plowden, chairman of the UKAEA, looked forward to 15,000 MW of nuclear power by 1975 (compared with the White Paper target of just 2,000 MW). He saw Calder Hall not only addressing the UK's enduring threat of fuel shortage, but providing an enduring base for the country's "true greatness" (Plowden, 1956).

Lord Citrine, chairman of the Central Electricity Authority, in his contribution to *The Times* quoted Sir Oliver Franks' recent Reith Lectures, describing the British quest for atomic energy thus: "We embarked on a full programme [of atomic energy] with nothing but green fields and grey matter" (Citrine, 1956). Citrine also tempted fate by adding that "The problems of building nuclear power stations will not differ materially from those met in the construction of conventionally fired stations."

But there was a touch of *The Wizard of Oz* about the proceedings. The future chairman of the privatised generator PowerGen, Ed Wallis, was among those who saw the ceremony and was inspired to make his career in nuclear energy. But Wallis found out some years later that when the Queen pressed the switch that sent power to the grid, the ten foot arrow that swept impressively round the dial showing the number of kilowatts generated was actually moved by a man turning a handle (private interview). And although *The Times* supplement made it quite clear that Calder Hall was "designed primarily to produce the fissile material, plutonium, and their function as power stations is purely secondary", (*The Times*, 1956a) there was no mention of this in Her Majesty's speech.

The Suez panic and dash for nuclear power

The UKAEA, having secured the first programme of nuclear power stations, quickly set about arguing for more. The new consortia, hungry for business, added their support to the lobbying in Whitehall of the UKAEA's chairman, Lord Plowden. The electricity industry's leaders were increasingly concerned at the speed with which they were being pushed into investing in an untried and costly new technology. But Lord Citrine, chairman of the CEA, was waiting to hear the government's plans for the next reorganisation of the power industry. The CEA had vigorously but unsuccessfully opposed the division of the industry between England and Wales on the one hand and Scotland on the other. Conservative MPs still regarded the industry as too concentrated and a committee under Sir Edwin Herbert was due to recommend further change. Fearful of antagonising the government at such a critical time, the CEA reluctantly agreed in October 1956 to a near doubling of the nuclear programme to 3,200 MW (Hannah, 1982 p. 177).

At about the same time that Calder Hall was being commissioned, the British, French and Israeli military became embroiled in the diplomatic mess that became known as the Suez Crisis. Egypt's President Nasser had nationalised the Suez Canal in July 1956 after the UK and US had withdrawn financial support for his Aswan dam project. Israel then invaded Egypt in late October, giving French and British troops a pretext to take control of the canal. The operation was a diplomatic disaster and the US government used financial pressure to force the UK to withdraw from Egypt.

Suez led to national humiliation for Britain and concern about future oil supplies. The pressures on Prime Minister Anthony Eden's health forced his resignation. He was replaced in January 1957 by Harold Macmillan, who believed that Britain must achieve greater energy independence. Macmillan took on personal responsibility for atomic policy and brought in a Birmingham industrialist, Sir Percy Mills (created Lord Mills on his entering the Cabinet), as his new Minister of Power. With public opinion fuelled by the Suez energy panic, and encouraged by strong press lobbying by the four construction consortia, the government shifted decisively in favour of more nuclear power. The UKAEA, which a few months before had argued that British resources of materials and labour were only just enough to build the 3,200 MW programme, now enthusiastically supported a huge expansion to 5,000–6,000 MW. If these stations all came on stream as scheduled in 1965, they would save about a quarter of the UK's total power station fuel needs, equivalent to some 18m tons of coal (Hannah, 1982 p. 179). The uranium would be imported but would be much cheaper than oil and would come from friendly countries such as Canada and South Africa. The electricity industry, even more concerned about the cost of the programme, still judged it wise not to oppose the programme.

So in March 1957 the government announced the expanded Magnox programme of 5,000–6,000 MW (British Government, 1957b). The Magnox design was a scaled-up and modified version of the brand new Calder Hall station, which had only been operating for six months. The government was planning a major investment in a type of nuclear reactor that had not actually been built yet, on the basis of a single working station that had barely been commissioned.

The Windscale fire in 1957

The most serious nuclear accident in UK history occurred seven months later. On 10 October 1957 the fuel cladding on some uranium fuel at Windscale's No. 1 pile was damaged; the fuel overheated and leaked radioactivity into the air (this was an air-cooled reactor). The graphite pile then caught fire. Local firemen brought the fire under control but only after a significant amount of atmospheric contamination. The Windscale fire was level five on the International Nuclear Event Scale and was the worst worldwide nuclear accident until the much more serious Chernobyl disaster in 1986, which was level seven (the highest).

The fire arose because of the poorly understood energy that had been discovered by the American scientist Eugene Wigner. The Windscale engineers regularly heated up the core to allow the graphite to release the Wigner energy that arose from atomic fission, a process known as annealing. It appears that this time the heating was too quick and a fuel canister ruptured, exposing uranium metal to the air. The uranium caught fire and set fire to other fuel and the core itself. At one point 8 tonnes of uranium were on fire. The reactor was open to the air but at a late stage in construction a set of filters had been added on the insistence of the scientist John Cockroft. These filters (known on the site as "Cockroft's follies") captured some of the radioactive particles, but some 20,000 curies of radioactivity were released, in the form of the radioactive isotope iodine-131. Without the filters the release would have been much worse (Hewitt and Collier, 2000 pp. 188–189).

Little was said locally, even when it was obvious that there was a serious incident. The people of Cumberland only officially learned what had happened from a press release by the UKAEA in London on the evening of 11 October. This lack of openness exacerbated the panic a few days later that followed the identification of potentially dangerous levels of radioactive iodine in cow's milk. Iodine-131 has a half life of only eight days so the problem was short term. Levels of iodine-131 in the grass were very low, so that fruit and vegetables grown locally were still regarded as safe to eat, but cows concentrate iodine in their milk. The Windscale authorities therefore decided to ban the consumption of milk over a 500 square kilometre area, affecting 600 farms. The milk ban caused more alarm than the original fire; it was only after a series of public meetings with the locally well-known and respected Windscale general manager H. G. Davey and promises of compensation for farmers that the furore died down (Pocock, 1977 ch.4).

An immediate UKAEA inquiry into the accident by Sir William Penney suggested that there had been faults both with personnel and with equipment, but commended the staff for their prompt and efficient steps to deal with the accident. Penney's team identified faults with the UKAEA (having too many responsibilities for the resources available); with the lack of an operating manual for dealing with Wigner energy releases; and with some of the instrumentation (Arnold, 1992 p. 79). Prime Minister Harold Macmillan saw the report on 29 October. He banned publication for fear of jeopardising a breakthrough in nuclear cooperation with the US, following alarm over the Sputnik launch. All but a few copies were destroyed, as was the type used at the printers (Horne, 1989 pp. 54–55). Even Sir Christopher Hinton, the new head of the CEGB and the former head of the industrial group at the UKAEA, was denied a copy. A full copy of the Penney report was only published in 1992 as part of Lorna Arnold's official history of the accident (Arnold, 1992 Appendix XI).

A shortened version of Penney's report was published as a White Paper on 8 November 1957 (British Government, 1957a). It included in Annex V a reassuring analysis of why the problem couldn't occur at Calder Hall or the Magnox stations under construction, all of which also had graphite moderators. But this reassurance was somewhat premature; understanding of the properties of graphite under irradiation was still limited. The Windscale accident "turned a searchlight on graphite and revealed the precarious foundation of knowledge on which the whole gas-graphite reactor programme rested" (Arnold, 1992 p. 90). The issue was as much economics as safety; some experts feared that the problem of Wigner energy might limit the lives of the new Magnox stations to only 7–14 years (Arnold, 1992 p. 90). This turned out to be far too pessimistic – Calder Hall operated for 46 years – but the scarcity of knowledge made such caution understandable.

A series of reports under Sir Alexander Fleck of ICI recommended that expensive repairs and additional monitors be fitted to the No. 2 pile (No. 1 was a write off). Modifications to Calder Hall and to the Magnoxes under construction were made, costing several million pounds. With new plutonium production at Calder Hall now established, the UKAEA decided to shut down No. 2 pile. Historian Lorna Arnold argues that the accident was probably inevitable and arose from the enormous pressure on the UKAEA from the combination of military and civil projects, relative to its resources, combined with a lack of knowledge about the effect of radiation on graphite. The new research that followed the accident helped in the operation and design of the Magnoxes. The "reactors in Britain were all undoubtedly safer as a result" (Arnold, 1992 p. 157).

The nuclear euphoria subsides

International oil prices, which had surged to a peak in 1957 after the Suez crisis, fell sharply in the next three years as new oil fields came on stream and larger tankers came into use that could avoid the Suez route by going round the Cape of Good Hope. The coal board was able to deliver a lot more coal than it had expected and there was now a forecast coal *surplus* of 16–20 million tons annually by the mid-1960s (Hannah, 1982 p. 232). The case for nuclear power in terms of energy security, which had seemed so compelling post-Suez, suddenly looked weak.

At the same time the cost of nuclear power compared with conventional coal stations was increasing, for several reasons. The first was that interest rates, to which nuclear costs are very sensitive because they are so capital intensive, had risen from 4 per cent at the time of the first nuclear programme decision in 1955, to 5.5 per cent in 1959. The plutonium credit, estimated at thousands of pounds per kilogramme in the 1955 White Paper, now looked questionable, owing to increasingly plentiful supplies of uranium from Canada and a lower price of enriched uranium available from the US. It was also clear by 1959 that plutonium could only be used as a fuel in fast breeder reactors, which were a long term prospect. The military need for plutonium would be met by Calder Hall and Chapelcross plus just one of the Magnoxes, Hinckley Point. In 1963 the plutonium credit was cut to zero.

Capital costs had also risen because of the need for new safety equipment following the report into the Windscale fire. Conventional coal power stations, by contrast, were becoming cheaper as a result of economies of scale, steadily improving thermal efficiency and cheaper siting of new stations closer to the coal fields that supplied them.

The electricity industry was reorganised in 1957 according to Sir Edwin Herbert's proposals, with the creation of the CEGB (Central Electricity Generating Board) which controlled electricity generation and the national grid in England and Wales. The industry's timidity in opposing the expanded nuclear programme now disappeared and the CEGB began to criticise what it saw as the tendency for both the government and the UKAEA to quote optimistic estimates of nuclear costs. The CEGB's own estimates showed nuclear costing 40 per cent more than coal in cheap coal areas and 20–25 per cent more elsewhere. Criticised for casting doubt on the programme and harming its export potential, the CEGB nonetheless advised civil servants privately that it believed that Parliament was being misled (Hannah, 1982 p. 235).

The first Chairman of the CEGB was Sir Christopher Hinton, who had overseen the Windscale reactor development and the building of Calder Hall and was one of the leading public figures on atomic energy. Having joined the Great Western Railway as an apprentice at 16, Hinton went on to a first-class degree in Mechanical Sciences at Cambridge. He was widely admired, although his "abrasive, dominating personality" (Hannah, 1982 p. 264) apparently limited his ability to build working relationships. He was described some years later in a House of Lords debate as both "the most brilliant engineer we have in this country" and "a little ruthless in pursuit of efficiency" (Williams, 1980 p. 102). His former colleagues at the UKAEA assumed, along with the government, that Hinton would naturally support the nuclear programme in his new job. This turned out to be a mistake. Although he was committed to the long term development of nuclear power, Hinton quickly came to agree with the electricity industry's pessimistic view of nuclear costs.

Sensing the risk of a public confrontation with a government that was still optimistic about nuclear, Hinton worked behind the scenes to reduce the CEGB's obligations, arguing that resources should be diverted into research for newer, superior designs to the Magnoxes. He succeeded in chipping away at the programme. First the target for completion was put back from 1965 to 1966. Then the UKAEA's own reactors (some 300 MW) were included in the 6,000 MW target (which amounted to a cut in planned new generation). And the CEGB delayed work on the fifth and sixth Magnox stations several times. The overall target had, in effect, been cut to 5,025 MW, still just within the stated programme of 5,000–6,000 MW. These moves were all kept secret for fear of political embarrassment to the government (Hannah, 1982 p. 236).

But then the Treasury added its weight against the expanded programme, concerned at the pressures on public spending going into the 1960s and the low prospective return on investment in the electricity industry. Coal scarcity had now become a problem of significant surplus, with unemployment among miners looking possible. By the spring of 1960 the CEGB's views won out over those of the UKAEA and the government accepted the need for a restatement of policy.

In its June 1960 White Paper "The Nuclear Power Programme", the government accepted that coal and oil supplies were no longer scarce and that conventional power was about 25 per cent cheaper than nuclear. The revised programme was to have 3,000 MW of nuclear plant in place by 1965, the original 5,000 MW target being postponed to 1968 (British Government, 1960). This still left Britain with the largest nuclear power programme in the world, with six Magnoxes under construction (five for the CEGB plus one in Scotland). The White Paper envisaged a further new station being ordered each year through the 1960s, but further CEGB pressure reined this back to just three more, for a total of nine Magnoxes in all (plus the original Calder Hall station and its near-twin at Chapelcross in south west Scotland).

Appraisal of the Magnox programme

Despite a family resemblance to the Calder Hall gas-cooled graphite-moderated reactor, each of the Magnoxes was, in effect, a prototype. This meant that the normal cost reductions associated with replicating a single design were lost. The Dungeness Magnox (construction started in 1960) achieved a higher gas outlet temperature (410°C) than Calder Hall (335°C), although still not high enough to drive the steam turbines used in the modern coal stations. Much older turbines had to be used, which meant lower thermal efficiency than the coal stations could achieve.

Construction of the Magnoxes took on average about 40 per cent longer than planned. Several had severe decommissioning problems. The problem of corrosion of steel components by the carbon dioxide gas, although identified as an inherent feature of the design, proved more serious than expected under the higher temperatures and pressures of the later reactors. In 1969 the power ratings of all the stations were reduced by about a fifth to keep the corrosion under control.

The Magnox programme was justified on fuel security grounds rather than cost. The fuel situation turned out by 1960 to be much less of a problem than was expected in the mid-1950s. But the extra cost of the nuclear stations was supposed to be only moderately more than coal stations. That conclusion rested on a mixture of wishful thinking on the plutonium credit, a lack of appreciation of the falling cost of coal generation, unrealistic hopes for the construction costs of the stations and a belief that interest rates would stay low. All of these conditions failed to hold and the economic cost of the Magnox programme was therefore substantially larger than the UKAEA and the government had expected.

There were other adjustments that artificially favoured the Magnox costs. First, none of the cost figures included any research and development costs. Second, the interest costs were too low. The rate applied in the late 1950s was typically 6 per cent. At the same time US nuclear construction economics assumed 14 per cent. The CEGB shifted to a 10 per cent figure only in the early 1960s (Williams, 1980 pp. 66–68). The higher the interest cost, the worse nuclear costs compare with coal.

In 1962 the CEGB estimated the operating cost of nuclear power, ranging from about 0.27p/kWh at Wylfa to 0.51p/kWh at Berkeley. This compared with 0.2p/kWh at the new Ferrybridge C coal station under construction. It estimated the total additional cost of nuclear power at £20 million per annum (House of Commons, 1963). Alex Henney (Henney, 1994) quotes the Ministry of Power as estimating the additional capital cost of building seven nuclear stations between 1962 and 1966 instead of conventional at around £360 million (Henney estimates £4 billion in 1993 money).

Perhaps the main problem with the Magnox programme was its size. It was at best optimistic to build so many stations so quickly, with so little operating experience of the prototype. But by the 1970s the Magnoxes came to be seen as reasonably successful. Their cost and construction over-runs were put into perspective by the atrocious performance of their successors, the AGRs. Magnox construction costs over-ran their budgets by 10–20 per cent, which compared well with nuclear construction in other countries. The stations settled down to reliable long term performance and far exceeded their original design lives (in part because there were run at lower than their designed power ratings). Calder Hall had its life extended repeatedly and only closed in March 2003, with over 46 years of operation. Some of the Magnoxes were still operating in 2007 exceeding by far their design life of 30 years. In the first attempt at nuclear privatisation in 1988–1989, the Magnoxes were routinely referred to as the "workhorses" of the nuclear power industry: steady, reliable and pretty trouble-free. Their close cousins the AGRs were not to enjoy any such praise.

Conclusion: lessons not learned

Britain became a pioneer in civil nuclear power because of a combination of its scientific heritage, the government's desire to build nuclear weapons and recurring fears over energy security. The choice of technology – gas-cooled, graphite-moderated reactors – was made through a lack of alternatives. Britain had no heavy water supplies so it couldn't copy the Canadian reactor design. The US water-cooled design was ruled out on safety grounds. And the prohibitive cost of enriched uranium forced a choice of natural uranium reactor. The French government adopted a similar reactor technology for the same reasons (Chapter 16).

The Magnox programme was an ambitious and hasty scaling up of the Calder Hall plutonium factory design. The atomic establishment showed its enthusiasm for technological advance ahead of proven prototypes and a worrying lack of conservatism in cost estimates. Economic arguments for building the stations were excessively reliant on a putative plutonium credit which then disappeared. The electricity industry was a bystander during most of the early important decisions. As it turned out the Magnoxes performed reliably and for many more years than expected, albeit at a lower power rating than designed. The lesson might have been learned from this period that nuclear technology was still in its infancy and that one should be cautious about forecasting costs and performance. The next chapter will show that it wasn't.

3　The AGRs and the reactor debates (1960–1978)

Introduction

The Magnoxes were never primarily justified on economic grounds and the over-ambitious building programme was largely a result of recurring panics over imported energy supplies during the early part of the Cold War. In other words there were good reasons for the decisions.

There were no such excuses for the second wave of gas-cooled reactors in the 1960s, the AGRs. This time the investment was supposed to have been based on economics. But it was one of the UK's worst industrial blunders. The UK went down a 30-year cul-de-sac in reactor development before abandoning hopes of an indigenous British reactor export industry in the late 1970s. The upshot was that when the CEGB was ready to be privatised in 1989, it had a poorly perform-ing and expensive fleet of nuclear stations and the public reputation of nuclear power had collapsed. The true costs only became clear at privatisation, as we shall see in the next chapter. In this chapter we tell the story of how Britain com-mitted itself to a unique type of reactor, at enormous cost.

UKAEA versus CEGB: the second nuclear programme

In the lead up to the second nuclear programme, Sir Christopher Hinton, as chairman of the CEGB and former Deputy Controller of the UKAEA, occupied an unusually influential position. In various speeches and articles, Hinton gave the impression that although he was committed to nuclear power, he might not want to buy the UKAEA's technology.

In a famous article in *Three Banks Review* in December 1961, Sir Christopher indicated strong doubts about the choice of the AGR for further power stations in Britain. Instead he seemed to be taking seriously the Canadian heavy water-moderated design, known as CANDU (Hinton, 1961). CEGB evidence given to the Select Committee on the Nationalised Industries (1962–1963) identified "defects in the existing structure and organisation" of nuclear policy making. The CEGB "harboured some resentment at the way they had been treated by the Authority" (Williams, 1980 p. 93). The CEGB also made it clear that it wouldn't order any new British reactor until its prototype had at least one year's operating experience (Williams, 1980 p. 96). With the prototype AGR only having reached full power in February 1963, this sent a clear signal that the CEGB would not just do what the UKAEA wanted.

The government was concerned that the UKAEA's investments in British reactor designs would hardly find export markets if their main customer rejected them. In its White Paper of April 1964 "The Second Nuclear Programme" (British Government, 1964), the government proposed a further 5,000 MW of nuclear plant, to be commissioned between 1970 and 1976. The Paper assumed that this plant would be economically competitive with coal. It also made clear that the CEGB would have some commercial freedom to choose the reactor type.

Immediately the CEGB invited tenders to build a 1,200 MW full scale power station (2 × 600 MW) at Dungeness, next to the existing Magnox. The tender was not limited to AGRs; the CEGB was interested in water-moderated reactors too. From a commercial point of view the CEGB had every reason to be interested in alternatives to the gas-cooled technology. The Magnoxes were showing that the gas-cooled approach might have severe development limits. And the US company General Electric had recently announced an order for a boiling water reactor (BWR) which it claimed would be cheaper than coal generation (Williams, 1980 p. 110). It also published a price list of reactors, giving every indication that it had brought the technology to the level of a normal manufacturing business. The Third Geneva Conference on Atomic Energy in 1964 was dominated by news of cost breakthroughs by US nuclear manufacturers, much to the annoyance of the UKAEA representatives (Williams, 1980 p. 115).

At the end of 1964 Sir Christopher Hinton retired from CEGB, to be replaced as chairman by his deputy, Stanley Brown. Hinton's departure seems to have coincided with the waning of any serious opposition at the CEGB to the AGR. With the tenders all in by the beginning of February 1965, rumours began to circulate in the press only six weeks later that the new Dungeness B would be an AGR after all. The CEGB sent their recommendation to the government in mid-May and the official decision was announced on 25 May 1965. In a now infamous statement, the Minister for Power Fred Lee told the House of Commons that he was happy to accept the joint recommendation of the CEGB and UKAEA in favour of the British designed AGR programme. He added: "I am quite sure we have won the jackpot this time.... Here we have the greatest breakthrough of all times" (cited in Burn, 1978 p. 10).

This "breakthrough" was to become the AGR disaster, possibly the greatest commercial failure in British history. The official historian of the CEGB was to call it "one of the major blunders of British industrial policy" (Hannah, 1982 p. 285).

Although nobody knew the scale of the problems ahead, there was concern about the way the previously sceptical CEGB had come back into the UKAEA fold, especially when it emerged that the winning tender had departed materially from the design specification. In an attempt to dispel these doubts, the CEGB published in July its "Appraisal of the Technical and Economic Aspects of Dungeness B Nuclear Power Station" (CEGB, 1965). Stanley Brown, chairman of the CEGB, insisted that the assessment was "a dispassionate study based only on hard commercial facts. No political pressure at all was put on the board" (*The Times*, 1965). But the document lacked enough detail to convince sceptics that the decision in favour of the AGR was soundly based. The CEGB figures showed the AGR costing about 7 per cent less than the American General Electric BWR design (submitted by the consortium Thermal Nuclear Power Group (TNPG)). But this was a comparison between a proven, even slightly obsolete American design and an unproven British one.

The cost difference between the AGR and BWR cost was explained entirely by the assumptions of how much of the time they would be available to produce power. The advantage of the AGR design was its claimed ability to refuel on-load (i.e. without having to be shut down). This meant more time producing power, for any given capital cost. The CEGB estimated this gave the AGR a cost advantage of £8.97/kW, compared with the overall cost difference of £8.81/kW (Pocock, 1977 p. 166).

There were two problems with the on-load refuelling argument. The first was that US designed LWRs had achieved high availability factors in the US and in Germany, without on-load refuelling, by making good use of the shut downs that are required for maintenance and safety checks. This operating experience was at least as good as the 75 per cent availability factor assumed by the CEGB for the AGR design (Williams, 1980 p. 131). The second problem was that on-load refuelling had not yet been shown to work. The AGR prototype at Windscale had achieved on-load refuelling on a small scale, despite problems of vibration. But the first full scale test of on-load refuelling in 1967 resulted in three fuel elements being shaken to pieces (Williams, 1980 p. 132). On-load refuelling was not satisfactorily achieved at some of the AGRs until the mid-1990s.

More generally the projected AGR costs were speculative, based on a year's operations of a much smaller pilot project, scaling it up by a factor of 20, increasing the operating temperature by more than 100°C and increasing circuit pressure from 300 psi to 450 psi at Dungeness and 600 psi for later AGRs. By comparison the first Magnox plant, Berkeley, was "only" four times the size of the Calder Hall prototype. The AGR design incorporated a concrete pressure vessel, another new technology that hadn't yet been built. The winning tender, from the consortium Atomic Power Construction (APC), departed from the original specification (moving from a 21-rod two ring fuel design used in the prototype to a 36-rod three ring cluster) in ways that suggested that the UKAEA had helped them push the design forward to ensure the AGR could beat the competing US BWR. But this raised the risk that the design would not work properly. It was also suggested that APC had bid low to secure the contract, which was vital to their commercial future (Pocock, 1977 p. 167).

The AGR capital cost was estimated at £78.40/kW, compared with £70.86 for the BWR. Yet Burn, in a trenchant critique of the appraisal, argued that the construction cost assumed for the BWR was 50 per cent above the expected cost of the Oyster Creek reactor in the US on which it was based (although actual construction costs at Oyster Creek rose well above the estimate) (Burn, 1978 p. 18).

So there were reasons to be doubtful that the CEGB had objectively chosen the AGR against the US competition. Sir Christopher Hinton was believed to be sceptical about the AGR – but he had conveniently retired from the CEGB just before the decision. The new Labour government, famously elected the previous autumn under the slogan of using "the white heat of technology" faced the political embarrassment at the beginning of April 1965 of cancelling the British TSR-2 advanced aircraft project in favour of the US F-111 fighter bomber. Perhaps choosing a US nuclear reactor over the British AGR just a month later would have been just too much to stomach (Williams, 1980 p. 143), although there is no evidence of linkage between the two – Harold Wilson doesn't mention the AGR in his memoirs. And at a time of recurring balance of payments difficulties there was the ever present argument for promoting a new British export industry. Nonetheless, in accepting the UKAEA's claims for the AGR, the CEGB and the government were taking a great deal on trust.

Enter the AGR: 1965

The Advanced Gas-cooled Reactor was, as the name implies, an improved version of the Magnox reactors, and used relatively similar technology. But the name masks the degree of difference between the two types. The key improvement in the AGRs was a much higher operating temperature, around 650°C, which would provide higher thermal efficiency, reducing the cost of electricity generated for a given fuel cost. But the first problem the AGR design met was that the magnesium alloy used to clad the fuel in the Magnoxes would melt at around 640°C. A search for a superior material turned out to be prolonged and costly. At first the UKAEA intended to use beryllium, an expensive and highly toxic material which had a high melting point and good thermal conductivity. Unfortunately, experiments showed that it tended to swell under irradiation and was prone to corrosion by the carbon dioxide coolant gas. After £10m of expenditure, beryllium was dropped in favour of stainless steel. The point about steel was that it required a degree of enrichment of the nuclear fuel, because of its poorer nuclear properties, but by 1961 this seemed to a cheaper overall solution to using beryllium (Pocock, 1977 p. 167).

Choosing the AGR meant continuing difficulties with the use of a graphite moderator. First was the already known tendency for the carbon dioxide gas to oxidise the graphite, decreasing the moderator's mechanical strength and possibly depositing carbon in the cooling system. Both processes could shorten the life of the reactor core. Experiments on the small 30 MW prototype AGR at Windscale established that mixing carbon monoxide and methane into the carbon dioxide could cut the graphite oxidisation to an acceptable level, but at the cost of some additional mechanical equipment.

The second known problem of using graphite was that under irradiation at high temperatures the graphite would undergo small but significant changes of shape and differential stresses that could lead to cracking. This was a potentially very serious problem; although the UKAEA became confident it could solve it using an improved form of graphite there was an understandable concern that the main – indeed only – customer, the CEGB, might need some further and independent reassurance. A committee was set up, chaired by Professor H. J. Eméleus and comprising three other professors. Three of the committee members were Fellows of the Royal Society and when the committee found that the AGRs should be able to operate satisfactorily at a design life of 30 years, this conclusion was regarded as final (Williams, 1980 p. 56).

In October 1965 the Labour government produced its own White Paper on fuel policy (British Government, 1965a). Confident that the AGRs would now be competitive with coal, the government increased the second nuclear programme from 5,000 MW to 8,000 MW, an average of one station a year to be commissioned between 1970 and 1975. It accepted that the hopes for nuclear costs matching coal set out in the 1955 White Paper had "been falsified, mainly by the unexpectedly high capital cost of the earlier nuclear stations and the steep fall in the cost per kilowatt of conventional generating sets, as these came to be built in ever larger sizes." It then estimated Dungeness B costs as 0.19p/kWh making the "cautious" assumptions of a 7.5 per cent discount rate, 75 per cent load factor and 20 year life. If instead one used a 30 year life and 85 per cent load factor, the unit cost would be only 0.16p. But there was no basis for assuming that the completely unproven AGR would ever reach 85 per cent (as indeed most of them by 2007 had not). The projected Dungeness costs were appreciably lower than those for the new coal stations at Drax (0.22p) and Cottam (0.23p) (British Government, 1965b para. 68). An unexpected cold spell in November brought power cuts and embarrassment to the CEGB but seemed to underline the need for new capacity. It would be a very long wait.

The Dungeness B disaster

The first AGR station, Dungeness B began construction in January 1966. It was to become "the single most disastrous engineering project undertaken in Britain" (Henney, 1994 p. 131). It was sited by the shingle beach of the Kent coast, near a dreary expanse of marsh much loved by wading birds and their admirers, next to the existing Magnox "A" station. Dungeness B was to become a by-word for everything that was wrong with the British nuclear industry and was still disappointing its owners into the late 1990s.

The first problems came to light in late 1966 when complex design problems arose with the boilers. When the House of Commons Select Committee on Science and Technology investigated in 1967, MPs were reassured by the head of the UKAEA, Sir William Penney, who told them: "It always happens in this kind of work that some emergency seems to arise, there is a great commotion about something, it looks of course as if it was not right, and then everything converges on it and it almost melts away" (House of Commons, 1965 p. 125). A dissenting opinion came from the Scientific Member of the National Coal Board, L. Grainger, a nuclear scientist who had previously worked at the UKAEA. Grainger warned the Committee that the technical difficulties had been underestimated and that it might be only after the station had been operating successfully for a few years that problems with the fuel could be properly judged. The Committee disregarded this advice (perhaps because he worked for the coal industry) and argued that "it could be against the national interest if decisions were taken in a spirit of fearing the worst from all new techniques" (Burn, 1978 p. 126). The "national interest" largely lay in the hope for future export orders. But later in 1967 the other main nuclear consortium TNPG (which admittedly had a business relationship with the US GE company) stated that the AGR design was unlikely ever to be exportable (Burn, 1978 p. 126).

The difficulties at Dungeness continued. By 1969 two serious problems had emerged. The first was that the steel liner to the inside of the concrete pressure vessel was distorted, leading to inadequate clearance for the boilers. The top halves of the liner walls had to be rebuilt, causing several months' delay. The second problem was that the boilers had to be fundamentally redesigned, owing to vibration caused by the high temperature gas (which was to cause problems at all AGRs). The delays and cost over-runs, compounded by strikes, led the CEGB to take over the APC construction consortium (and get compensation from shareholders). Dungeness B was to take 19 years to commission its first reactor in 1983, with the second not commissioned until 1988.

After commissioning, defects were discovered in the steam pipes and the station's load factor reached 50 per cent only in 1991. In 1999 weld defects were found that forced the closure of both reactors. Something close to full load was achieved in 2004, 38 years after construction began. The station was given a ten year life extension in September 2005, in part because the key life-limiting equipment, the boilers and graphite core, had been so little used in earlier years (British Energy Group, 2005).

The fight with coal: 1965–1970

Dungeness B combined the problems of an unproven and flawed design with a weak construction consortium, poor labour relations and recurring manufacturing defects. Of greatest importance was the inherent design weakness, which was to undermine the whole AGR programme. The CEGB, having committed itself to the AGR, didn't want to reopen the discussion. Any criticism by the parliamentary Science and Technology Committee was constrained by the desire not to damage the increasingly illusory export prospects of the AGR. This left the only serious source of criticism of the AGR programme as the National Coal Board (NCB).

It may seem surprising that a traditionally pro-coal Labour government should not merely support but expand the previous Conservative government's nuclear programme. More nuclear build meant fewer coal mining jobs. But the coal industry didn't really start to fight until the mid-1960s, for two reasons (Williams, 1980 ch. 7). First, the original demand for nuclear power was driven by a fear of coal scarcity in the 1960s and beyond. The 1955 White Paper launching the first nuclear programme stated that: "The provision of enough men for the mines is one of our most intractable problems. . . . Any relief that can come from other sources of energy such as nuclear will do no more than ease the problem of finding and maintaining an adequate labour force. There can be no question of its creating redundancy" (British Government, 1955 para. 47).

Second, despite the early hopes of the authors of the 1955 White Paper, the Magnox stations were clearly not competitive with the modern coal stations coming on stream in the 1960s, so nuclear appeared to pose no threat to coal on economic grounds. So it was only in 1965 when the CEGB threw itself so enthusiastically behind the AGRs, and nuclear expansion on a grand scale, that the coal industry realised it had a problem.

In July 1967 Lord Robens, the chairman of the NCB told the annual conference of the National Union of Mineworkers that the Magnoxes had cost 28,000 miners' jobs and £525 million more capital spending than coal stations would have cost (Williams, 1980 p. 158). Robens, a former member of the Labour shadow cabinet, had served his time as a trade union official before becoming an MP in 1945. He was appointed by the Conservative Prime Minister Harold Macmillan as chairman of the NCB in 1961 to oversee an orderly contraction of the coal industry. Over the next decade he would supervise the closure of 406 pits with the loss of 315,000 jobs (Powell, 1993 p. 178). But he was not going to accept what he saw as untested claims by the nuclear industry. Over the next few years the NCB offered some of the most serious criticism of the AGRs. While obviously partisan, its emphasis on the unproven nature of AGR performance was both fair and unfortunately unusual, when so many other analysts were happy to accept grossed up extrapolations from the relatively small Windscale AGR prototype.

Robens' attack failed. Sir Ronald Edwards, chairman of the Electricity Council, insisted that there was no pro-nuclear bias in the industry and that Dungeness B would produce power at 0.22p/kWh in 1970, including royalties to the UKAEA. Its successor station, Hinckley Point B, would produce at 0.2p/kWh in 1972. The best coal cost was 0.23p/kWh (*The Times*, 1967). *The Times Business News* decided that "unless the nation is being taken for a gigantic ride by its technocrats, the age of cheap nuclear power has, after several false starts, now arrived" (cited in Williams, 1980 p. 159). These figures were confirmed in the government's next White Paper on Fuel Policy in October 1967. The White Paper, which was published following the discovery of North Sea gas, described nuclear power as "proven and increasingly competitive". It put the costs of nuclear power at about 0.2p/kWh, compared with 0.22p/kWh for the best coal station then operating, Cottam (British Government, 1967 Appendix III, table F). The figures for nuclear were for two stations that had only just started construction (Dungeness B and Hartlepool B).

Meanwhile the CEGB announced in March 1967 that the next AGR was to be sited, provocatively, in Hartlepool, on the edge of the Durham minefield. The NCB repeatedly called for an independent enquiry into the claims that nuclear costs were lower than coal. Support for the coal industry came from an unlikely source in 1968 when a report by a team of American economists from the

Brookings Institution criticised the speed of nuclear substitution for coal. The report, published as a book titled *Britain's Economic Prospects*, argued that "the latest plans probably exceed the optimal rate of substitution of, in effect, nuclear power for coal; they involve an exceptionally and unnecessarily capital intensive method. ... The investment programme for electricity (especially nuclear generation) should be substantially reduced" (Caves, 1968 p. 193).

The unfolding AGR fiasco 1967–1978

The CEGB awarded another AGR contract, for Heysham 1, in 1969. This was despite increasing evidence of problems at Dungeness. On 12 August 1968 Robens pointed out in another letter to *The Times* that the cost of a unit of electricity had gone from 0.19p in the original White Paper of 1965, to 0.21p in 1967, then 0.24p in January 1968. These changes were a mixture of inflation, a higher discount rate, the devaluation of sterling and higher uranium prices. He backed the call by the Select Committee on Science and Technology for an independent comparison with coal costs, which he argued were falling. Nothing happened. The government stated in February 1969 that it had been assured by the CEGB that the problems at Dungeness B had no implications for other AGRs, so there was no reason for an independent enquiry into their costs or the delays (Williams, 1980 p. 169).

But the problems continued. In 1970 the nuclear safety regulator, the Nuclear Installations Inspectorate, decided that the AGR designs at Hartlepool and Heysham must be modified on safety grounds, at a cost of some £25m (Williams, 1980 pp. 204–205). In 1971 the discovery of corrosion of reactor components by gas in the Magnoxes led to costly changes to Dungeness B. The restraint coupling which allows the graphite core to expand within the reactor might be liable to similar corrosion, so it was replaced (*The Times*, 1971). Then in 1972 new steel corrosion problems were found with the chrome steel of the boiler tubes. Dungeness B and Hinckley Point B were too advanced in construction for substitute steel to be used so their power rating was cut instead.

It had also become clear by now that the use of methane in the cooling gas to control graphite erosion was leading to carbon deposition on the fuel pins, with a loss of performance. And the on-load refuelling wasn't working properly. In April 1972, Dungeness B was afflicted with a problem with the thermocouples attached to the steel tubes in the boilers. *The Times* reported that the construction cost had now reached £170 million, from the original £89 million (*The Times*, 1972).

On 26 May 1978, the CEGB revealed that Dungeness would now cost £344 million, a rise of £255m over the original budget, of which £150m was caused by inflation. The target for operation was now early 1980. The CEGB's director of projects, Mr C. E. Pugh, when asked about the original decision to accept the Atomic Power Construction consortium's design said "Yes, with hindsight it was foolish to accept it." The station project manager, Mr F. W. Coates summed up the lessons learned: "You don't place a contract with a contractor of doubtful viability. You don't place orders for three designs of AGR. You don't extrapolate the data and jump 200 degrees C without extensive pre-site work. And you do enough research work not to find unpleasant surprises halfway through the project" (*The Times*, 1978c).

The problems of Dungeness B need to be put in context; the CEGB's record on power station construction and design was generally poor in the 1960s. An authoritative and generally critical study of the nationalised industries by Richard Pryke published in 1981 noted that low productivity and long delays were endemic in large construction projects in the UK but argued the problem was worse in electricity. It quoted evidence from the National Economic Development Office that large industrial projects in the UK generally took about 40 per cent longer to complete than abroad; but for power stations the figure was 90 per cent (Pryke, 1981 p. 27). Pryke also pointed out that the CEGB's record with their conventional 500 MW turbo generator sets had been very poor owing to defective design and bad workmanship (Pryke, 1981 p. 28). But the problems were worst in nuclear stations. The AGR capital costs were some 15–30 per cent higher than a comparable US-designed PWR. By the spring of 1979 some £700 million of extra capital cost had been incurred by choosing the AGRs for little or no compensating advantage (Pryke, 1981 p. 29).

The 1970s: reactor wars

By the early 1970s the CEGB was losing faith in the AGR but not with nuclear power. Nuclear output was running well behind forecasts because of delays in the AGR programme. With a rising oil price the CEGB stopped converting coal stations to run on oil, so coal burn was running higher than expected. Coal costs too were rising and there was a major mining strike in February 1972. By the end of the following year, oil prices had trebled after the October Yom Kippur Middle East war and there was another coal miners' strike, which lasted four months.

As the first generation of nuclear stations, the Magnoxes, came on stream, the CEGB was understandably keen on shifting the energy mix away from fossil fuels. Once fully commissioned, the Magnoxes operated well and their operating costs (excluding capital costs and future nuclear liabilities) looked quite reasonable compared with increasingly costly oil and coal.

The CEGB therefore wanted more nuclear power but faced the question, what reactor should supply it? The period from 1972 to 1978 was one of intense, repeated arguments about the choice of reactor. There were four contenders: i) the AGR; ii) a US-designed light water reactor (increasingly the choice was the Westinghouse PWR); iii) the Steam Generating Heavy Water Reactor (SGHWR); and iv) the High Temperature Reactor (HTR). A fifth design, the Fast Breeder Reactor (FBR) was seen by the CEGB and the UKAEA as the longer term choice, since it offered great economies in the use of uranium. The AGR, SGHWR, HTR and FBR were all UKAEA designs. The criteria for the choice were: the cost; the possible export potential for the UK; and safety.

The CEGB had become disillusioned with the AGR. In 1969 it told the Select Committee that it saw both the HTR and the SGHWR as offering greater potential than the AGR (Williams, 1980 pp. 201–202). The following year the CEGB invited tenders for a new HTR reactor at Oldbury. The HTR was a further development of gas-cooled reactors, a prototype of which had been running at Winfrith in Dorset since 1964. Development delays led to the tender being cancelled. And meanwhile the worldwide dominance of the US LWR design was beginning to influence CEGB thinking.

In August 1972 the new CEGB chairman Arthur Hawkins told the Parliamentary Science Committee in 1972 that with electricity demand having grown much less than forecast, because of slow economic growth, there was no immediate need for new nuclear capacity. When the time did come though, it would not be an AGR. He described the AGR as an "inherently difficult system" and that with £600m–£700m tied up in four stations under construction, the CEGB refused to order any more, at least until one had been brought successfully into operation. He confirmed the suspicions of many when he told the Committee that the AGR had been adopted too quickly and that the CEGB had been very strongly advised by the UKAEA, which now appeared over-confident in its design (Williams, 1980 p. 207).

Perhaps surprisingly, the CEGB appeared still to have confidence in the UKAEA's other designs, and wanted to pursue the HTR, but only as part of a broader programme of LWRs. It saw little point in going for the UK-designed SGHWR if it was going to choose a water-moderated reactor type. The PWR was now the leading choice internationally, was achieving good construction times and could be built in such a way as to have only 10 per cent import content. In December 1973 the CEGB put forward figures for reactor costs for a 1,320 MW station for the different types. The AGR was 0.57p/kWh; the SGHWR 0.51p/kWh; but cheapest was the PWR at 0.46p/kWh (Burn, 1978 table 9.2). None of these figures could be regarded as proven, because even the PWR had relatively few operating years of history at this stage.

The CEGB asserted its preference for the PWR over the next few years, although it still held out support for the long term development of the British HTR and eventually the fast breeder. But the MPs of the 1972 Science Committee (House of Commons, 1973) backed the UKAEA in arguing for the British SGHWR. This was mainly on the grounds of support for British industry, since it was hard to see how the UK could gain much advantage from a belated joining of the PWR club – although the French had done just that (see Chapter 16).

The ultimate decision on what new reactor to build lay with the government but the Conservative government lost power in the election in February 1974 following the winter miners' strike. In May the new House of Commons debated the question in great depth. The views came down to the following. The CEGB and others in favour of the PWR said it would bring the UK into the reactor mainstream, while still allowing development of the HTR and the FBR. They saw the SGHWR as another unusual British design, facing more problems of scaling up from a limited prototype, which would delay further nuclear production, while diverting resources from developing the more promising HTR (Williams, 1980 p. 231).

Proponents of the SGHWR believed the prototype could be successfully commercialised and that this would open the possibility of cooperation with Canada (whose CANDU reactors also used heavy water as a moderator). They emphasised safety concerns around the PWR pressure vessel, while acknowledging that the SGHWR's heavy water supplies would have to be imported, at some cost to the balance of payments. The South of Scotland Electricity Board (SSEB) disagreed with the CEGB by backing the SGHWR, which meant there was no united electricity industry voice. A PWR would have accounted for nearly 20 per cent of capacity in the isolated Scottish system, leading to difficulties of security of supply and system flexibility. But there may also have been an assertion of Scottish independence in the SSEB's opinion.

In July 1974 the government decided at last in favour of the British SGHWR. The grounds given were reactor reliability, public acceptability and the boost to British technology (Williams, 1980 pp. 233–234). The HTR was discontinued when the foreign partners in the Winfrith prototype venture decided not to continue their financial support. Two SGHWR stations were approved in early 1975, one for Sizewell for the CEGB and a smaller one for Torness near Edinburgh for the SSEB. But this decision lasted less than a year. By the summer of 1976 electricity demand was running so far below forecasts that the two new stations were postponed (Williams, 1980 p. 241).

By 1976 the PWR was back in contention. In January Westinghouse was reported to be willing to build a PWR for £200 million, compared with their estimate of the £370 million cost of a SGHWR. A CEGB board member in May 1976 compared the SGHWR's development difficulties with those of Concorde (Williams, 1980 p. 241). Meanwhile the concerns over the PWR pressure vessel integrity had been largely laid to rest by a special report by Walter Marshall, the Deputy Head of the UKAEA. The UKAEA chairman, Sir John Hill, and Marshall visited Energy Secretary Tony Benn on 3 June 1976 to say that they wanted to cancel the SGHWR: it was expensive, had only a small market and the customer [the CEGB] didn't want it. The PWR was now safe and the UK should concentrate on the fast breeder reactor for the longer term. Benn didn't want the SGHWR but was even more opposed to the US PWR design (Benn, 1989 p. 573). In August Benn told the Science and Technology Select Committee that the SGHWR was being deferred – not cancelled – because of pressure on public spending and technical slippage in developing a commercial SGHWR design. The same committee was told by the Electrical Power Engineers Association, representing 95 per cent of engineers, scientists and managers in the electrical supply industry, that they were not in favour of the SGHWR (Williams, 1980 p. 250).

In the autumn of 1976 Benn began another review of the reactor choices. The National Nuclear Corporation (set up in 1973 as the single nuclear design and construction company, with minority ownership by the UKAEA and the rest by private industry) published its report in July 1977. It concluded that there was no case for the SGHWR, which would take another decade of development, had no foreseeable export prospects and was the most expensive option (including the balance of payments costs of heavy water imports). It further argued that the PWR might be cheaper than the AGR but that lack of UK experience with it might mean a damaging delay for the construction industry. But the AGR had no export prospects. So it recommended choosing the PWR *and* the AGR (Williams, 1980 p. 254).

On 25 January 1978 Benn told the House of Commons that the SGHWR was to be discontinued. This was after £145 million of spending – about £1 billion in 1994 prices (Henney, 1994 p. 132). Instead the CEGB in England and the SSEB in Scotland would each be authorised to build another AGR. But, Benn continued, the government believed that "the United Kingdom's thermal reactor strategy should not be dependent on or exclusively committed to any one reactor system and that in addition to the AGR we must develop the option of adopting the PWR system in the early 1980s" (*The Times*, 1978b) – a truly British compromise.

But the delay had been costly, not only because of the money wasted on developing the SGHWR. Sir Arnold Weinstock, the chairman of GEC, which owned 30 per cent of the National Nuclear Company design and construction company, told *The Times* in June 1978: "Had we gone for the PWR in 1974, we had a comprehensive and detailed plan for collaboration with the French to develop a nuclear industry. . . . That was ruined by the choice of the SGHWR" (*The Times*, 1978a).

The two new AGRs were to be at Torness in Scotland and Heysham (next to the existing AGR under construction) in Lancashire. By the late 1970s it was generally accepted that one of the lessons learned from the AGR programme was the lack of any replicable standard design. Apparently not. In July 1979 the CEGB awarded a design contract for its last AGR, Heysham B, to Parsons Engineering for a 660 MW generating set with six exhausts. For the supposed sister station to Heysham B at Torness, the South of Scotland Electricity board then chose GEC's rival four-exhaust design. Even the last two AGRs were different from each other (Patterson, 1985 p. 54).

The Windscale inquiry 1977

The other development in the mid-1970s that would influence the future nuclear power industry was the building by British Nuclear Fuels Limited (BNFL) of a large spent fuel reprocessing plant and the associated public inquiry.

The origins of BNFL and Britain's role in fuel reprocessing lay in the nature of the Magnox reactors and in the scarcity of fuel. Magnox fuel, with its reactive magnesium oxide container, cannot be stored in dry air for long without a risk of combustion. It can be stored under water for short periods, but the container eventually reacts with the water to produce magnesium hydroxide, possibly leading to failure of the canister. Although this can be controlled by appropriate chemical treatment of the water there is a risk with long term water storage that the dangerous fission products inside are exposed (Hewitt and Collier, 2000 pp. 243–244). So from an early stage it was clear that the spent Magnox fuel had to be reprocessed.

The shortage of uranium also offered an economic case for reclaiming the unused uranium and plutonium from the spent fuel. A very small proportion of the uranium fuel is actually "burned up" in the reactor so that most of the spent fuel is potentially reusable. There is also plutonium, which has military value and was expected until the 1990s to be used as fuel in a fast breeder reactor programme. The uranium and plutonium are mixed up with the volatile and highly radioactive fission products that arise during the burning up of the uranium. Reprocessing is the physical separation of useful uranium and plutonium from the pure waste products that must be stored and eventually disposed of.

The AGR fuel need not be reprocessed because the fuel cans are stable in air. The case for reprocessing was therefore mainly economic. In the mid-1970s, as the AGRs began to come on line and with uranium prices high, this case seemed strong. There was spare capacity in the original military reprocessing plant used for the Magnoxes, using an additional piece of equipment called the head end unit. After a leak was found, the head end unit was shut in 1973, leaving BNFL with fuel piling up and nowhere to reprocess it.

BNFL's answer was to build a new plant, specifically designed for the AGR (and PWR) mixed oxide fuel. BNFL was trying, with government support, to capture a big part of the profitable foreign nuclear fuel reprocessing market (Bolter, 1996 p. 65). Building one large plant for both domestic and foreign use would bring economies of scale and spread the fixed costs to the benefit of the British reactors. This was to become THORP (thermal oxide reprocessing plant), which became the subject of a public inquiry announced by Environment Secretary Peter Shore on 22 December 1996.

The inquiry, chaired by Mr Justice Parker, ran from 14 June 1977 to 4 November 1977. Parker's report recommending that THORP proceed was published on 6 March 1978. Inevitably the conclusion was controversial and was to provide something of a rehearsal for the much longer inquiry into the building of a PWR at Sizewell a decade later. The important thing for the British nuclear power industry was that the decision to build THORP meant that the nuclear fuel must now be reprocessed; and the future cost of nuclear power would now depend heavily on BNFL's costs and on THORP in particular.

Public opinion had already started turning against nuclear power following publication in September 1976 of the Royal Commission on Environmental Pollution's sixth report "Nuclear Power and the Environment", often referred to as the Flowers report, after its chairman, Sir Brian (later Lord) Flowers. Flowers, a previous part-time member of the UKAEA, put the arguments for and against nuclear power "on a basis which thereafter made reasoned criticism of fission energy almost orthodox" (Williams, 1980 p. 279). In particular the report helped to focus doubts about the fast breeder reactor, which used plutonium fuel. The Commission warned of the dangers of a "plutonium economy", namely the risk of terrorism and the problems of long term disposal of nuclear waste. But use of plutonium in breeder reactors was an important justification for reprocessing the AGR spent fuel.

The other major influence on public opinion ahead of the Windscale inquiry came from the US. In March 1977 the Ford Foundation published a study "Nuclear Power Issues and Choices" (Ford Foundation, 1977) which recommended that the US stop reprocessing nuclear fuel because of the risk of nuclear weapons proliferation, the risk of terrorism and because it was barely economic. The report led President Carter to announce on 7 April 1977 the end of federal support for reprocessing and in effect the end of US development of fast breeder reactors. The UK and France nonetheless pressed ahead with reprocessing.

Causes of the AGR mistakes

The reasons for the AGR disaster boil down to: unwarranted optimism about technology; a centralised decision process that stifled free debate; and an understandable but excessive preference for indigenous British designs over superior foreign ones. Lord Hinton told the House of Lords in January 1976 that the public image of nuclear power had deteriorated in the previous decade partly because of an "over-ambitious extrapolation of designs" (Williams, 1980 p. 103).

In an influential article published in 1977, the economist P. D. Henderson suggested some reasons for the British tendency to errors in large scale technology ventures like the AGR and Concorde (Henderson, 1977). Henderson estimated the excess costs of the AGR programme (i.e. the additional cost relative to a hypothetical PWR programme instead) at some £2.1 billion in 1975/1976 prices (compared with £2.3 billion for the Concorde programme) when discounted at the Treasury's test discount rate of 10 per cent. In 2005 money, Henderson's estimate comes to about £12 billion. The figures are sensitive to assumptions but Henderson notes that the sum of all university-based research and development in 1975 was about £200 million; the probable size of the two errors was a waste of national resources equivalent to the cost of all British university research for 12 years (Henderson, 1977 p. 185). We now know that the AGR costs grew even further – at the time of Henderson's article Dungeness B was supposed to be completed in 1978; it didn't produce any power until April 1983.

Henderson saw the problem in the nature of British administrative process, in four respects. First, *decorum* – an excessive formality, impersonality and administrative tidiness which "are so much prized that they are sometimes equated with good administration" (p. 188). Second, *unbalanced incentives* – the relative unimportance of whether a civil servant's advice has been any good. These problems were then compounded by *anonymity* and *secrecy*. The overall effect, Henderson argued, was to undermine personal responsibility.

More generally Henderson argued for greater pluralism in public decision making. He saw the conventional thrust of policy as being precisely in the opposite direction, citing the recent Plowden report for the Department of Energy on the structure of the electricity industry (Plowden, 1976). Lord Plowden, the former central planner and former chairman of the UKAEA, argued it was difficult for the electricity industry as a whole to speak with one voice. Henderson argued that the search for administrative tidiness meant the crowding out of varied and different voices, which might result in fewer such errors as the AGR and Concorde.

Support for this sort of explanation came from Burn, the leading critic of the AGR programme. He contrasted the centralised decision making in the UK with the more diverse range of decision makers in West Germany, Sweden and Japan. In varying degrees in each of these countries the electric utilities (both in the private and public sectors) had some autonomy in their choices and there was nothing resembling the UKAEA–CEGB–government axis of the UK (Burn, 1978 ch.7). Admittedly the French model closely resembled the British one but the French appeared to show more realism in their adoption of the PWR; possibly they had less of an investment in their own technology than the AEA did.

Henderson also suggested but didn't investigate another reason for the AGR failure, which he called a *bipartisan technological chauvinism* – "uncritical acceptance of the idea that indigenous research and development, and indigenous technology developed from it, will necessarily yield substantial benefits to society" (Henderson, 1977 p. 186). This seems a reasonable description of the attitude of MPs and of government ministers throughout the 1960s and 1970s.

Conclusion

As a new Conservative government took office in May 1979, nearly a quarter of a century of British nuclear power had passed. From a position of apparent early leadership Britain had pioneered practical nuclear electricity. The Magnox stations had been costly to build and needed expensive fuel reprocessing but they were reliable and would operate comfortably into the next decade and beyond. But the successor AGRs had been dreadfully expensive, had destroyed any hope of a British export industry and had contributed to growing public disillusion with nuclear power. If nuclear power had any future in the UK after 1979 it was only going to be with the world industry standard Pressurised Water Reactor.

4   The first privatisation attempt (1979–1989)

Introduction

It was the attempted privatisation of Britain's nuclear power stations in the late 1980s which revealed at last their atrocious economics. The stations couldn't be sold because of concerns over the unquantified liabilities and their high operating costs. But by the time the stations were withdrawn from the privatisation, the generating industry in England and Wales had been restructured into a duopoly that would inhibit competition for nearly a decade. This duopoly led to power prices being higher than they would have been under competition, which meant that nuclear power, reconstituted as British Energy plc in 1996, could at last be privatised. But the rapid unwinding of the duopoly in the late 1990s brought about a power price collapse that led to British Energy's financial crisis in 2002. The roots of the company's crisis therefore lay in the failure of the original attempt in 1989 to privatise nuclear power, which is the subject of this chapter.

Political support for the PWR

The election of the Conservative government under Margaret Thatcher in May 1979 influenced the path of nuclear power in three ways. First, the Conservatives instinctively supported nuclear power as an insurance policy against the political power of the coal miners. As former Energy Secretary Nigel Lawson put it, nuclear was seen "as the means of emancipation from Arthur Scargill [President of the National Union of Mineworkers]" (Lawson, 1992 p. 166). Second, the government was determined to bring more market forces into energy policy. And third, later in the Thatcher period the government would decide to privatise the utilities, although this wasn't yet policy in 1979.

Margaret Thatcher personally supported nuclear power, not only because of its value against the coal miners but because as a scientist she admired the technology. She later came to value nuclear power's contribution to avoiding carbon dioxide emissions. So long as nuclear power was economically competitive with other fuels then it would not be threatened by market liberalisation. The government at first seemed to believe there was no conflict. Energy Secretary

David Howell told the House of Commons in December 1979 that "[nuclear power] is a cheaper form of electricity generation than any known to man" (Helm, 2003 p. 89).

It was widely assumed too that fossil fuel prices would remain high in the 1980s after the second oil price shock in 1979 following the Iranian Revolution. So when Howell announced a policy of building ten PWRs amounting to 15GW of capacity, it seemed to combine economic and political logic.

But change was in the air. The early 1980s recession, which hit manufacturing very badly, led to a fall in electricity consumption of 19 per cent from 1979 to 1982. In Scotland the SSEB had a staggering 73 per cent excess capacity. In 1981 the House of Commons Energy Select Committee recognised that there was a strong economic case for cancelling the two new AGRs at Heysham and Torness. Construction costs had risen 25 per cent in real terms in just one year, owing to tougher safety requirements and tight markets for materials (House of Commons, 1981).

As the pressure for public spending cuts grew, the government started to scale back the PWR programme. Under Secretary of State John Moore told MPs in February 1982 that the government no longer projected a 15GW ten year programme (Helm, 2003 p. 101). But the political case for nuclear power remained. The new Energy Secretary in September 1981 was Nigel Lawson, one of the core Thatcher radicals. Lawson had been appointed to replace David Howell after the government had been forced to cave in to a threatened miners' strike over pit closures in February 1981. Lawson wanted to introduce market forces into energy policy and believed that the CEGB's optimistic demand forecasts were symptomatic of a futile government policy of attempting to plan the future. Instead he wanted liberalisation, to get the price of energy set by the market (Helm, 2003 ch.3). At first Lawson saw no conflict between his liberalisation strategy and nuclear power, though his support for nuclear was largely political. "The PWR was vital to demonstrate to the NUM that coal was not fundamental to the economy any longer", he later wrote; "The need for 'diversification' of energy sources, the argument I used to justify the PWR, was code for freedom from NUM blackmail" (Lawson, 1992 p. 168).

When the term of the previous CEGB chairman Glyn England ran out, Lawson took the opportunity to find a more suitable leader for the electricity industry. He needed someone to keep the power stations running in a coal strike and to cooperate with the government in planning for such a strike. He chose for this role Walter Marshall. Marshall was eminently qualified technically and, of equal importance, he had been previously sacked from his position as chief scientific advisor to the government by the Labour Energy Secretary Tony Benn. Benn hadn't liked Marshall, whom he had described in his diaries as "conceited" and "self-satisfied and pompous". Benn also believed Marshall was the head of a nuclear lobby that was intent on pushing the American PWR design on the UK (Benn, 1989 pp. 570, 620, 625; 1990 pp. 100, 140). At least this last part was apparently accurate. Lawson concluded from this history that Marshall would be reliable in the fight against Scargill and the miners. Lawson knew also that

Marshall was popular with Margaret Thatcher, who shared his enthusiasm for nuclear power (Lawson, 1992 p. 154).

Lawson remained somewhat innocent about nuclear economics. When told by his staff that the Dungeness B AGR would be on stream in six months he believed them, not knowing that this was something of a standing joke among civil servants. When he told Margaret Thatcher this news she, having heard it before, laughed and bet him £10 that it wouldn't. Lawson took the bet and lost (Lawson, 1992 p. 167).

Sizewell B

Marshall's immediate task as head of the CEGB was to get the first PWR built in Britain, at Sizewell in Suffolk, next to the Magnox station. As Sizewell B would be the first PWR in the UK there had to be a planning inquiry. The terms were vague, partly because the government wanted the inquiry to examine the case for a switch to PWRs in general for future British nuclear policy (Helm, 2003 p. 102). The Sizewell Inquiry began on 11 January 1983 and lasted till March 1985. At a cost of over £25 million and at more than 3,000 pages, the inquiry set records.

The CEGB case was put by John Baker, who later became the chief executive of privatised generator National Power. Whatever doubts about nuclear economics Baker later came to have in the private sector, he enthusiastically put the case for the public sector to build a British PWR. As Helm (2003 p. 103) put it, the CEGB's "role was not to present balanced evidence, but rather to gather all the arguments in favour and rubbish the opposition." The first justification the CEGB put forward was on the grounds of increasing fossil fuel prices. But the MMC inquiry of 1981 had severely criticised the CEGB's forecasting methods and further damaging testimony came from Gordon McKerron of Sussex University (McKerron, 1984). This part of the CEGB's argument was discredited and the inspector, Sir Frank Layfield QC, a leading planning barrister, noted in his report that the Board's argument in this area "fell short of what I could reasonably expect" (quoted in Henney, 1994 p. 135). The CEGB then had to argue that there was a need for new capacity and that a PWR would be the cheapest way to meet it. Alex Henney, a vocal critic of the PWR, lists the various ways in which the inquiry failed to get at the real cost comparison with coal and sums up the process as, "the inquiry was not economics – it was politics" (Henney, 1994 p. 137).

Layfield's report was delivered to the government on 5 December 1987. Unsurprisingly, given her enthusiasm for nuclear power, Margaret Thatcher did nothing to block the report's conclusion that "Sizewell B is likely to be the least cost choice for new generating plant" (Department of Energy, 1987). Remarkably, the report only considered the case of coal; the dominant source of new generation in the 1990s, gas-fired stations, were ignored because the CEGB saw no prospect for gas generation.

By the time it was published, oil prices had fallen sharply but its recommendation that Sizewell B go ahead was accepted by the latest Energy Secretary, Peter Walker, an enthusiast for PWRs (Walker, 1991 p. 117).

The Nuclear Installations Inspectorate (NII) had been working in parallel with the inquiry to prepare licensing, which was finalised in 1987. The first concrete was poured at Sizewell B in July 1988, about ten years after the first decision in principle to build a PWR in Britain. It was intended to be the first of four identical plants, the others to be at Hinckley Point, Sizewell (station "C") and Wylfa in Anglesey (to replace the Magnox there). None of these other plants was built.

Nuclear and the miners' strike

Walter Marshall's other key job was to help beat the miners. The Conservative government's defeat of the long and bitter coal strike of 1984–1985 boiled down to the ability to keep electricity supplies running. Marshall, having been picked as chairman of the CEGB in part for his cooperation in this expected task, did not disappoint, although the CEGB would probably have felt responsible to keep the lights on in any case (Ledger and Sallis, 1995 pp. 102–103). Nuclear power played a relatively small part but still gained additional credibility with a government that was in most other respects dismantling the conventional wisdom of post-war energy policy (Helm, 2003 pp. 44–66).

The origins of the strike lay in the sharp fall in coal demand because of the early 1980s recession. With the NCB losing money, the chairman, Derek Ezra told the NUM leaders in February 1981 that some 20–50 pits were at risk, with the loss of around 30,000 jobs. The union threatened strike action and the government, realising that it was ill-prepared to win a strike in the middle of winter, withdrew the threatened cuts on 18 February 1981. An angry Margaret Thatcher decided that the government must prepare to win the next battle, whenever it came. A major coal stocking programme began in June 1981 (Powell, 1993 p. 217).

In September 1983 the NUM called an overtime ban from 31 October after the NCB rejected a call for a substantial wage increase. About the same time the new head of the NCB, Ian MacGregor began work on plans to accelerate the existing gradual run down of the industry, with cuts of 44,000 jobs in the next two years, albeit with generous redundancy compensation. The combination of pit closures and disruption arising from the overtime ban worsened industrial relations, leading to strikes first in Yorkshire then in Scotland in March 1984. Miners in Kent, Lancashire and Wales then either joined the strike or had their collieries shut by picketing during the next two months (Parker, 2000 pp. 37–40).

But the strike took place on very unfavourable terms for the miners: coal stocks were exceptionally high (partly because of their earlier success in preventing pit closures; demand had fallen sharply because of the 1980–1982 recession; and the strike began in spring, when electricity demand was falling and would not reach its seasonal peak for nine or ten months. There were other reasons why the strike failed, including the decision of the Nottinghamshire miners to keep working, the lack of broader trade union support and the tougher labour laws passed by the Thatcher government in the previous few years. But the touchstone was whether the government could avoid the three day week of Edward Heath in 1974, when power supplies were widely cut. The answer was yes. Walter Marshall and his team managed to keep power available by switching to oil (using the mostly idle oil fired capacity built during the late 1960s), avoiding summer maintenance outages at the nuclear stations and running down coal stocks.

The switch to oil saved the equivalent of 38m tonnes of coal, at an extra cost of about £2 billion (Ledger and Sallis, 1995 p. 177). The industry began the strike with 8,000 MW of oil burning capacity available but by the winter demand peak of January 1985 had raised this to 17,600 MW. Nuclear's contribution was much smaller, saving the equivalent of 2.5m tonnes of coal, but that margin helped to keep the lights on (Ledger and Sallis, 1995 p. 230). The nuclear power stations were operated for the maximum two years allowed between statutory safety inspections, instead of the typical 18–20 months. They generated annual output of 36.9 TWh, up from 31.3 TWh the previous year.

Nuclear had proven its value against coal, reinforcing Margaret Thatcher's enthusiasm for it. Ironically, the miners' power having been broken, the insurance value of nuclear now declined. But as the idea of privatising electricity grew during the later 1980s, nobody wanted to challenge the Prime Minister on the question of nuclear power, even though it would nearly wreck the whole privatisation. Walter Marshall received a peerage for his work in keeping the lights on. Having done so much to support the government's goals so far, he was to find himself at the end of the decade in direct opposition to them.

The decision to privatise electricity

In 1988, on the brink of privatisation of the electricity industry, the CEGB and SSEB had 11 nuclear power stations. There was a fleet of nine Magnox stations which were sturdy, reliable but expensive. There were two completed AGRs, one of which had performed quite well (Hunterston B) and one of which was still far from proven (Hinckley Point B). There were five other AGRs at various states of construction and a building site that would become the UK's first (and, as of 2007, only) PWR.

Margaret Thatcher's Conservative government came to power in 1979 with the intention of privatising only the state enterprises, companies like British Airways and British Steel that operated in competitive markets and for which the argument for public ownership was, at best, strategic. The political benefits of privatising monopoly utilities became apparent in 1985 with the successful privatisation of British Telecom. The Conservative manifesto for the 1987 general election included a promise to privatise the electricity industry, the largest in the public portfolio.

Cecil Parkinson, having rejoined the Cabinet after the Conservatives' 1987 election victory, was appointed by Margaret Thatcher as Secretary of State for

Energy. Astute, hugely loyal to the Prime Minister and a political realist, Parkinson was the right person to push through the most difficult privatisation yet, though he almost certainly underestimated just how problematic it would be. The industry was not only very large (£37 billion of assets and 240,000 people) but privatisation was opposed by the generally quiescent but potentially very powerful industry unions and by a large segment of the industry management. There were also some formidable technical issues to resolve around using the National Grid for competitive power markets, without jeopardising security of supply.

Having twice privatised two monopoly industries largely intact (British Telecom in 1985 and British Gas in 1986), the government this time wanted to change the structure of the industry in order to increase competition. In England and Wales, the industry consisted of two components: 12 regional electricity companies (RECs) that operated the local distribution monopoly; and a giant monolith called the Central Electricity Generating Board (CEGB) which owned all the power stations plus the national grid that transported power to the RECs. In Scotland the industry was organised into two vertically integrated monopolies, each of which owned generation and distribution, one covering the lowland urban region and the other the Highlands. These two companies were privatised largely intact in 1991. The RECs could be privatised as they were, subject only to having a new regulator to oversee them (OFFER – the Office of Electricity Regulation). The CEGB was more problematic.

Electricity generation is not what economists call a natural monopoly, meaning it lacked the special characteristics of water and electricity distribution activities which can only efficiently be provided by one firm. While it makes economic sense to have a single electricity wire coming into your house, there is no reason why the power the wire carries can't come from a number of competing generators. Such competition was rare but not unknown in other countries. So there was a good competition policy case for breaking up the generation part of the CEGB into five or six competing companies (Parkinson, 1992 p. 265). There were two formidable obstacles to this sound economic policy. The first was the CEGB itself, under Lord Marshall. The second was the existence of the nuclear power stations, with their enormous but poorly quantified liabilities.

Taking on the CEGB

The CEGB was probably the most powerful of several non-governmental public sector entities that once loomed large in the British political system. With its scale (47,000 employees), financial strength and the prestige that accompanied its undoubted engineering excellence, the CEGB's leaders saw themselves as having a duty to the public interest. This interest usually entailed building ever more power stations, with the CEGB confident in the willingness of a captive monopoly customer to pay for them. A former senior manager at the CEGB told this author that the key functions of the Board were: i) to prop up the coal industry; ii) to support the British electrical engineering industry; iii) to support the rail industry; and iv) to provide cheap power to ICI (the leading British manufacturing company in the 1970s and 1980s). All of these worthy goals were accomplished by forcing the consequently expensive electricity down the wires of a captive customer base (private interview February 2006).

The CEGB Chairman, Lord Walter Marshall of Goring, was a brilliant physicist of forceful personality who inspired devotion bordering on hero worship in his employees (private interview with Ed Wallis, former Director of Operations, CEGB, 2 November 2005). Marshall had at the age of only 28 been made division head of theoretical physics at the Atomic Energy Authority (AEA) laboratory at Harwell, rising to be overall director of Harwell in 1968. As Deputy Director of the AEA in the 1970s he also became part-time Chief Scientific Advisor to the government. He was abruptly fired by Labour Energy Secretary Tony Benn from this role in 1977 for being too enthusiastic about nuclear power. With his curiously hard to define accent, which Marshall attributed to having been taught by mid-European émigré mathematicians at Birmingham University, on top of his native Welsh, he was a highly articulate enthusiast for science. Lawson described him as opinionated, articulate, with a caustic wit, large and shambling (Lawson, 1992 p. 154). Benn's view was that he was "a self-satisfied and pompous man with poor political judgement" (Benn, 1990 p. 100).

The government had ducked the issue of breaking up a national monopoly when it privatised British Gas intact (a company led by another dominant leader in the form of Sir Dennis Rooke). This failure to act had led the company into a decade of costly and acrimonious wrangling with the regulator, Ofgas. The view in Whitehall was that the government had given in to Denis Rooke over keeping British Gas intact and there was some apprehension as to whether Lord Marshall would pull off a similar victory in electricity. But ministers were prepared for more of a fight this time, since the idea of a single privatised generation company was absurd. Parkinson was clear that he would enforce competition on electricity, even if it meant a fight with Marshall.

He told the Conservative Party conference in Blackpool that service to the customer would be the top priority in privatisation, a pledge that it would be hard to argue was kept. Parkinson records in his memoirs how Marshall offered him a series of personal seminars on the workings of the electricity industry and that he developed a great liking and respect for Marshall. But the underlying message was, leave the CEGB alone (Parkinson, 1992 p. 263). Marshall let it be known that he and the whole board would resign if any attempt were made to break up the CEGB (Parkinson, 1992 p. 269). Parkinson successfully called their bluff. But the degree of structural change forced on the CEGB turned out to be rather less than they had feared. For the intransigence of the CEGB management was not the only obstacle to breaking up the generation industry.

The greater obstacle was the problem of what do with the nuclear power stations. Cecil Parkinson, so dedicated to the principle of competition in electricity, was also trying to keep alive Margaret Thatcher's increasingly lone support for nuclear power. These two goals, competition and the preservation of nuclear power, were in conflict and the nuclear policy won.

Although operationally there was no reason in principle why the nuclear power stations couldn't be parcelled out into two or more separate, competing companies, there was a serious financial obstacle. All of the stations faced future liabilities in the form of decommissioning and fuel reprocessing costs. These costs ran into billions of pounds. The CEGB, supported by the government's financial advisers, Rothschilds, argued it was essential to create a large enough generation company that the nuclear costs would be manageable. It was therefore agreed that the CEGB's generation assets would be split into just two companies, known initially as "Big G" and "Little G", with the latter taking just 30 per cent of the total. The enormous "Big G", later renamed National Power, would be obviously the dominant player in the market but would, it was hoped, be strong enough to handle the nuclear liabilities.

The compromise plan was outlined in a short White Paper in February 1988. Lord Marshall, while still annoyed that the CEGB was to be restructured at all, was happy enough with a proposal that left him Chairman of Big G and made no secret of his contempt for Little G, which later became PowerGen. Ed Wallis, Director of Operations at the CEGB who became the chief executive of PowerGen, recalls Marshall calling a meeting of the future board of Big G and joking that the Little G team would have their meeting in a telephone box. Marshall also indicated that he expected National Power to drive PowerGen out of business, thereby restoring the monopoly position of the old CEGB (private interview 2 November 2005). The privatisation of nuclear power would evidently be incompatible with competition.

The first nuclear retreat

But even this severely compromised plan was not enough to solve the nuclear problem. Once National Power had been constituted as a separate entity within the CEGB and the countdown to privatisation had begun, the new company's board began to take fright at the liabilities. The problem was that nobody really knew with any accuracy just what they were. Nowhere in the world had a nuclear power station been fully decommissioned, mainly because it would take decades to do. The provisions that the CEGB had made each year for decommissioning were therefore somewhat rough and ready.

But private shareholders needed to know accurately their liability and the risks of it rising in a way that might wipe out their equity in the company. As the privatisation bill neared its late parliamentary stages, Parkinson was advised that the CEGB's auditors could only offer an estimate of the nuclear liabilities between £8 billion and £13 billion. The risk was therefore that if National Power could be privatised at all, it would only be on a very pessimistic view of the liabilities that would amount to a severe under-pricing of the company.

Nigel Lawson, now Chancellor of the Exchequer, had heard from his Treasury civil servants that the decommissioning costs might now be £15 billion, compared with the CEGB's figure of £3.7 billion just a year before. The government was prepared only to provide a subsidy of £2.5 billion. Lawson argued with Parkinson that he should withdraw the Magnoxes from the sale. These older reactors were due to close soon and therefore accounted for the bulk of the decommissioning costs. Their liabilities would give the privatised company a negative net worth, not to mention the huge uncertainty around the numbers. Parkinson at first disagreed because he feared that Margaret Thatcher wouldn't like it but eventually gave in (Lawson, 1992 p. 169).

On Monday 24 July 1989 Parkinson told the House of Commons that the Magnox reactors would have to be withdrawn from the privatisation. But the more modern AGRs were to be retained in the sale. Parkinson felt there was no reason why these nuclear stations could not have been successfully privatised (Parkinson, 1992 p. 279). National Power publicly reaffirmed its intention to build three more PWRs like the one under construction at Sizewell. PowerGen was supporting a new, smaller Anglo-US PWR type called the Safe Integral Reactor (SIR), backed by Rolls-Royce, the Atomic Energy Authority and some of the regional electricity companies. There was a general sense that the Magnoxes had been the only problem with privatisation of nuclear power and that their withdrawal from the privatisation had solved it.

The second retreat and the new duopoly

Soon after his speech to Parliament on the Magnox withdrawal, Cecil Parkinson was moved to the post of Transport Secretary. His replacement as Energy Secretary, John Wakeham, quickly grasped the dilemma of electricity privatisation: competition versus nuclear privatisation. As the autumn of 1989 drew on, investors began to scrutinise the erratic operating record of the AGR power stations. There was still uncertainty over AGR liabilities too, but the numbers were much more manageable because the stations were at least a decade or more from closure. But equally problematic was the fact that these expensive stations couldn't demonstrate a satisfactory operating record. National Power's management did nothing to discourage the City from lobbying the government to reopen the nuclear question.

The company was being advised that the banks wanted full government guarantees of the debt as well as assurances that all significant risks would either be passed through to consumers or carried by government itself. These demands were not politically realistic and Lord Wakeham realised that the nuclear assets would make the privatisation impossible. At the same time the already questionable costs of building new PWRs were becoming utterly uncompetitive when a higher, private sector rate of return was applied to them. Nuclear plants, being very capital intensive, are especially sensitive to the required rate of return on that capital. It was increasingly obvious that new PWRs would simply not make economic sense.

On 8 November 1989 Margaret Thatcher made a speech at the United Nations in New York on the part that nuclear power could play in mitigating global warming (*The Times*, 1989). The following day in London, Lord Wakeham made a statement to Parliament that finally brought the nuclear power industry down to earth. He withdrew all the remaining nuclear power stations from the electricity privatisation, including the new PWR under construction at Sizewell. He also suspended all National Power's plans for additional PWRs, pending a nuclear review in 1994. Margaret Thatcher had wanted to continue with the plan to build three more PWRs but Wakeham and the Chancellor of the Exchequer Nigel Lawson refused to support her (Henney, 1994 p. 143). Wakeham and the Treasury would have preferred to have stopped construction even of Sizewell B, believing that it would have been cheaper than continuing, but this would have been too much of a political embarrassment for Margaret Thatcher. The faltering forward march of nuclear power in the UK was halted.

Wakeham's decision to pull the remaining nuclear power stations out of the privatisation was based on a letter from John Baker, the managing director of the CEGB and chief executive of the new National Power. Dated 11 October the letter apparently laid out the CEGB's best estimates of the future costs of the AGRs and of the proposed new PWRs. The base figure for the new PWRs given to the Hinckley Point inquiry was 2.24p/kWh. But this assumed the CEGB's existing 5 per cent real return on capital. As had been explained to the Hinckley Inquiry, the CEGB would need to raise its required return to 8 per cent and a privatised National Power would require at least 10 per cent. That would raise costs from 2.24p/kWh to 3.8p/kWh. Adding two years of inflation took the figure to 4.2p/kWh. Then the period of depreciating the capital cost would have to be cut to 20 years, from 40 years, which took the figure to 4.7p/kWh. Reallocating the nuclear-specific overheads of the CEGB would push the costs up by a further 0.7p to 5.4p. A new appraisal of decommissioning costs, plus a shift to fixed price from cost-plus contracts for fuel services from BNFL would add a further 0.2p, for a running total of 5.6p. Finally, contingencies for output not reaching its design target and for cost over-runs in construction would put the grand total up to 6.25p/kWh. By comparison a modern coal station would cost 3.7p/kWh. These figures were later confirmed by Lord Marshall (Marshall, 1989).

The final financial statements of the CEGB, released in November 1989, made it clear why nuclear couldn't be sold. Annual profits had been some £600 million below target because of extra provisions made for nuclear costs. The expected cost of decommissioning the Magnoxes had doubled over the year to £600 million each. The cost of paying BNFL for reprocessing the spent fuel from the Magnoxes had also doubled to over £6 billion. Clearly nuclear costs were unreliable and private shareholders were right to have rejected them.

A new corporate entity was carved out of National Power to own and run the England and Wales nuclear power stations, Nuclear Electric plc. Its first set of accounts showed the current cost value of the nuclear power stations (net of long term provisions) as having fallen from £6.3 billion in March 1988 to £0.4 billion at the end of March 1989 and then *minus* £1.6 billion on the first of April 1989 (Nuclear Electric, 1989). In Scotland the two AGRs were put into a new company called Scottish Nuclear Limited.

After signing the last set of accounts, Lord Marshall resigned from the CEGB and from the new National Power board. He was, in effect, fired. The government saw the huge increase in nuclear liabilities as evidence on the CEGB's part either of incompetence or of deception (private interviews with former CEGB management). Either way Marshall had to go. His life's work seemed to have been wasted. Never really interested in fossil fuel generation, Marshall's great quest over the 1980s had been for a major new programme of PWR power stations in Britain. Only Sizewell B was now going to be built.

Always sceptical that nuclear power could be privatised, Marshall had been proven right – but at the price of creating a monstrous new electricity generation duopoly. It was too late to restructure the privatisation if it was to be completed in the current parliament, which would end in 1992 at the latest. National Power and PowerGen, the two new generation companies, dominated the England and Wales power market. Even though the nuclear stations accounted for some 15 per cent of market share, none of them set the marginal price of electricity because they all ran continuously (i.e. at base load). All of the future price setting power lay with just two companies which divided generation in a roughly 60/40 split between them, a structure which nobody can possibly have believed would lead to competition.

This legacy of the first, failed attempt to privatise nuclear power would ultimately be enormously important for the successfully privatised company British Energy more than a decade later. For the new electricity regulator saw it as his key goal to find a way to introduce competition to the power market to bring prices down to customers, for whose benefit the whole privatisation had supposedly been carried out. He was to be successful but only after several years of being frustrated by the coal lobby, and the intransigence of the power companies themselves. When competition finally did come, at the turn of the century, it came with a speed and a vigour that ruined several power companies, including British Energy.

Conclusion

Henney, in his authoritative analysis of the privatisation of the electricity industry, lists several ways in which the AEA, the CEGB and the government disguised the true costs of nuclear power: ignoring research and development costs (about £1.5 billion for the AGR, £0.5 billion for the PWR in 1994 prices); understating operations and maintenance costs by assuming PWR costs would be similar to those of coal, even though in the US they were double that of coal; ignoring post-operational capital spending needed to keep the nuclear plant running, which was some 0.15p/kWh in the US; overstating the cost of competing fuels, by assuming ever increasing coal costs, against the long term international trend (until the early 2000s); ignoring the cost of corporate overheads which are far higher for nuclear than coal; understating the discount rate, against Treasury views; understating fuel reprocessing costs – witness the increase in the CEGB's annual long term provision from £117 million in 1983/1984 to £1,049 million in 1988/1989; understating decommissioning costs, for which the CEGB made no provision at all until 1976; using historic cost accounting which flattered the capital intensive nuclear stations during years of high inflation (Henney, 1994 p. 135).

Even without accepting every one of Henney's points, the impression remains of an organisation that had decided on the answer – nuclear power – and then worked backwards to the questions. The attempted privatisation of Britain's nuclear power stations brought into the light for the first time the enormous economic cost of the public sector nuclear programme. The reputation of nuclear seemed irretrievably damaged. Certainly nobody expected that putting the nuclear stations into separate companies would bring about a dramatic improvement in their performance that would resurrect the possibility of private ownership once again. But that is what happened.

Part II

A focused industry (1990–1995)

5 Humiliation and transformation (1990–1994)

Introduction

In 1990 the reputation of nuclear power in Britain was at an all time low. The existing nuclear power stations had been publicly exposed as uneconomic. The government had given every indication that it wanted no more after Sizewell B was completed. In the two companies hurriedly created after the failed privatisation, the employees were demoralised. As the rest of the electricity industry entered the private sector world of commercial freedom and competition, Scottish Nuclear and Nuclear Electric faced an uncertain future.

But out of this uncertainty and despair, two highly effective companies emerged. Against all expectations, they transformed the performance and profitability of the British nuclear power stations and finally got to grips with the AGR technology. Largely friendless at the beginning of the 1990s, the two nuclear companies built a grudging respect among their customers, competitors and eventually the government. The performance improvements were so successful that by 1994 it was a realistic possibility that nuclear power might be privatised, without any state financial support. This chapter explains what the companies achieved and how they did it.

Aftermath of the failed privatisation

Several senior employees of what became Nuclear Electric later described the day that the AGRs were pulled from privatisation as the worst of their lives. They had spent months reconciling themselves to the advantages of the private sector; after some initial doubts most had come to see privatisation as an opportunity. Now they were being held back in the public sector. Worse was the sense of public humiliation. Workers on the nuclear side of the CEGB had tended to think of themselves as the elite. Yet now they were being told that nuclear was an embarrassment; that it couldn't be sold because it was expensive and had unquantifiable liabilities; and that the now-defunct CEGB had been less than straight with the public about the true costs of nuclear power. They had been told for over a year that the private sector was the arbiter of efficiency, value and productivity. And the private sector had apparently decided that it didn't want nuclear power (private interviews).

Two new organisations were created. In England and Wales, Nuclear Electric (NE) was created from the "company within a company" that was to have been National Power Nuclear. It had five AGRs and seven Magnox stations, plus the nuclear research and development overhead from the CEGB. In Scotland, Scottish Nuclear Limited (SNL) had been carved out of Scottish Power, to run the two AGR stations at Hunterston and Torness. SNL also had the job of managing the decommissioning of the recently closed Magnox station at Hunterston.

Neither company had any proper marching orders. Certainly nobody was thinking about future privatisation. Managers felt that the government just wanted them to keep quiet, avoid further political embarrassment and lose as little money as possible. Civil servants gave the impression that they hoped the nuclear industry would just die (private interviews).

Yet in the next five years, both companies were to achieve a dramatic improvement in costs, productivity and above all in the operating performance of the AGRs. It is natural to assume that these improvements, which took place in the public sector, were spurred by the incentive of privatisation, but this is not so, at least in the years from 1990 to 1992. Privatisation was not an explicit goal of NE for at least the first two years of its life. Even in 1993 and 1994, the government discouraged the idea that NE would be privatised. SNL's team didn't even want to be sold. By the time privatisation began to look feasible, in 1995, both companies had made their greatest improvements.

So where did the inspiration for this management transformation come from? Both companies were lucky to have talented staff who found exceptional leadership. John Collier in England and Wales, and James Hann in Scotland, picked up the demoralised workforces they found and breathed new self confidence and self belief into them, with remarkable results.

Nuclear Electric

Nuclear Electric had the greater challenge because it had inherited a lot more power stations (five AGRs and seven Magnoxes, plus one being decommissioned), including the notoriously problematic Dungeness B, and the whole CEGB nuclear bureaucracy. The CEGB had been a regional organisation with no centralised accounting for nuclear resources. When National Power Nuclear (NPN) was first created in 1988 as the designated owner and operator of the nuclear stations within National Power, senior managers were alarmed at just how many nuclear related staff there seemed to be (private interview). There were three separate CEGB research laboratories at Leatherhead, Marchwood and Berkeley. There was a generation design and construction division, most of which was concerned with nuclear stations. And there were five regional laboratories. NPN would have some 3,000 people in central technology, i.e. not running power stations.

Even before the stations were pulled out of privatisation, work had begun on commercialisation. A team under Ray Hall, who was to become NE's future executive board member for production, started the process of turning power stations into profit centres and driving down costs. Members of this team were shocked at the uncommercial attitude of many staff. The CEGB was evidently full of highly qualified people who were interested in complex problems. But they mostly had no concept of customers or of cashflow (private interviews).

Hall's team introduced the idea of an internal supply chain, in which the company's resources were dedicated to helping the power stations. The status of power station managers (who previously could authorise payments only up to £5,000) rose greatly and that of the researchers and problem solvers correspondingly fell. Many staff found this fall in status hard to accept.

But the emphasis on profit centres became clearer once NE became a stand-alone company. The staff were dismayed when they heard that all nuclear power stations were to be pulled out of the privatisation. The main impetus behind CEGB policy for more than a decade had been the promise of nuclear power and many staff felt as if years of effort had been wasted.

Turning this disillusioned workforce into a motivated, cohesive company would take great leadership. Luckily this was found in the form of John Collier, who was appointed chairman of NE. Collier was a nuclear man through and through, a protégé of Walter Marshall. Like Marshall, he was both physically very large, at six feet five inches, and academically distinguished. But unlike Marshall, he was an engineer rather than a physicist and had a down to earth and gentle, even humble manner.

Collier had left St. Paul's School, Hammersmith, with an engineering scholarship – much to the disapproval of his headmaster – to go to the atomic research centre at Harwell. He then got an engineering scholarship to University College, London, where he received a first-class degree in chemical engineering, later joining the UKAEA as director of technical studies. In 1983 Marshall had recruited him to be the director general of the general development and construction division of the CEGB. He apparently told his team at his first meeting that "the biggest thing I have ever built is a sandcastle" (*The Times*, 1995c).

John Wakeham summoned Collier in November 1989 and told him to set up a new, state-owned nuclear power company, Nuclear Electric. Collier's "warmth and sense of humility" helped him build a strong team during the 22 weeks he had before NE was officially born (*Independent*, 1995b). Collier set out six goals for NE to reach by 1994: i) increased generation output; ii) increased turnover; iii) progressive reduction in the nuclear levy on fossil fuels; iv) increased profits; v) completion of the new PWR under construction at Sizewell B to current cost estimates; and vi) resolving the uncertainty over waste management and decommissioning costs (Nuclear Electric, 1991).

There was no talk of future privatisation at this stage. The main goal was to rescue the reputation of nuclear power and make the case for new nuclear stations, in effect to resurrect the plan for three more PWRs that had been cancelled by John Wakeham. The senior management of NE had committed much of their careers to the British nuclear power industry and were keen to show that it hadn't all been pointless. But the immediate challenge was to turn NE into a commercial company (private interviews).

The first year of NE's life was largely about developing the pre-privatisation work done on profit centres and efficiency. Collier provided the inspiration and his team provided the execution. A key member of the team was accountant Mike Kirwan, who had been seconded from Coopers and Lybrand Deloitte to advise on setting up National Power Nuclear. He had then joined NNN in a permanent capacity as Finance Director. Kirwan introduced the finance and planning structures that would provide the skeleton on which the operational performance improvement could be carried. With his distinctive reddish, closely trimmed beard, Kirwan was affable and charming. But he had a determined and stubborn side that would become evident during the privatisation of British Energy several years later. Another former member of the early NE management team told this author that Kirwan was "an excellent hire for us, I don't know what we would have done without him" (private interview).

Collier and Kirwan set the framework for NE's efficiency gains but others drove the operational transformation. During 1990–1991 there was relatively little focus on cost cutting, although a generous severance programme had been set up. The company had 14,164 staff on average in 1990, falling to 13,542 in 1991. This was still far too many for profitability. Collier had targeted improved profitability and his corporate planning team had constructed a scenario – not yet a proper plan – in which the company could be genuinely in the black by 1996.

"Genuinely" because NE was receiving income of some £1.2 billion from the so-called Fossil Fuel Levy, a charge on electricity customers the great bulk of which went to NE, to pay for the nuclear liabilities inherited from pre-privatisation operations. Unofficially but universally it was known simply as the "nuclear levy" and was slightly more than NE's ordinary income from selling electricity into the market. The levy had been set up as part of the original privatisation planning to provide an income to National Power, to compensate it for taking on the nuclear liabilities of the Magnox stations. Including the levy, NE was technically profitable but without it the company was running a loss of about £1 billion. Collier was clear that the company must plan to do without the levy eventually, anticipating that customers and politicians would seek to end it.

But the emphasis on NE's profitability really took hold when Bob Hawley joined the company in June 1992 as chief executive. Collier had hitherto been both chairman and chief executive and was under pressure to split the role according to the conventional wisdom of good corporate governance. Hawley brought a new, relentless focus on execution, leaving Collier to concentrate on safety, running the board and government relations.

Formerly the managing director of the Newcastle-based engineering group NEI, Hawley was another life time engineer. Having left school at 16 and gone to night school, he was awarded a first-class degree in electrical engineering at Durham University before joining the engineering firm Parsons. Parsons was absorbed first into NEI then into the Rolls Royce group, with Hawley progressing to be head of the NEI subsidiary. A tall, self confident and direct man, Hawley had been brought in to provide private sector expertise and a degree of executive granite that had perhaps been lacking before. John Collier explained with characteristic candour that "I was a research engineer. I had no idea of how to form a company.... Because [Bob's] been in the private sector, he's a little sharper than I am on some things. Really the combination works very well" (*The Times*, 1994a).

Hawley had been a supplier to the CEGB in his Parsons/NEI days and had not been very impressed by his main customer. His assessment of NE when he joined it was that it had "more PhDs per square foot than a university. Ask a question and you'd get a 15 page answer" (*The Times*, 1994a). One of Hawley's new colleagues described him as "a breath of fresh air – well, more like an icy blast; his commercialism shocked some people" (private interview). Hawley brought the goal of genuine profitability forward to 1995. This meant improving profits by about £250 million a year from 1992 onwards.

Hawley's message to employees over the next couple of years was the need to get the company into the best possible financial state ahead of the government's nuclear review in 1994. Collier and Kirwan had set the framework and the goals for NE. But Hawley brought urgency, enthusiasm – and toughness. Staff at NE had been forced in 1990–1992 to adapt to working in a business rather than a public service corporation. Now they would have to learn to make that business profitable. It is not the job of a chief executive to be popular. But Hawley was to win the respect, not only of his employees, but of the government and later of the shareholders in British Energy.

The transformation of NE

The improvement in output at NE during the first half of the 1990s was remarkable; arguably this was the most successful phase in the whole history of British nuclear power. The average load factor (percentage capacity use) in 1990 for the English stations was 47 per cent – a dreadful figure, even allowing for the inclusion of the wretched Dungeness B station's mere 12 per cent result. In the year to March 1996, the last full year before privatisation, the figure was 76 per cent. (For comparison, the two Scottish stations had gone from 57 per cent to 84 per cent). By dragging the AGRs up to an acceptable international operating standard, NE had generated extra output of some 13.8 TWh, a rise of 64 per cent. This was the equivalent of two brand new stations' worth of output. How did this transformation come about?

It always helps if somebody has done it first. Privatisation of the electricity industry was followed by several years of dramatic cost cutting, both in generation and in distribution. The two privatised non-nuclear generators, National Power and PowerGen, cut manning levels at coal power stations by more than a half, and head office staff numbers were pruned repeatedly. This gave an example to Nuclear Electric management but nuclear power stations are very different from coal. And the British nuclear stations were unlike any others in the world so there was no best practice to copy.

But there was a source of inspiration and NE managers found it, thanks to a visit to the US organised by IBM. In 1992 George Jenkins, the director of AGR operations, and Mark Baker, board director for corporate affairs, were invited to join a group of British utility executives to see examples of the best US utility companies. Utilities in the US were not universally well run, not least because the cost-of-service-based regulation tended to discourage efficiency improvements. But the best of US practice was very good indeed. When Jenkins and Baker were taken to one particular company they were "knocked out" by what they found (private interviews). The company was FPL – Florida Power and Light.

FPL is the electric utility serving eastern and southern Florida. The company's top management had been involved in the setting up under President Ronald Reagan of the Malcolm Baldridge National Quality Award. In 1989 FPL became the first ever non-Japanese company to be awarded the Deming Prize for quality, awarded by the Union of Japanese Scientists and Engineers. Japanese working practices had been much scrutinised in the 1980s, as American and British companies tried to compete against what seemed the unstoppable success of the Japanese. FPL was one of the few that appeared to grasp the true principles of quality control and of continuous improvement.

The British utility managers were impressed by what the FPL management told them about quality achievements and the company's productivity record. But what really motivated them was evidence that the line workers in the power stations bought into the quality method, when a fitter's mate gave a convincing presentation of what quality management meant for him. Jenkins and Baker came back to NE enthused by what they had seen and ready to start applying it to their own company. With full support from John Collier, Bob Hawley and Ray Hall, they began to introduce a quality-based, continuous improvement business model to the nuclear power stations. This "quality improvement process" (QIP) was based on the FPL experience and was based on four principles – respect for people, customer satisfaction, management by fact and plan-do-check-act (PDCA). The QIP was led by a quality council chaired by chief executive Bob Hawley (British Energy, 1993).

The flow of information about best practices was also helped by the growing involvement of BE in international nuclear organisations. The first was INPO, the Institute of Nuclear Power Operators, which was set up after the Three Mile Island accident in Pennsylvania in 1979 to drive improvements in nuclear performance. INPO had an international participation advisory committee, which met two or three times a year in Atlanta, to provide a forum for more international information sharing. Although the US had the greatest overall number of nuclear reactors, the best operating results were still typically in Europe. George Jenkins of NE became chairman of the international committee and ensured that NE was fully plugged into the improving experience of nuclear operations.

A second organisation was WANO, the World Organisation of Nuclear Operators, set up after the far more serious Chernobyl disaster in 1986. WANO worked with INPO but was able to achieve greater international cooperation by virtue of not being American. Walter Marshall had become the head of WANO after leaving the CEGB. During the 1990s WANO became an increasingly authoritative source of industry benchmarking. It organised detailed peer-review groups that would visit a nuclear operator and assess it against world best practice. WANO was to become involved with NE's successor British Energy several years later, by which time the British performance was falling well behind world best practice (see Chapter 14).

In a high fixed cost industry like nuclear generation, the key to performance is raising output. The essence of the quality management approach to the AGR's performance was to identify the source of every shortfall in output from the theoretical maximum. At that stage a percentage load factor in the high 80s was regarded as about the best that could be realistically achieved, given the need for refuelling and maintenance shutdowns. In 1991/1992 the average AGR load factor had risen from 47 per cent in 1990 to a still unacceptable 66 per cent. NE harnessed the skills of the employees who worked on the stations and could see how processes could be simplified and shortened. NE used financial incentives, but the essence of the Japanese approach they had imported via the US was to motivate individual staff out of a sense of pride in their work. As Figure 5.1 shows, the AGRs began to operate at increasingly respectable load factors.

The output improvement arose not from a single magic formula but from a process of multiple incremental improvements, with the station teams sharing their lessons with each other. The biggest single problem with the AGR design had been the fuelling process. The AGRs had been designed to refuel at full load, with a consequent saving in lost power compared with the Magnoxes and PWRs that had to shut down to refuel. But the process was complex and involved crucial bits of equipment being buffeted by very hot carbon dioxide gas. Gradually the NE team found ways to improve the movements of the fuel rods in and out of the reactor. Even then the lessons from one station weren't always applicable to the others because no two were exactly alike.

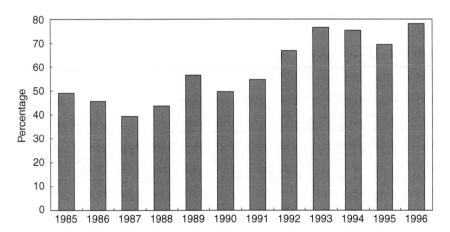

Figure 5.1 AGR load factors, 1985–1996 (source: company accounts, IAEA, author's calculations).

In principle these improvements might have been made under the CEGB but several former NE executives have emphasised to this author that the key to success was focus (private interviews). The CEGB, with its regional structure and huge scale, lacked the incentives to get the AGRs right. NE simply had to get them working properly if it was to become profitable, and the management aim was to incentivise all levels of staff to contribute to greater output, while sharing the results of each success. Most of the increase in output was achieved before there was any serious prospect of privatisation.

Productivity gains could not be at the cost of safety. The nuclear regulator, the Nuclear Installations Inspectorate, would not allow any change in procedure that might jeopardise safety. So it was an important breakthrough when in August 1993 NE was given permission by the NII for its Hartlepool AGR to move to statutory safety shutdowns every three years instead of two. Since a typical safety shutdown took ten weeks and cost around £20 million in lost electricity sales, this was a significant achievement, especially if it could be repeated at the other seven AGRs, as it subsequently was.

Hawley and cost control

The other aspect of improved profitability was cost control. Here it was chief executive Bob Hawley who led the charge. In his first comment in the company newspaper, in June 1992, he insisted: "My job is NOT, repeat NOT, as a hatchet man" (British Energy, 1992). No doubt this smacked to some readers of protesting too much, as one of Hawley's main achievements over the next few years was a sharp fall in costs. When he arrived, the company still had over 13,000 employees and two major overhead centres, which Hawley referred to menacingly in meetings as two head offices. One was the official HQ at Barnwood, near Gloucester; the other was the operational centre at the former CEGB regional HQ in Bristol. On his arrival at NE, Hawley found that the senior management accepted that there was a need for rationalisation and had come up with a plan to build a brand new HQ roughly mid-way between the two. This plan didn't survive Hawley's scrutiny very long and the Bristol office was closed.

Hawley's first speech to a conference of managers on 27 August 1992 was called "The Wolf at the Door", a metaphor for the competitive pressures the company was increasingly facing. Hawley very soon began to impose his vision on the company. He used the company newspaper, the *Nuclear Times*, to tell the workforce in July 1992 that the company would have to be cut from the 12,400 it was on schedule for in 1992 to 9,500 by 1995. He told the *Financial Times* the same month that "This is not a doomed industry. This is a growth industry" (*Financial Times*, 1992). The news that SNL had moved into the black in July 1992 increased the pressure. The *Nuclear Times* was no longer posted to employees' homes from August, saving £35,000 a year. In September Hawley turned up the pressure. Amid rumours that the government nuclear review might be brought forward from 1994, the company now had just one year to show that it could impress ministers. "We are business and business is war" he told readers in

September, who were presumably now reading it at work. "Watch every penny, challenge every overhead, monitor and push people" (British Energy, 1992).

Each month *Nuclear Times* emphasised the cost cutting message. All photo-copiers were to have double sided copying ability. The company's use of chauf-feurs was cut back. Business lunches were made less generous. Plants in the atrium at the Barnwood HQ would now have to be watered by staff, instead of by outside contractors.

The combination of output improvement and cost control worked; NE's oper-ating loss fell from £1.1 billion in 1990/1991 to just £33 million in 1994/1995. And that loss was fully accounted for by the high cost Magnox stations and the start-up losses at the new Sizewell PWR. Taken on their own the AGRs were in the black by March 1995, just as Hawley had wanted.

Scottish Nuclear Limited

SNL was to have been a ring fenced subsidiary of the larger Scottish electricity company, Scottish Power. It would have been relatively small, buying in ser-vices from the rest of the company. Tearing out the nuclear stations meant build-ing a major new company. SNL was born with about 2,000 employees and two major assets. Hunterston B was one of the better performing AGRs, sited in Ayrshire on the west coast. The brand new Torness station near Dunbar in East Lothian on the east coast had started generating in 1988 and was still being fully commissioned in 1990–1991. SNL also had one major liability, the Hunterston A Magnox station that had been closed in March 1990 and would now have to be decommissioned.

The electricity industry in Scotland had always been vertically integrated, that is the two main companies, Scottish Power and Scottish Hydro Electric, each ran generation, transmission and distribution of power. This contrasted with England and Wales, where the CEGB controlled generation and transmis-sion but the twelve area boards (which on privatisation became the regional electricity companies) owned the local distribution and the mass customer base. Scotland's structure arose from the smaller scale of the system, which was built and run quite separately, although it was connected to the English one.

The advantage of a vertically integrated system was that it removed a source of tension and turf fighting that afflicted England and Wales. SNL's managers believed that SNL inherited from Scottish Power a more consensual and friendly culture than that of the CEGB. The smaller scale helped too. SNL had only two operating power stations to Nuclear Electric's 12, which also had the big research teams. SNL's staff had a readiness to get round a table to sort problems out that they saw as lacking in the larger and more fragmented English power system (private interviews).

Even with these advantages, SNL faced a battle to build a successful new organisation, and the appointment of James Hann in 1990 as chairman was a very important reason why it was successful. Hann was new to the nuclear industry. But he showed a commitment to nuclear which underpinned his remotivation of the workforce. "Dynamic and inspirational" (*The Times*, 2004), his message to employees and to the government was that the SNL must demonstrate that nuclear power could be both safe and economic. He identified early on that part of the nuclear industry's problem was public suspicion about its activities. So he began a long running "come and see" programme to get the Scottish people comfortable with the source of a third of its electricity. This programme involved a large programme of site visits from schools, councils and politicians, even royalty when Princess Anne opened the new head office at Peel Park in 1992. SNL opened visitors' centres at the Hunterston and Torness AGR stations. The company published a safety review for the first time to explain just how the plants were managed. Hann was good with the media and spent a lot of time building a new, positive profile for the company.

All of this helped to make the staff feel less like pariahs and prepared the ground for major improvements in costs and productivity. Hann identified early on the potential for improved output from the power stations. He and his team also squared up to BNFL, the provider of the company's nuclear fuel services. In SNL's first annual report, published in June 1991, Hann stated that "based on present costs reprocessing is an uneconomic and unnecessary part of the fuel cycle at this time. As an alternative we have developed proposals in collaboration with others for on-site storage which has a number of environmental and economic benefits" (Scottish Nuclear Limited, 1991 p. 5). This was a direct challenge to the long standing basis of British nuclear waste management policy, and would have consequences for NE and for the future British Energy.

The impetus for improving operating performance grew with the arrival of Robin Jeffery as chief executive in February 1992. Jeffrey had worked for many years in Scottish Power and its predecessor the South of Scotland Electricity Board (SSEB). He had joined boiler makers Babcock and Wilcox as an engineering apprentice, completed a PhD at Cambridge and joined the electricity industry in 1979 as a technical trouble-shooter. He had also spent seven years as SSEB's project manager for the construction of the Torness AGR station, which was being commissioned when he joined. Jeffery commanded great authority as an engineer and would show that he was an effective chief executive.

When Jeffrey joined the SNL team saw their key challenges as: i) profitability; ii) preparation for the government's nuclear review in 1994; and iii) continuing to build public acceptability. The company made a net loss of £32.5 million in 1990/1991, excluding the costs of decommissioning Hunterston A Magnox station. This figure was struck after a "revalorisation" charge for increasing the value of the future nuclear liabilities (caused by inflation and by the unwinding of one year's discounting, since they were one year closer to crystallising). The AGR stations made an operating profit of £52 million, before interest charges; by 1995 it was £182 million. Another measure of improvement is net cashflow generated, after investments, a rough proxy for free cashflow. In 1990/1991 this was £171 million; in 1994/1995 it was £353 million.

The company's improved finances came, as at NE, from a combination of higher output and lower costs. Jeffrey and his team used a scheme called Target

Outstanding Performance (TOP) to encourage staff to come up with ideas to cut station outages (periods not producing power). Some outages are essential for refuelling, safety inspections and maintenance. The trick is to achieve as much as possible when the station is closed so that it can be kept running as long as possible. TOP led the staff to identify complex and irrelevant processes that kept the outages longer than necessary. Hunterston B had already achieved an overall load factor of 79 per cent in 1990/1991, one of the best AGR performances to date. Over the next few years, Torness overcame some commissioning teething problems to achieve 79 per cent in 1995 and a remarkable 87 per cent in 1996.

TOP motivated cost cutting too, but SNL also borrowed a scheme from Nuclear Electric to provide direct financial incentives for cost control. The "Gainshare" scheme was applied to all aspects of the company's operations, including the head office. Each of the company's three main sites (Torness and Hunterston power stations plus Peel Park head office) had its own team, run by the workforce directly with minimal management involvement. Bonuses of up to £2,000 a year were payable for a combination of output improvements, cost cutting and improvements in safety, quality and excellence. There were staff cuts too: the company's payroll fell from a peak of 2,200 in 1992/1993 to 1,860 in 1994/1995, a cut of 15 per cent

The overall result of the Jeffery–Hann leadership team was to cut the company's unit cost of production from £33/MWh in 1990/1991 to £22/MWh in 1994/1995, which meant SNL was profitable at the then wholesale power price of about £24/MWh.

NE and commercial freedom

The nuclear power stations were kept in the public sector only because they threatened to wreck the privatisation of the rest of the electricity generation industry. The government lacked any plan for nuclear and had pushed policy decisions into the nuclear review scheduled for 1994. But the creation of SNL and NE as government owned corporations meant that they might enjoy more operational freedom than in the past. Both companies sought to test and use this freedom. But the management came to feel that the government regarded the nuclear sector as a place to dump problems that would otherwise cause political difficulties for the privatised companies or, most seriously, for the nuclear industry's old adversary, coal.

As public limited companies, albeit owned entirely by the government, NE and SNL had a duty to maximise the value of their operations. SNL's market freedom was constrained by the fact that the two non-nuclear Scottish power companies had to buy all of SNL's output under a contract known as the Nuclear Energy Agreement (NEA). SNL's emphasis was on establishing more commercial arrangements with its suppliers, especially BNFL.

NE, on the other hand, had potentially more to gain from commercial freedom. As the biggest supplier of base load (continuous demand) electricity, NE was a major player in the electricity contract market, in which generators dealt with the regional electricity companies (RECs) and big industrial customers to buy and sell power.

The early electricity trading in England and Wales was fairly simple. Power was mostly sold in the form of contracts for difference – CFDs. These amounted to fixed price contracts, typically for one year, in which both buyer and seller knew exactly what the price would be, cutting out the volatility of the half hourly price in the spot market, the pool. The market mainly consisted of the three major generators selling and twelve RECs buying.

With 17 per cent of the total England and Wales power market in 1991, NE looked like a powerful player. But under the post-privatisation rules NE was forced to sell all of its power to the 12 RECs, with no access to the large industrial customers who were now allowed to buy direct from generators, cutting out the RECs as intermediaries. NE's commercial team feared it would be a forced seller to the RECs, who were also keen to diversify away from the existing generators by building their own new gas power stations. So NE faced a shrinking, captive market.

Despite its large market share, NE couldn't influence the marginal price of power, the pool price, which was set almost entirely by National Power and PowerGen. NE in practice had little scope for commercial behaviour and found that when it did try to behave like a normal profit seeking company it was rapped over the knuckles by the regulator, OFFER. For example, in March 1992 OFFER forced the company to halt its auction of CFDs because it feared that NE was being too aggressive (private interview). On another occasion OFFER put out a press release saying that NE must cut its price, right in the middle of an auction, which NE understandably regarded as unacceptable interference with the commercial market.

As a pure commodity power producer, NE's strategic focus was on production. The company had a commercial director, Mike Townsend, but he wasn't on the board. It also had a director of trading, Andy Clements, who constantly tried to improve the prices at which the company sold power to the RECs. But he was hemmed in by the regulator on one side and a senior management dominated by engineers on the other. NE's engineering-based culture was a strength during the first half of the 1990s but the lack of a strong commercial culture was to become a source of weakness in the later 1990s.

Nuclear versus coal again

Nuclear power's dismal public reputation became important with the coal crisis of 1992/1993. The expiring of the first set of privatisation power contracts for coal created an unexpected political problem for the ailing Major government. National Power and PowerGen had contracted before privatisation to buy a volume of coal from British Coal and to sell an equivalent amount of power to the RECs, in a "back-to-back" arrangement that left the generators with little risk and a guaranteed profit. The coal was priced high enough to keep British Coal profitable, meaning it was well above the price of imported coal.

So long as this extra cost was passed on to the RECs (and then to the captive customers) the generators were happy. But with the expiry of the contracts on 31 March 1993, National Power and PowerGen were looking for much lower prices to match imported coal costs – or another set of contracts to protect their profits. But the RECs were much less keen to buy high priced power now because part of their guaranteed market, known as the "franchise", was to disappear in 1994, when medium sized businesses would be free to buy power directly from generators. If they couldn't pass on the expensive coal-based power to captive customers, the RECs would refuse to buy it.

The underlying problem was British Coal's uncompetitive cost structure, compared with increasingly cheap imported coal. In theory, the Conservative government was happy to let market forces flow, which would mean several coal pit closures, accelerating the trend that had been continuing since the 1960s. But when British Coal announced in November 1992 that it would be forced to close 31 out of 50 pits, there was a national outcry. Michael Heseltine, President of the Board of Trade, announced an immediate government enquiry and the House of Commons Trade and Industry Select Committee (TISC) set up a parallel public investigation.

The crisis was foreseeable and it is odd that the government was so surprised. The enquiries revealed what was obvious to industry insiders, which was that a free market in energy would doom British Coal to further contraction and the power generators would import most of their coal, using the new import facilities they had recently been building. On top of this, a wave of new gas power stations being built by the RECs would further squeeze the demand for coal.

MPs cast around for some way to make more space for coal. They found it in nuclear power. NE was suddenly under pressure to shut down its older Magnox power stations to make space for more coal burning (at the price of a sharp rise in atmospheric pollution and greenhouse gases). Since NE was in the public sector it could be forced to do things that the privatised generators could refuse to do on commercial grounds. Nobody much liked nuclear and it was easy for the rest of the power industry to gang up on nuclear as a way of solving the problem. Ed Wallis, chief executive of PowerGen, and a former senior CEGB executive, suggested in a speech to the Coal Industry Society that the Magnoxes be closed early in order to help coal (*Financial Times*, 1993d).

NE had seen this threat coming; Bob Hawley had already argued that coal and nuclear were complementary because nuclear's low emissions allowed high emission coal to be environmentally acceptable (Nuclear Electric, 1992). This argument made little headway, partly because the general view was that NE was subsidised, just like coal, so the question was simply where the public subsidy should be put. What the general view missed was that the "subsidy" to NE was payment for unavoidable decommissioning and fuel reprocessing costs arising from previous nuclear generation – most of these costs would exist whether or not the Magnoxes were shut down.

NE made its submission to both reviews in November 1992, the TISC evidence being public (House of Commons, 1992). The company argued that the plight of British Coal was a result of its high costs, made worse by the structure of the generation market and the incentives of the RECs to build new gas power stations that were only viable because National Power and PowerGen were preventing a truly competitive generation market from emerging. All of this was largely correct, but hard to do much about. NE then argued that the Magnox nuclear stations had avoidable costs of only £12/MWh, well below the current power price of about £23/MWh. This meant that closing the Magnoxes would entail a substantial cash cost, while leaving the taxpayer to pick up the unavoidable liabilities.

Given the dismal history of nuclear power economics MPs and the public were naturally sceptical about NE's claims. But independent accountants Ernst and Young found that NE's figures were sound, possibly the first time that the nuclear industry had won such an argument (*Financial Times*, 1993b). This didn't swing every MP against Magnox closure but it ensured the support of the Treasury, which understood the costs to the taxpayer of bailing out coal by sacrificing the Magnoxes. The TISC report was published in January 1993 (House of Commons, 1993). It recommended a number of measures to widen the market for coal, but stopped short of calling for Magnox closures.

The government published its White Paper on coal in March 1993 (DTI, 1993) and definitely killed off the early nuclear closure scheme. But NE wasn't completely safe yet. The White Paper, having reasserted the government's commitment to free, competitive energy markets then approved a further set of back-to-back contracts between British Coal, the RECs and the two generators National Power and PowerGen. Since privatised companies couldn't be forced, they had to be bribed, and the profit margins on these new contracts were very generous to the power companies. The only problem was that the contracts were for five years, running until the complete ending of the RECs' franchises in March 1998. But the RECs had already contracted for some of their future power with NE, through CFDs which had two years or more to run. At this point the government started to put pressure on NE to give up these contracts (which were at good prices from NE's point of view) in order to free up the RECs to buy more coal-based power. NE quite properly refused – it was after all a public limited company subject to ordinary company law, which meant its directors must operate commercially.

Furious at this refusal, senior civil servants in the Department of Trade and Industry summoned NE's executives to London on a Friday afternoon. Chief Executive Bob Hawley insisted that the board couldn't do something obviously against the interests of their shareholder without the shareholder giving written approval. Eventually a civil servant, on behalf of the government as sole shareholder in NE, gave the authorisation and the REC contracts were terminated (private interviews). This show of principled independence from NE did nothing to improve the company's relationship with the government.

The nuclear review and the end of plans for new stations

In 1993 and 1994 it was increasingly the goal of John Collier and Bob Hawley at NE and of James Hann and Robin Jeffrey at SNL to position their companies as effectively as possible for whatever options the government's nuclear review might offer. Although the government's March 1993 White Paper on coal had called for the review to be brought forward, the rest of the year passed with no announcement. NE was keen to present its case to the review, to show what dramatic changes it had achieved since the humiliating days of 1989. It was therefore a blow when the government announced in September that the review would be put back again to 1994. The reason given was that the review might complicate the current public consultation about whether to switch on the THORP plant at Sellafield and the possible review of planning permission for a new PWR at Sizewell (station C).

But the real reason appeared to be that the government was deeply split on the whole issue of the review. There were three government departments involved. The DTI wanted a narrow review that concentrated on the question of whether the private sector would finance nuclear power stations. The Treasury wanted a thorough examination of future nuclear liabilities and whether privatisation would be feasible. And the Department of Environment wanted the emphasis to be on environmental factors (Helm, 2003 pp. 195–196).

The management's frustration had grown as their finances improved. In July 1993 they had released their results for the year 1992/1993. John Collier stated that, with output up 17 per cent, the company was on track for operating profitability without the nuclear levy in the year 1995/1996. He added, "I can see Nuclear Electric carrying its commercial success through to the point where a move out of the state sector is recognised as feasible and desirable" (Nuclear Electric, 1993c).

In October 1993 NE formally submitted planning application for a 2,600 MW twin PWR, Sizewell C. But the submission lacked conviction. NE's executives had been gradually changing their goals. In the early 1990s there had been no talk of privatisation. The goal was to make the company financially viable in order to preserve the option of building more PWRs. The nuclear review would be the time to make this case. But from 1992 some of the corporate team had privately begun to think that privatisation might be possible, if the company could be made profitable without subsidy (private interviews). Privatisation would mean much tougher scrutiny of the economic case for new nuclear build, including a higher cost of capital to reflect the risks. So privatisation seemed to conflict with a goal of new nuclear build. But it was also increasingly obvious that the government wouldn't contemplate funding new nuclear power stations in the public sector. One benefit of the privatisation of the public utilities – gas, water, telecoms and electricity – was to push the cost of major capital spending off the government's books. It was most unlikely the government would make an exception for the politically unpopular nuclear sector.

The government's response to the Sizewell C application was duly frosty. A DTI statement noted that it was a purely commercial decision by NE and that the government did not encourage the application (*Financial Times*, 1993c). In fact NE only made the application to make sure that the question of new nuclear plant was considered in the review (private interview). The balance of opinion on the board of NE was swinging behind the view that seeking privatisation was not only the best option for commercial freedom but also the only way to keep any hope of new nuclear power stations alive, albeit in the longer term (private interviews).

On 20 September 1993 NE launched another front in its public relations campaign by publishing its first annual Environmental Report. At the press conference Bob Hawley produced a box of chocolate Brazil nuts and passed them round the bemused journalists. His message was that the radioactive dose from eating one was about 0.3 microsieverts, about the same as the annual average dose to the public from nuclear power in the UK (Nuclear Electric, 1993a). Most of the journalists chose not to eat the Brazils, presumably drawing the conclusion, not that nuclear power was safe but that chocolate Brazils were dangerous.

Frustrated that the review had been pushed into the indefinite future, NE let it be known publicly that it had in any case told the government it wanted to be privatised and believed it would be profitable by 1995/1996. An exasperated Tim Eggar, in an unusual rebuke to a state owned entity, said it was for ministers to decide whether to privatise, not companies. He softened the blow by saying he nonetheless saw the long term future of the company in the private sector and that it was "not a question of whether, but how and when it gets there" (*Financial Times*, 1993a) Chairman John Collier refused to be silenced, and when announcing the interim results (which showed another strong improvement in performance) in December repeated his view that the future lay in privatisation (Nuclear Electric, 1993b).

In Scotland, SNL had been preparing for the nuclear review too, but the board had different goals. Chairman James Hann and chief executive Robin Jeffrey had not wanted privatisation for SNL but were increasingly aware that NE was pushing for it. Hann had made clear in the SNL annual reports for 1992 and 1993 that he saw the review as a chance to get some long term energy policy in place, not least to avoid the UK becoming too dependent on gas power stations (a view that anticipated a key theme of the government's energy review of 2006). By making SNL profitable and delivering consistently high output from their AGR stations, the team hoped to convince the government that nuclear should have a permanent place in energy policy, including at some point new stations to replace the Magnoxes.

SNL launched a media campaign in December 1993 promoting energy policy, including what they called "long term sustainability". This term was a not very veiled criticism of the accelerating "dash for gas" that was taking place, with new gas power stations set to take about a fifth of the British generation market. The company ran large newspaper advertisements and sent a 20-page document to MPs and to the boards of large companies. The campaign was widely seen as an attempt to lobby ahead of the nuclear review to prevent it becoming simply a discussion on privatisation.

By contrast, NE had begun a round of City briefings to educate potential investors about the company and its financial progress, with a conference for analysts on 26 October 1993. In February 1994 it announced that NE was on target to meet its future decommissioning liabilities without the nuclear levy from 1998. It also said that the first stage of decommissioning the Berkeley Magnox station had been completed £30m below budget and that a move to the longer term "safestore" decommissioning strategy would cut the total bill to below £2 billion (Nuclear Electric, 1994c p. 1).

In fact, the conditions for a future privatisation were coming together. The Public Accounts Committee of the House of Commons argued in February for a "visible" fund for eventual decommissioning. This idea was fleshed out in more detail a few months later in a report commissioned by the Radioactive Waste Management Advisory Committee from the Science Policy Research Unit at Sussex University (*Financial Times*, 1994f). It was accepted that the decommissioning costs for the Magnox reactors (put at some £2.9 billion) would remain with the taxpayer. But a privatised nuclear industry would pay for its own decommissioning costs.

Also in February energy minister Tim Eggar confirmed the government's intention to privatise part of the UK Atomic Energy Authority (*The Times*, 1994b). The following month the High Court finally gave the go-ahead to BNFL's long troubled THORP plant at Sellafield. While neither of these directly concerned NE, it seemed that nuclear matters were gaining pace. Approaching the spring of 1994, NE was increasingly impatient for the review to begin. The flow of good news was increasingly a gush. The February 1994 edition of *Nuclear Times* (Nuclear Electric, 1994b) revealed that the company had been profitable before the nuclear levy in the month of December (when electricity prices admittedly were at their seasonal high). Then in March a *Financial Times* article claimed the Treasury was keen to see an early sale of the nuclear industry (*Financial Times*, 1994e). At the end of March NE announced proudly that their AGRs had achieved the best operating performance of any nuclear reactor type in the world with a load factor of 73.68 per cent. The US designed PWRs had achieved on average only 73.16 per cent. Three years before, the AGRs had been by far the *worst* in the world, performing at about 50 per cent (Nuclear Electric, 1994a).

The flow of cost cutting measures at NE continued. It was reported that at the company's London office a female member of staff had decided to reject a contractor's offer of £100 to unwrap the company flag from its pole and do it herself for nothing using her husband's fishing rod (*Daily Telegraph*, 1994). Hawley's message had got through.

Energy Minister Tim Eggar announced the terms of the nuclear review on 19 May 1994. There would be three areas of investigation: i) the economic and commercial viability of nuclear power stations, including the prospects for privately financed new stations; ii) the options for bringing private finance into the existing nuclear industry; and iii) the financing of the full costs of nuclear power, centring on the nuclear levy. Eggar showed the way the political wind was blowing by telling the House of Commons that in his view the privatisation of British Energy in this parliament was unlikely (*The Times*, 1994c).

In its submission to the review on 20 June 1994 (Nuclear Electric, 1994d), NE's argument amounted to backing the privatisation horse and recognising at last the brutal economics of new nuclear power stations. The company proudly announced its record since 1990: output up 45 per cent; productivity doubled; market share up from 17 per cent to 23 per cent; and the successful completion, on time and (revised) budget, of the PWR at Sizewell B.

The company also confirmed what everybody already knew, that the old Magnox stations might well be suitable for life extensions but the uncertainties over this and their decommissioning costs made them unsuitable for privatisation. NE saw them being carved out into a separate ownership entity, though possibly still managed by NE.

On new build, NE argued that the heavy one-off investment in Sizewell B could best be exploited by building two more PWRs, Sizewell C and Hinckley Point C. Their financial advisor Price Waterhouse suggested that these new stations would yield a real return in the range 5–9 per cent but that the private sector would require at least 11 per cent real. Only the state could bridge the gap. The "gap" for Sizewell C alone amounted to about £1 billion, assuming power prices continuing at their current level of 2.7p/kWh (a most unrealistic assumption). Finance Director Mike Kirwan put a nuanced interpretation on the message to the government. "We are not asking for government money to build Sizewell C", he told the *Financial Times*, "we are just explaining the possibilities for building it" (*Financial Times*, 1994c) .

In July Nuclear Electric revealed that its AGR power stations were producing power at 2.6p/kWh – below the 2.7p/kWh price of electricity. The Magnoxes were producing at 3.8p/kWh. The company's annual report showed that the AGRs had made an operating profit of £47 million before any levy income, against a loss of £107 million in 1992/1993 (Nuclear Electric, 1994a p. 31).

SNL's much shorter submission, written by the company's chief executive, Robin Jeffrey, put the emphasis on building new nuclear power stations, chiefly a replacement for the closed Magnox at Hunterston. But it made a case for commercial freedom from the government too, in what seemed a change of policy. SNL hadn't wanted privatisation but saw the success of Bob Hawley and John Collier's campaign for privatisation of NE. If NE was going to be sold then SNL had to make sure it wasn't left disadvantaged as the only state owned generator (private interview).

There was unease among NE staff about the top management's pursuit of privatisation. The September 1994 *Nuclear Times* had Bob Hawley responding to employee concerns that NE was abandoning its "nuclear heritage". Hawley insisted there was absolutely no chance of building new nuclear stations in the public sector so privatisation was the only way to give new build a chance. The board, he said is "dedicated to a nuclear future, provided that nuclear power stations can be built on a fully commercial basis" (Nuclear Electric, 1994b).

The electricity regulator, Stephen Littlechild, supported nuclear privatisation in his evidence to the government nuclear review (*Financial Times*, 1994a). But he wanted Nuclear Electric split up into a number of smaller entities, to dilute its 23 per cent market share. NE responded by pointing out, not for the first time, that although the company had a large total market share, none of its power stations set the marginal price so it had no anti-competitive influence on the market.

In another hopeful sign, the government appointed in September the British investment bank BZW to advise it on options for privatisation. Soon afterwards, US investment bank Morgan Stanley published a report that suggested that NE could be privatised and that it would be comparable to the higher quality US nuclear electric companies (*Financial Times*, 1994b). The report noted that private ownership of nuclear power was not new; US, Asian and continental European investors had long experience of owning shares in companies with nuclear operations. What would make NE unusual was only that it would be wholly nuclear, but conceptually investors understood the risks and rewards.

While the government digested the submissions to its review (including some that were deeply hostile to the nuclear industry) NE had the satisfaction of seeing its new PWR, Sizewell B, begin fuel loading, the penultimate stage of construction. NE showed its increasing grasp of public relations by publishing its latest environmental report, adorned with charming pictures of golden haired children in green meadows, a large close up of a bee and not a single image of a power station.

The year 1994 ended with mixed feelings for NE's management. In early November Her Majesty's Inspectorate of Pollution gave the final approval for radioactive discharges at Sizewell B, allowing the station to proceed finally to start-up. Yet at the interim results later in the month, the management appeared downcast and close to abandoning hope that privatisation could be achieved before the election. With a growing prospect of an anti-privatisation Labour government being returned at that election, the management feared that time was against them (*Financial Times*, 1994d).

Whatever the nuclear review concluded, the two companies had a lot to be proud of. Tables 5.1 and 5.2 summarise the key financial and operating results since the companies had been carved out of the old CEGB.

The figures for the companies are not exactly comparable but give a similar sense of improvement. SNL's employee number is distorted by an increase in 1993 of permanent employees to replace contract staff. NE's larger proportionate increase in AGR output reflects the worse state of its stations at the end of the CEGB period; by contrast SNL's Hunterston B was already running pretty well. But even in 1994/1995 NE's unit operating costs were dragged down by the continued poor performance of Dungeness B. NE was still making an operating loss in 1994/1995 but the AGRs alone were making an operating profit of £62 million with the loss fully accounted for by the Magnoxes; SNL had no Magnoxes by this time.

Table 5.1 Summary data for Nuclear Electric Ltd, 1991–1995 (£m)

Year ending 31 March	1991	1992	1993	1994	1995
Output (TWh)	45.0	48.4	55.0	61.0	59.2
AGR	22.5	27.5	34.6	39.3	37.2
Magnox	22.5	20.9	20.4	21.7	22.0
Market share (%)	17.4	18.5	21.6	23.2	22.3
Average no. of employees	13,542	12,674	11,323	9,454	8,900
Output per employee (GWh)	3.2	3.6	4.5	5.7	6.3
AGR unit operating cost (p/kWh*)	4.4	3.5	2.8	2.6	2.3
Operating loss	(1,101)	(1,033)	(616)	(434)	(33)

Source: Nuclear Electric company accounts.

Note
* 1993/1994 prices.

Table 5.2 Summary data for Scottish Nuclear Ltd, 1991–1995 (£m)

Year end March	1991	1992	1993	1994	1995
Output (TWh)	12.17	12.69	14.34	14.17	16.85
Average no. of employees	1,976	2,047	2,202	2,060	1,860
AGR unit cost of generation (p/kWh*)	3.2	3.1	2.9	2.8	2.2
Operating profit	52	69	97	99	182

Source: Scottish Nuclear company accounts and author's estimates.

Note
* 1993/1994 prices.

Conclusion

Economists tend to argue that incentives matter and so the conventional reason for the remarkable improvements in performance of the British nuclear stations is the carrot of future privatisation. Other companies have shown strong performance in the same circumstances (e.g. British Airways). But this argument is wrong in the case of NE and SNL. The incentive of privatisation was weak or non-existent before 1994 and even then it looked as if the companies might never leave the private sector. SNL's management didn't even seek privatisation until 1994.

As former finance director Mike Kirwan put it to the author, this story shows the importance of focus rather than ownership (private interview 12 December 2005). NE's performance was entirely about nuclear stations. Nuclear had been only one part of the giant CEGB, in which its losses and poor performance could be hidden indefinitely. Once SNL and NE had been carved out as specialised nuclear power generators, the talented leaders they then acquired were able to transform the operations and cut costs, turning a demoralised group of engineers and scientists into the world's leading nuclear operators. All of this was done while still in the public sector. Soon both companies would find out if privatisation could lead to even better results.

6　The birth of British Energy (1995)

Introduction

The year 1995 was one of transition. The two companies that emerged out of the failed privatisation in 1989 were merged to form British Energy, which would be sold to private investors in 1996. The key questions of 1995 were political; whether selling nuclear power was worth doing, and if so, whether the Scots would accept a merger with the English. The upshot was that BE was born as a political creature with a divided board and a culture of suspicion between the English and Scottish subsidiaries. These tensions were to become an enduring feature of BE's board.

The decision to privatise and the Scottish question

In early 1995 the government was tired and facing a general election that looked increasingly hard to win. The cabinet was split on the politics of privatising nuclear. The "consolidators" wanted to avoid any contentious policies, especially those that would reignite back-bench rebellions. The "radicals" wanted to try the privatisation magic one more time: lots of happy shareholders and some extra funds for tax cuts. The press reported that Michael Heseltine (President of the Board of Trade) was cautious about another controversial privatisation, having been forced to stop the privatisation of the Royal Mail in 1994. But Chancellor of the Exchequer Ken Clarke was said to be in favour mainly because of the expected £2 billion proceeds, which he saw as funding tax cuts (*Daily Telegraph*, 1995a; *The Times*, 1995b).

The Treasury was said to be pushing privatisation as a matter of urgency because they had missed their government borrowing target for the fiscal year just finished by £1.2 billion. Investment bank BZW had advised the government that NE could be privatised, but only if it were combined with SNL to make a more attractive investment. Cabinet opinion appears to have swung behind privatisation during April 1995. The decision in favour of privatisation owed something to the lobbying of former Conservative MP Francis Maude, who was now running the privatisation unit at investment bank Morgan Stanley. It may also have been helped by NE's commercial director, Peter Warry, who had long standing links with the Downing Street Policy Unit (private interviews).

Whatever the industrial merits of merging NE and SNL, the idea revived a long standing controversy in Scotland. When Scottish companies had merged with English ones in the past there tended to be a loss of jobs and influence in Scotland. Most infamous was the case of Britoil, a Scottish-based oil company taken over by BP in 1988. BP had promised to keep a head office in Glasgow but in 1992 had shut the Glasgow office with the loss of 350 jobs (*The Times*, 1992). SNL staff were dismayed at the idea of being merged into NE, believing that it would mean the end of the Scottish head office and of Scottish jobs.

The years of lobbying by SNL chairman James Hann now became critical. Key Scottish Labour MPs like Brian Wilson (shadow spokesman for Trade and Industry and in whose constituency the Hunterston AGR lay) and George Robertson (shadow spokesman for Scotland) were brought into the campaign. The Conservative Party, seldom very strong in Scotland at the best of times, could hardly afford to see one of Scotland's largest companies consumed by an English one, just ahead of a difficult general election. Ian Lang, Secretary for Scotland, squared up for a fight with the Department of Trade and Industry.

As NE management learned that privatisation was a real possibility but that Scotland was an issue, they began to lobby too. Chief executive Bob Hawley told the DTI that he was quite happy to have any combined company styled as "Scottish" if that made privatisation feasible. If it meant having a symbolic head office in Scotland, then so be it (private interview).

SNL, having decided that privatisation now looked inevitable, moved onto the front foot by promoting what became known as the "4 plus 4" option. In this scheme, NE would lose two of its most northerly AGRs to SNL and there would be two competing nuclear companies, each with four stations. NE management was appalled at the idea of dismembering their company and Mark Baker, board member for corporate affairs, told the *Daily Telegraph* on 31 March 1995 that a break up "would be so bad for the company and so bad for nuclear power that, if it is the price which we would have to pay for privatisation, we would not wish to pay it" (*Daily Telegraph*, 1995b).

Instead he tried to reassure the Scots that in the event of a single company privatisation, NE would preserve the SNL's "Scottishness". This was received in disbelief by SNL's chief executive Robin Jeffrey, who was reported to have asked: "What's that mean? That they'll have us working in kilts?" (*The Herald*, 1995).

In England, the NE workers were just as alarmed at the prospect of becoming part of a Scottish company. A spoof memo was circulated among employees:

Nuclear Electric/SNL
In order to avoid a last minute rush/total chaos, it is the company's intention to allow personnel who feel they may be going 'North of the Border', to purchase the correct dress for this chapter in their lives. To this end the company has arranged for: KILT EXPRESS to visit on 8 May. Thermal

underwear will also be available at advantageous prices and staff are advised to take advantage of this offer now, while it lasts. If you have any queries on the above please contact the undermentioned. A. Windup.

Some 50 SNL executives and managers lobbied MPs in London on 2 May 1995 to protect Scottish jobs. The Scottish press was full of articles warning of betrayal. Ian Lang used this pressure to get some concrete guarantees from Heseltine that would ensure there would not be "another Britoil".

A deal was done. The Cabinet approved the policy on 4 May (*The Times*, 1995a) and five days later, in an announcement timed for the imminent Scottish Conservative Conference, Michael Heseltine told the House of Commons that the government had decided to privatise the more modern nuclear power stations – the seven AGRs plus the Sizewell PWR. The liabilities associated with the stations would be transferred to the private sector. A new corporate structure would be designed to "preserve the identities of Scottish Nuclear and Nuclear Electric and to establish a significant holding company to be registered in Scotland, where its headquarters will be located. The headquarters will include all key group functions. A chairman independent of both Nuclear Electric and Scottish Nuclear will be appointed." He went on to say that engineering functions within the group will "be reorganised to bring more jobs to Scotland. In all, these developments are expected to bring at least 100 jobs to Scotland." The part of the fossil fuel levy to which Nuclear Electric is entitled would cease, 18 months early, ensuring an earlier cut in electricity prices (Reuters, 1995).

The White Paper accompanying Heseltine's statement was far from friendly to nuclear power. It rejected the case for a new PWR compared with the new combined cycle gas turbine stations (CCGTs) that were being built by existing private generators. It even doubted the argument for any environmental case for helping nuclear power. In his authoritative account of British energy policy Dieter Helm points out that the government could ignore nuclear's contribution to avoiding carbon dioxide emissions because these were set to fall in the UK in any case, as dirty coal stations were rapidly being replaced by much cleaner CCGT stations (Helm, 2003 p. 198). On the economics of privatisation itself, Helm makes the argument that was widely accepted at the time, that the DTI started with the conclusion that it would sell British Energy and then worked out the numbers to justify it (Helm, 2003 p. 199).

The same day as Heseltine's statement, the Scottish Office defended the merger of SNL with NE by saying that investment bank BZW had provided "strong and clear advice that there were considerable risks for the taxpayer associated with separate privatisation of SNL" (Scottish Office, 1995).

The Scottish Secretary Ian Lang had secured what became known as the "triple lock": i) a head office retained in Scotland; ii) SNL's separate operation and function would be written into the new holding company's memorandum and articles of association; and iii) the Scottish Office would retain a "golden share" in SNL that would allow it to veto any significant changes in structure of which it disapproved. SNL insiders felt the Scottish Office had run a good campaign. Labour MPs remained hostile to privatisation and refused to believe the guarantees.

The case for privatising a single company was not at all obvious. Nobody claimed there were significant economies of scale – although the *dis*economies of the three-headed structure of British Energy were clear enough. SNL had always drawn on the research and development base of NE and duplication of this would have been wasteful, but much of that base was shut down over the next five years in any case. A better reason was that SNL's guaranteed income from the Nuclear Energy Agreement would expire in 1998 when full competition was to be introduced in electricity supply across Great Britain. SNL could still have sold its power but it would have faced new uncertainty over the price. This risk might be easier to deal with as part of a larger nuclear company.

Creating the new holding company

The next task was to thrash out the board of the new company, delicately preserving the national balance in a manner more familiar to company boards in Belgium than the UK. The chairman of course must be Scottish, and on 17 May Ian Lang announced John Robb as new chairman of the holding company (DTI, 1995). There were to be two deputy chairmen, one from each subsidiary. It was widely assumed that these would be the two current chairmen of SNL and NE, respectively James Hann and John Collier. Neither was in fact to make it to the board of what became British Energy, but for very different reasons.

The next problem was who to make chief executive? There was one job and two existing chief executives: Bob Hawley and Robin Jeffrey. Both very able in their different ways, the two men had recently met when Jeffrey invited Hawley to watch Scotland play Wales at rugby. Jeffrey had reportedly won a bet over the margin of Scotland's victory, the actual result being presumably not in doubt (*Independent*, 1995a). Hawley had the upper hand in two respects: NE was a much larger company; and the chairman was Scottish so an English chief executive seemed only fair. In fact the DTI had, in effect, already offered Hawley the job as part of the deal in accepting a Scottish HQ for the new holding company. As a leading Scottish paper put it, "Bob Hawley . . . now appears the favourite if the merger is not to seem a Scottish takeover" (*The Scotsman*, 1995a). But this would leave Jeffrey without a job.

To widespread surprise though, it was Jeffrey who became deputy chairman of the holding company, not James Hann. On 19 July Hann said "I was asked and agreed to stand down as Chairman [of SNL] in the autumn so that the senior executive team in place at the privatisation would have the right balance of skills and age profile for the longer term" (Scottish Nuclear Limited, 1995b). Staff at SNL were shocked. Hann personified the recovery of SNL from the demoralised lows of 1989 to the flourishing, self confident and profitable company that SNL had become in 1995.

So why did Hann go? The new chairman of the holding company John Robb told the press that he was keen to harness Jeffrey's skills as an engineer in the nuclear industry and was determined to bring on younger directors (*Guardian*, 1995). He added that Hann had been appointed by the government before he (Robb) had arrived and that he wanted a management team that he was comfortable with "rather than one I had inherited". Robb claimed the same day that Hann had not been fired (*The Scotsman*, 1995c). But this was a nicety; Hann had been utterly surprised to be asked to go, though former colleagues remark on his great dignity at the time. Robb was surely right to find room on the board for Jeffrey, who had more practical nuclear engineering expertise even than John Collier. There was a widespread feeling that Hann earned the knighthood he received the following year.

The rest of the executive board of the holding company was announced. NE's finance director Mike Kirwan would become finance director of the holding company. And Robert Armour moved from SNL's board to become company secretary for the whole group. Fears about an English takeover refused to go away. *The Scotsman* ran an editorial suggesting that real power in a company lay with the chief executive and finance director and that Hawley and Kirwan would "continue to be a formidable team" (*The Scotsman*, 1995c). In light of future board developments at British Energy this was to prove rather ironic.

The holding company had a board and structure. In early September it acquired a name: British Energy. John Robb commented that the name showed "we are creating a group with the potential to succeed in wider energy markets", a slightly ominous message to future investors anxious about diversification (Scottish Nuclear Limited, 1995c). The company would have an initial staff of 50 people, based in Edinburgh Park, on the edge of the city.

The battle for privatisation had been won then, but at some cost. In truth British Energy was an unwieldy creature: three separate boards; three head offices (plus a London office); and hostility between the English and Scottish companies. What was less clear to outsiders was the antagonism within the board.

The new chairman John Robb was the former chairman and chief executive of the British pharmaceuticals company, Wellcome plc. He had been educated at Daniel Stewart's College, Edinburgh and then started with Heinz, before working his way up the corporate ladder at Beecham's Products. Widely expected to become chief executive of Beecham, Robb had lost out to a boardroom coup that brought in Bob Bauman. He had left Wellcome when it had been taken over by the leading British pharmaceutical company Glaxo. He had high level board experience, he had gravitas and he was Scottish.

A blitz of newspaper interviews revealed something of Robb's character. A *Financial Times* profile described him as "tall and angular, looks every inch an aristocrat" before then revealing that his father was a factory worker. He was credited with injecting much needed commercialism into Wellcome and driving up its operating margin from 21 per cent in 1990 to 36 per cent in 1994. But there were some concerns about his management style; he was described by some former colleagues as arrogant and difficult to work with, a bully and even "Neanderthal" (*Financial Times*, 1995b). *The Scotsman* (1995a) noted that

"Mr Robb, whose reputation for dour certainly goes before him, appears not to have been the first-choice Scot to head the company." Robb's "dour" approach was to be helpful in future meetings with investors, who liked the idea of a downbeat, cautious chairman able to rein in a possibly over-enthusiastic chief executive. This was indeed the double act that Robb and chief executive Bob Hawley were to perform.

Preparing for privatisation

One of the biggest obstacles to the first attempt at nuclear privatisation had been the uncertainty over nuclear liabilities and the relations with BNFL, the government owned fuel reprocessing company at Sellafield. SNL had been already been asserting its independence from BNFL by researching into the possibility of "drystore". Drystore (so-called to distinguish it from the storage in water of the spent fuel of the earlier Magnox stations, the containers of which were unstable in air) meant storing spent nuclear fuel in a shallow underground bunker for up to 100 years, rather than sending it to Sellafield for reprocessing. The reprocessing route had two problems. First, it was very costly; and second, it involved the physical transfer of highly radioactive material from the power stations to Sellafield. SNL had estimated that drystore would save the company around £45m a year (Scottish Nuclear Limited, 1993 p. 14).

Drystore was a serious threat to BNFL's business model. In December 1994 BNFL's German utility customers had sought to cancel their contracts for reprocessing at Sellafield after a change in German law to permit dry storage for the first time. Although it wasn't convinced that SNL was serious about dry storage, BNFL had to respond. SNL were able to drive down the cost of fuel services with BNFL in a new contract under which the fuel was still delivered to BNFL but not necessarily reprocessed.

What BNFL didn't know was that the SNL board had concluded that drystore was probably not workable. The costs of building the new repository were potentially very high and there was a risk that planning permission wouldn't be granted. But the new BNFL contract offered most of the projected cost savings of drystore, so SNL's negotiating bluff had worked (private interviews). SNL's annual report stated that the BNFL contracts for all aspects of the fuel cycle fixed the costs at 0.9/kWh, a saving of 0.3p/kWh on the previous contract (Scottish Nuclear Limited, 1995a p. 7). By comparison the cost of decommissioning the stations was only 0.07p/kWh.

The new £4 billion BNFL contract with SNL was announced at the end of March 1995, at the same time as a new long term deal with NE. The NE deal was headlined at £14 billion, but like the SNL deal it covered contracts that ran decades into the future. About £4 billion of this was for reprocessing of spent fuel from the Magnox stations and was on the old cost-plus basis. The remaining £10 billion was for BNFL to reprocess the spent fuel arising from the AGRs from 1989. Importantly this contract was on a fixed cost basis (but indexed to the retail price level), which should reassure potential future investors that the nuclear liabilities were clearly pinned down and there would be no open ended risk.

In June 1995 SNL and Nuclear Electric both revealed impressive sets of results. SNL raised its operating profit by 84 per cent to £182 million. It also hit a new unit operating cost of 2.2p/kWh and reaffirmed its target of 2.0p/kWh. The staff total was down to 1,737 from a peak of 2,100 in March 1993 (Scottish Nuclear Limited, 1995a pp. 12, 40). NE had raised operating profit by 53 per cent including revenue from the nuclear levy and achieved a loss of only £33 million without it (the loss was £90 million excluding a one off pension credit). The modern AGR reactors achieved a unit operating costs of 2.4p/kWh and made a profit of £62 million; the loss lay with the Magnoxes and the start-up costs of Sizewell B (Nuclear Electric, 1995a p. 27).

NE's results were despite lower electricity prices and two lengthy power station shutdowns. Hawley's relentless focus on costs had cut operating costs by 24 per cent, with output per employee up 11 per cent. In recognition of his good work and with one eye on possible future privatisation salary expectations, Hawley was given a 22 per cent increase in his basic salary to £200,000 in July, excluding bonuses and other benefits.

Creating the new British Energy entailed a divorce between the Magnox operations and the AGRs. Although the two types of power stations had been managed separately for two years under Ray Hall (Magnoxes) and George Jenkins (AGRs), the employees had all felt part of one successful team. Carving out Magnox Electric was an unhappy process, although it did allow an element of self selection among staff; those seeking a privatised life under Bob Hawley would try to join British Energy, while those suspicious of the private sector or preferring to work under Ray Hall (who became chief executive of Magnox Electric) chose to stay in the public sector. Out of a workforce of about 9,000 only 100 employees appealed against their allocation and only four of these took their appeal further (House of Commons, 1995 Q.128).

The arrangements were complicated by the fact that so many of the reactors shared a site. At stations such as Sizewell and Dungeness, new contracts had to be devised to allocate rights and responsibilities over shared facilities. The final vesting day process of creating the new British Energy involved a heap of paperwork several metres high. The day long process of signing the contracts was halted at one point by a dispute about the exact terms of access to the Dungeness social club by Magnox employees.

Conclusion

The creation of British Energy heralded a new future for the modern British nuclear power stations. But it also marked the end of any immediate hope of building new ones. In December 1995 the new British Energy board announced that it would not use its planning consent for a third nuclear station at Hinckley Point in Somerset. It was also withdrawing its application for planning permission to build Sizewell C. Privatisation had forced the company to recognise the impossible economics of new nuclear build. BE in its press release said that the announcement "clears the air" and "allows potential investors to judge our core business without trying to assess the prospects of our involvement in a large capital intensive project in an uncertain market" (British Energy, 1995). Patrick Green of Friends of the Earth was jubilant, telling the *Financial Times* "This is the final nail in the nuclear coffin. . . . No more nuclear power stations will be built in the UK" (*Financial Times*, 1995a).

Part III

Life in the private sector (1996–2002)

7   Privatisation (1996)

Introduction

The government decision in 1995 to privatise British Energy fired the starting gun. But there were many hurdles ahead before the company could be sold to private investors. Many of those involved in the privatisation of British Energy recall it as one of the most difficult flotations they had ever worked on. These difficulties arose in three areas: i) investor ignorance and suspicion about nuclear power; ii) the unusual level of antagonism between the company's executives and the government and its advisor, BZW; and iii) the unfortunate timing of a key station shutdown late in the privatisation process. Although the company was eventually sold, its early days in the private sector were coloured by the controversy over the flotation and a lack of interest from the main British investment institutions.

Finding an agent

Having decided to offer British Energy plc for sale, the next job for the Department of Trade and Industry (DTI) was to appoint an advisor and agent for the sale. The Treasury, who controlled the financial side of these things, had a record of giving privatisation contracts to British investment banks, as part of an unstated "national champions" policy. In this way, former leading merchant banks Warburg and Kleinwort Benson had benefited both from the fees and the global prestige of transacting the British government's high profile asset sale programme.

But by 1996 Warburgs had been bought by Swiss Bank and Kleinwort Benson was part of the German Dresdner Bank group. The only British investment bank of any scale left was BZW, a subsidiary of the high street bank Barclays. BZW had already been advising the government on the possible sale of BE so it was the natural choice for the actual sale. But BZW had just become involved in controversy over the previous electricity privatisation, the sale of the government's remaining 40 per cent stake in National Power and PowerGen ("the Gencos") which took place in June 1995.

The "Gencos 2" offer, as it became known, was a secondary offering – a sale of shares in existing companies which were well known to investors. But on the first day of trading for the new shares after the sale was finished, the electricity regulator Stephen Littlechild announced a review of power prices. The share prices of the gencos fell to below the price that investors had just paid for them and there was an angry reaction from investors, MPs and the Stock Exchange. BZW, one of the two global coordinators for the sale, was heavily criticised for not making this highly material information available to investors before they decided to buy the shares. Whatever BZW's responsibility for what happened, its damaged reputation with investors (especially American ones who had bought a large chunk of the Gencos 2 offering) put it in doubt as sponsor for the sale of another British government owned generator.

But faced with the choice between a tarnished British investment bank and a spotless foreign one, the government chose the former and BZW was confirmed in July as advisor on the privatisation of British Energy. In BZW's favour was that it knew more about the company and its finances than any other bank. Any reputational damage done by the Gencos 2 fiasco would probably attach to the government in any case, whoever the advisor was.

BZW assembled what become known as the "nuclear team" under the leadership of Lynda Rouse, a former civil servant, and one of a handful of senior women in the City. The team spanned corporate finance advice, equity capital markets (the people who advise on selling new shares), the lending experts and the equity research analysts.

In 1996 it was still legal and normal for equity research to be directly involved with the transaction team before the actual sale took place. The only constraint was that the analysts should not be given any non-public "inside" information about the company that would give them an unfair advantage once the shares began trading. The analysts benefited from closer access to the company management and a fuller immersion in the accounts than their competitors would enjoy. In return they provided evidence to the capital markets team and to the government about the level of interest by investors in the forthcoming transaction. This information would help BZW address any real or perceived obstacles to the successful sale and guide the government on likely pricing.

BZW, to be clear, was advising the government, who owned BE. Meanwhile the company had taken on its own financial advisors, Lazards, part of the Anglo-US-French Lazard investment banking organisation, and former advisor to SNL. Why would BE have its own advisor? At this stage the firm was completely owned by the government. The board's legal duty was to look out for the interests of the shareholders. So whose interests were being served by Lazards?

The reality of any privatisation is that once the decision to privatise (on which they agree) has been taken, the interests of the managers and the government diverge. The government, as owner, wants the highest possible sale price. The management, who will have to live with the longer term challenge of meeting and beating investor expectations, would prefer a lower sale price, so long as it's consistent with a viable company. The lower the investors' financial and operating expectations, the easier it would be to beat them in future.

Lazards' role therefore became, in effect, to advise the management of the company how best to criticise the advice being given by BZW and in particular to talk up the risks facing the company and talk down its prospects. In other words, BZW's people – especially the equity analysts – found that they were most likely to have their analysis and forecast challenged by BE itself.

Educating the investors

As Morgan Stanley, another international investment bank and former advisor to NE, had argued in 1995, international investors were already familiar with nuclear power, through ownership of partly-nuclear utilities in the US, Germany, Belgium, Korea and Japan. But one would normally expect a privatisation to be sold mainly to investors in the home market. And British investors not only had little experience of owning nuclear assets but also shared many of the prejudices of the general public about nuclear matters.

Even for experienced foreign investors British Energy raised new questions. The company's power stations were mostly of a unique British type with, until recently, a poor track record. The treatment of liabilities was much more complex than in most other countries, where the state assumed the final liability for nuclear waste (see Chapter 16). And above all British Energy was a wholly nuclear generator in the world's most deregulated power market. All of this meant that BZW had a big job of educating investors around the world, if it was to get a fair price for the company. Unusually for an offering of this size, the BZW analysts did an international pre-sale roadshow to investors some months before the flotation.

BZW's first research document, in October 1995, contained no financial projections or valuation. Instead it explained the company's assets, detailed the track record of operating improvements and cost cutting and analysed the prospects for continued financial improvement (BZW Research, 1995). The goal was to get investors to the point where they saw British Energy as just another company and assessed it on its financial merits. International investors were, on the whole, sanguine about investing in nuclear power, even if they had reservations about buying anything second-hand from Her Majesty's government.

In the UK, however, investors were more ignorant – and more hostile. Equity investors shared the general public fear of nuclear radiation and tended to overestimate dramatically the actual risks of nuclear power and the history of accidents. The most important reassurance to potential investors on this score was the fact that BE, like all nuclear power companies in the world, faced a limited liability on any damage arising from a nuclear accident, under a series of international treaties which were reflected in British law under the Nuclear Installations Act of 1965.

The second issue British investors demanded reassurance on was the nuclear liabilities. Investors needed first to grasp that the biggest liabilities were concerned with fuel reprocessing, not decommissioning. Second they needed to understand that the great majority of future liability risk had been transferred to

BNFL through the long term contracts signed in the spring. The matter of fuel reprocessing was quite obscure to most investors, who, if they had any notion of nuclear power at all, typically had some concern about the cost of closing down the stations after they stopped operating, namely decommissioning. And decommissioning did raise an awkward question: how can a commercial company satisfy the public that it has adequately provided for costs that will not fall due for decades to come, possibly long after the company has ceased to exist? A cynical member of the public (or a greedy investor) might suspect that the company would simply pay out all of its profits while the stations were operating then declare itself unable to pay for decommissioning and throw the problem onto the taxpayer.

This is analogous to the problem of company-sponsored pension schemes, and the accounting and valuation issues are very similar (see Chapter 11). The solution, as recommended by MPs and by the Radioactive Waste Management Advisory Committee (see Chapter 6) was to set up an independently managed fund. The privatised company would pay regularly to this fund, with the amounts chosen so as to grow over the very long time periods involved to provide enough money to decommission the power stations. The fund would be a "pension fund" for retired nuclear power stations.

British investors were familiar with the idea of long term pension funds – many of them worked for pension fund management companies, one of the largest sources of institutional investment in the UK. They also understood the power of compound interest. BZW's calculations suggested that the annual contributions to such a decommissioning fund might be only of the order of £25m–30m, quite modest enough to leave room for a decent dividend payment.

How could such relatively small sums roll up to the roughly £5 *billion* estimated cost of decommissioning? It was the magic of compounding. Under the new strategy known as "safestore", some decommissioning costs were postponed until up to 70 years after the power station closed. With such enormous time scales even relatively modest sums today would grow to substantial amounts, so long as they were invested sensibly and there was no catastrophic fall in financial markets. At the time both of these assumptions seemed reasonable, just as the security of company pension schemes was taken for granted.

With decommissioning made palatable, investors could then focus on the much larger costs of dealing with the irradiated spent fuel. These costs were captured through the contracts with BNFL. The contracts had two purposes from an investor's point of view: i) they quantified the amounts both now and into the future (in real terms); and ii) they contracted with a reliable third party for the future costs. In other words, the greatest concern for potential investors, that the liabilities would turn out to be far greater than expected and destroy any value for shareholders, was taken care of. BNFL was, in effect, providing insurance for British Energy that a large part of its costs would be fixed. This was only feasible because BNFL was fully owned by the government, so the ultimate provider of this insurance was the taxpayer.

Realistically there was no other way in which these risks could be handled. In every country with nuclear power, the government provides some form of guarantee for long term waste fuel costs. In the US for example, nuclear utilities pay the government a fixed 1¢ per kWh of energy produced, then hand over responsibility to the Department of Energy. But some commentators suspected that the BNFL contracts were a backdoor way of breaking the government's solemn promise that at privatisation the liabilities would follow the assets (Helm, 2003 p. 198 n. 19).

Fight over debts and liabilities

A key point of financial strategy is the capital structure, the ratio of debt to equity on the balance sheet. BE's management wanted the company sold with a strong balance sheet, meaning little or no debt. The government wanted to load as much debt onto the company at privatisation as possible. The argument was further complicated by the question of what liabilities would be taken by BE and which would be left with the government. Hawley and Robb fought a long and bitter fight with civil servants and BZW on these issues.

The temperature began rising in January 1996. BZW's corporate finance team had advised the government that BE could be sold for about £2.6 billion, including debt. The government was broadly indifferent as to what mix of debt and equity made up the £2.6 billion so long as it got its money. There are tax advantages in using debt as a source of capital because the interest payments are tax deductible, whereas dividend payments on equity capital are not. But debt brings a risk that the company may get into financial difficulties and face "financial distress", meaning the company can't make the investments it wants and ultimately may lose control to the banks. In principle there is a debt/equity mix for any company that would maximise its overall value – which was the government's goal.

BE was unusual in having a further balance sheet complication, the nuclear liabilities. These are similar to debt in that they represent obligations to third parties in future, but unlike debt pay no interest. But a company with lots of liabilities for future payments would, all else being equal, want to carry less debt than one without liabilities. The debate about British company pension fund deficits in the early 2000s was resolved in favour of treating these deficits – which are analogous to nuclear liabilities – as equivalent to debt for valuation purposes (see Chapter 11). The government and BE became locked in a negotiation about the combination of debt, equity and liabilities.

Energy Minister Tim Eggar had affirmed that the liabilities would follow the assets (House of Commons, 1996 p. 66). But BE objected to about £1 billion of costs associated with reprocessing fuel from operations before the creation of BE. This was fuel which had been burned years before but was sitting in storage tanks waiting to be reprocessed at BNFL's Sellafield-based THORP plant. BE was, in effect, a new corporate entity with a new balance sheet. Agreed, the current and future costs of operations should be fully reflected in the books, but previous operations? Surely these belonged to the public sector – the taxpayer?

These arguments were generally had in private because it was in nobody's interest to jeopardise the sale. But news of the impasse leaked out. In January the *Financial Times* reported that "A senior member of the government and a BE executive both said yesterday that privatisation could be jeopardised by the impasse." A minister was quoted as saying "These people [at BE] are being bloody silly." Whereas the government thought BE was worth £2.6 billion, the company thought it might be worth only £500 million, a fraction of the £2.7 billion cost of building Sizewell B (*Financial Times*, 1996e).

Exasperated at the company's intransigence, the government pulled out a weapon it had used successfully in the run up to the privatisation of PowerGen in 1990: the threat of a trade sale to another company. On 21 January the papers were full of rumours that the American electricity company Duke Power had made an offer to the government to buy BE. Energy Minister Tim Eggar told the *Financial Times* that the government had received an indirect offer from a company, but of a very preliminary nature, which must be considered in the interests of the taxpayer (*Financial Times*, 1996d). The clear intention was to scare the BE management into backing down for fear that they would lose their jobs in a takeover.

The problem was that there was no bid, nor even an indirect expression of interest. Duke Power's spokesperson "emphatically and vehemently" denied any expression of interest to the UK government (*Daily Telegraph*, 1996). It emerged that the only grain of truth in the story was that the British merchant bank Schroders had informally contacted a number of its corporate clients in the US about BE and was furious at the misrepresentation of its role.

The Duke "news" coincided with a House of Commons Trade and Industry Select Committee report, which was mildly critical of the proposed segregated decommissioning fund but which otherwise gave grudging support to the privatisation This was despite taking evidence from Richard Killick, a former director of safety at SNL, who argued that commercial attitudes could threaten safety (House of Commons, 1996 p. 18). The Committee concluded that "We are therefore satisfied that privatisation of British Energy, together with continuing rigorous scrutiny by the NII, need not result in any reduction in nuclear safety" (House of Commons, 1996 p. 21).

Having failed to threaten the BE management into backing down, the government opted for character assassination. The *Sunday Times* reported on 25 February that BE directors were coming under pressure to "rein in their chief executive, Bob Hawley" who had "incensed" government officials Hawley was described as "stubborn as a mule", a description he probably relished (*Sunday Times*, 1996). Other newspapers stories that referred to Hawley as "eccentric" and "awkward" were widely seen as government-sourced.

But the liabilities were decided in favour of the government: BE would have to accept the £1 billion of pre-privatisation liabilities – an apparent injustice that the company would revisit in its negotiations with the government in 2002. But this meant little without a decision on the level of debt. As March rolled on, the positions emerged through press leaks: the company wanted a maximum of

£500 million and the government wanted £1,000 million. This did not mean that the privatization proceeds might vary by £500 million because the equity value of the company (the amount that investors would pay for the ordinary shares) would be higher if the debt was lower. Roughly speaking, if BZW's overall valuation of £2.6 billion was correct, then £500 million of debt meant an equity value of £2.1 billion and £1 billion of debt meant an equity value of £1.6 billion. A higher level of debt would raise the value of the company by the value of the "tax shield", the tax benefit of higher future interest payments. But this gain would be partly offset by the greater risk of financial distress with a higher level of debt, so the broader point remained, that the government wasn't at risk of losing £500 million. It is likely that it was the sheer intransigence of the board – not just Hawley but Chairman John Robb – that annoyed civil servants.

The final resolution of BE's balance sheet came in the discussion of the new segregated decommissioning fund. This fund would require annual payments by the company to provide for the "retirement" of the reactors. The more cash the fund started with, the lower the future payments would need to be. The government agreed that the fund would start with £230 million of cash, which could be seen as a partial reversal of its position that the company must shoulder all future liabilities. The company would accept gross debt of £700 million but netting off the cash injection into the fund, this fell to net debt of £470 million. The company's annual payments into the fund would be just £16 million, compared with the £22 million that BZW's analysts had originally estimated. Hardly a problem for a company that would generate £427 million of free cashflow (*after* dividends) in its first year in the private sector. It is hard to see the outcome of these negotiations as anything other than a victory for Hawley's stubbornness.

The last change to the balance sheet took place in May when BE showed in its accounts for the year to 31 March 1996 that it had taken a £2 billion write down in the value of its assets. Of this, £800 million was on the first-of-a-kind costs at Sizewell B, which would not now be amortised over future additional PWRs. The remaining £1.2 billion was a write down on the rest of the company's assets owing to lower forecast power prices. The size of this charge naturally generated a lot of comment. For the anti-nuclear lobby it showed that privatisation was, as they had hoped, forcing the industry to come clean about the economic waste of the past. But for investors these write downs referred to the past; what mattered to them were future cashflows.

Valuing the company – assumptions on output and prices

Having overcome much of the initial hostility to investing in nuclear power, BZW's analysts emphasised the two things which would determine BE's value: its electricity output, and the market price of electricity. BZW's second research report, published in March 1996 made it clear that this was a highly operationally geared company, meaning that a small change in revenue would lead to a disproportionate change in profits (BZW Research, 1996a). This is good news when revenues are growing, which they had been in the previous few years.

BZW expected continued growth on the back of further rises in output. Of course when revenue falls, operational gearing becomes very unpleasant, as BE was to find out in the years after 2000.

BE was not a utility in the conventional sense of having stable, predictable and regulated earnings. It was more like a commodity producer, such as a copper mine or an oil exploration company. The first two items in BZW's list of "Key threats" were pricing and plant reliability. Both the volume of output and the selling price of that output were likely to be volatile. And while the company could have a significant degree of influence over the former, it was powerless to influence the latter; BE was a "price-taker".

BZW's goal was to achieve the highest sale price for the company, by maximising demand from investors. BZW's views were purely suggestive though; investors would be free to disagree with BZW's analysts and set the value of the company in line with their own forecasts for output and price.

BZW volume forecasts were challenged by BE management's tendency to play down expectations of future output. On the one hand, BE and its predecessor companies had achieved a remarkable improvement in the load factor of the AGRs, which suggested that good, motivated management might raise output further in future. On the other hand, argued BE's management, improvements from now on would be much harder to achieve and so it would be unwise to bank on any significant further rise.

BZW's base case assumed the company raised load factors to a long term steady state of 82.5 per cent, although in any one year the figure would oscillate around this target because station outages were unevenly spaced. As Table 7.1 shows the out turn was reasonably close to this forecast until 1999, after which output fell sharply.

On electricity prices, the company's view was of less significance because it arguably had little more expertise in forecasting the future than did BZW's analysts (or anybody else). BZW's research showed three scenarios: a base scenario of wholesale power prices remaining flat in real terms for five years; a high scenario in which they rose in real terms; and a low scenario in which they fell sharply to 2.0p/kWh in 1998/1999 (in 1996 prices) and then rose back to the base case level by 2003/2004. These scenarios generated different valuations for the company and investors could choose for themselves. Roughly speaking a 0.1p/kWh change in the average long term power price (which was then about 2.4p/kWh) altered the company's total equity value by about £250 million.

BE's management publicly distanced themselves from BZW's valuations.

Table 7.1 BZW forecast and actual nuclear output, 1995–2003 (TWh)

Year ending 31 March	1995	1996	1996	1998	1999	2000	2001	2002	2003
BZW forecast	55.1	59.5	67.9	68.6	69.0	69.0	69.0	69.0	69.0
Actual	55.1	61.2	67.2	66.7	69.1	62.2	62.5	67.6	63.8

Source: BZW Research, 1996 Appendix Two; BE annual reports.

When the pathfinder (i.e. provisional) prospectus was published on 10 June it contained a statement from the company that they expected power prices to fall (*The Times*, 1996a). Two unrelated Monopolies and Mergers Commission reports on the conventional generators, National Power and PowerGen, published in April revealed that both companies forecast a steady fall in power prices over the next four years. On one scenario, National Power saw the price below 2p/kWh by 2000 (MMC, 1996 figure 5.11). Both conventional generators had a strong interest in pessimistic price expectations because they wanted to discourage new entrants to the power sector, but their forecasts were widely noted. Not much time was spent on BZW's high scenario and in practice the debate was about the degree to which prices would fall (Table 7.2).

Crucial to the BZW view was that even in the low scenario the company would have enough cashflow to pay a growing dividend stream. Operating cashflow before interest and tax in this scenario would be around £150 million–£170 million in the years 1998–1999 compared with about £400 million in the base case. The company would show accounting losses in these years but would still have a discounted cash flow (DCF) value of about £1.8 billion, compared with the £2.6 billion base valuation (BZW Research, 1996a p. 61).

For most investors it was the dividend potential that mattered and BZW's argument was therefore persuasive. Indeed, some investors began to see that if the company was sold at a price that reflected this modestly pessimistic scenario then the actual out-turn might easily be a bit better and the difference would translate into markedly higher cashflows and a higher future share price. This is pretty much what happened.

The sale process began with an advertising campaign on 30 May 1996. Under the line "A final burst of energy" shots of javelin throwers and other vigorous athletes were featured in TV commercials that appeared more than a little coy about the source of this energy. A director of public relations company Dewe Rogerson was quoted as saying that power stations were not seen as strong advertising (*Financial Times*, 1996c). Whether retail investors ever actually realised they were buying shares in a nuclear power company remains unclear.

The privatisation attracted a great deal of press attention. The prejudices, suspicions and fears of the public were aroused by media commentators keenly aware of the political difficulties the government already faced. The mainstream press was divided on the privatisation, feeling that it was clearly unsatisfactory but not being quite sure just why. One common point of view was that the

Table 7.2 BZW forecast for British Energy average sales price (p/kWh)

Year ending 31 March	1996	1997	1998	1999	2000	2001	2002
BZW base forecast	2.52	2.56	2.60	2.67	2.76	2.84	2.92
BZW low scenario	2.52	2.35	2.17	2.30	2.45	2.60	2.76
Actual	2.57	2.54	2.63	2.66	2.56	2.26	1.56

Source: BZW Research Appendix Two; British Energy Annual Reports.

company would be sold off at too low a price to canny private shareholders, so the taxpayer would be ripped off. The alternative view was that the ignorant shareholders would be buying a completely worthless company from a scheming government and so it was the investors who were going to be ripped off.

The sale

An asset sale is a game of poker. The advisor puts out an indicative price range in the hope that it will influence investor demand. Investors provide conservative indications of interest. The job of the equity capital markets experts in the advising bank is to peer through the smokescreen and form a realistic view of what the asset will really fetch. And it became clear that BE would raise rather less than originally hoped. BZW's equity analysts wearily touring the world in search of demand were reporting back that investor appetite was weak unless BE was priced cheaply. It wasn't seen as a "must have" privatisation, partly because it wasn't large enough to go into the FTSE 100 index of leading UK shares, which meant many investment institutions felt no obligation to have even a small holding in it.

The pathfinder prospectus was published on 10 June, which included the all-important first year dividend forecast of £96 million. Several analysts were valuing the company crudely on a gross yield of over 7 per cent (i.e. including the tax credit on the dividend that was then received by most institutional shareholders, until abolition by the Labour government in 1997). The dividend forecast therefore implied an equity valuation of about £1.4 billion. With net debt of £470 million that gave a total value to the government of around £1.9 billion, rather less than the £2.5 billion the government had publicly touted some six months before.

The pathfinder prospectus contained some of the most cautious risk analysis of a UK company offered for sale ever made by the directors. They emphasised that the company was at the mercy of its operating environment and stated that the dividend policy would need to be reconsidered if prices fell more than 5 per cent in real terms (*The Times*, 1996a).

More positively the company confirmed that it was seeking permission from the Nuclear Installations Inspectorate for life extensions for four of its eight AGR stations. BZW estimated that each extension added about £100 million of value, since it meant a longer period of cashflow generation and the delaying of the decommissioning costs, but excluded these benefits from its base valuation. The prospectus also mentioned that new nuclear power stations were not ruled out but not planned in the near future.

In press interviews following the prospectus launch, the senior management fleshed out their vision of the company's future. Chairman John Robb asserted that the company would seek growth rather than steady liquidation. Lest this awaken investor fears of diversifying utilities he added that the management had "no intention of squandering cash. We are going to take things very steadily" (*Financial Times*, 1996a). CEO Bob Hawley ruled out any significant investment in the over-supplied UK generation industry. He also suggested there was no case for the company to buy a REC (regional electricity company) because after the liberalisation of supply in 1998 (when the RECs would lose their geographically guaranteed or "franchise" market to smaller customers) there would be no point. The company would look at overseas investments but would avoid being "foolhardy or macho", unlike, Hawley couldn't resist pointing out, a certain water company (a reference to Thames Water's recent £75 million write-off on overseas investments). Hawley showed his roots as an engineer rather than an economist when he told the interviewer, "I don't like debt and I want to be rid of it." These words seem ironic indeed in light of the company's later history (*Financial Times*, 1996a).

The final and official prospectus appeared on 26 June and showed an unusually wide indicative valuation range, from £1.26 billion to £1.96 billion. The upper end looked increasingly fanciful as another major investment bank, Salomon Brothers, advised investors a few days later not to buy the shares even if priced at the bottom of the range. Another influential broker Credit Lyonnais Lang thought the shares were worth only 198p (*Daily Mail*, 1996).

BE's shares were sold using a bookbuilding procedure, a technique imported from the US. This means building up a demand curve for the shares. If you ask a group of potential investors what they would be willing to pay for something they will have an incentive to underplay their interest in the hope of getting it cheap. So to overcome this, the bookbuilder – in this case BZW – offers the incentive that an early, firm bid will be rewarded with a higher likelihood of a good allocation of shares in the event that the bid is successful. This relies on the fact that a successful sale will be "oversubscribed" – demand exceeds supply so that most bids will be only met in part. Bidders are incentivised to place real and honest bids for the shares and these bids gradually build up into a demand curve for the shares.

BE's book of demand was building up reasonably comfortably until the evening of Wednesday 11 July, two working days before the weekend when the price would be set. BE then announced that Hinckley Point B station had been shut down and a second unit would close at Hunterston B for two weeks following the discovery of hairline cracks in steam pipes during a statutory outage at the first Hunterston B reactor unit. The two stations were twin designs and a fault at one might imply a fault at the other. Cracks can be trivial or serious and Nuclear Electric's boss, Peter Warry, advised the BE board that the stations must close for checks (private interview).

The timing could hardly have been worse. Retail investors had had to make their final decision by Wednesday afternoon. The BE press release appeared just after this deadline, on Wednesday evening. BE insisted that there was nothing suspicious about this, it was the earliest time at which they could confirm the problem, but there were angry letters and questions in the House of Commons. The BE board met on Friday to discuss the cracks. The company had poor records from the constructors on the details of the original welds, which made diagnosis difficult. The board decided that if one more crack was found the privatisation would proceed, as the board would feel the prospectus statements on risk would still be valid. But if more than one was found the sale would have to be pulled (private interview).

BZW's poker-faced head of equity capital markets, Amir Eilon, told the *Independent* newspaper on 12 July that "we have had interest from high-quality institutions around the world" (*Independent*, 1996a). This is the sort of bland statement that bankers running deals are expected to make. The paper said that there were "indications" that the share price would be about 230p, a figure probably leaked from BZW to try to drum up last minute demand. The truth was the Hinckley Point cracks had hit investor confidence. Institutional investors were still free to withdraw their bids and some did.

One last piece of bad news appeared on Sunday 14 July, the day the shares were being priced. Engineers at the new PWR at Sizewell B found leaks in fuel pins that might delay the station's return to power (it had been closed for its first routine annual maintenance check). A BE spokesman told the *Observer* (1996) newspaper "This is not significant and has no safety or economic impact." But the company couldn't *categorically* deny the possibility that Sizewell would be shut for longer than the planned 45 days, even though the risk was minimal. The *Observer* took this as tantamount to an admission that something terrible had happened.

But it was too late for investors to withdraw now and the price of BE shares was finalised at 203p for institutions, equivalent to a gross yield of 8.4 per cent (both figures on a fully paid basis). This was close to the bottom end of the indicative pricing range. The government would receive £1.4 billion from the equity proceeds plus £470 million from the debt it had placed in the company (net of the cash in the segregated fund), a total of £1.9 billion, much less than the £2.6 billion that BZW's bankers had originally estimated. Even at 203p the book was barely adequately covered, at only three times (private interviews).

The truth was that the offer had been unpopular, and many key British and American institutional investors had not bid. The offering was held together by one large US institutional bid and a few substantial orders from some German institutions. This was a testimony to the effectiveness of the small German equity sales team at BZW, who had exploited the fact that many German investors were already comfortable with owning nuclear power through the big three German utilities, VEBA, RWE and Viag (private interview).

Luckily for the government and for BZW, the retail private investors had more than twice subscribed for the 30 per cent tranche allocated to them and so the retail part of the offering was raised to 50 per cent.

Opening trading

The opening trading was terrible. Some investors in equity offerings buy with the intention of selling at the first opportunity, hoping to lock in a modest but rapid and safe return; this is known as "flipping" the deal. Normally other investors are buying shares in the opening market to make up for the fact that they have received rather less than they had bid for, which offsets the flippers.

But in BE's case, the combination of unenthusiastic demand concentrated in a small number of big investors made for a fragile market. One large US investor, alarmed by the Sizewell B leak news, decided it had had enough of this accident prone company and tried to sell at the first opportunity. But there was not enough demand from other investors to offset this sell order. So, uniquely in the history of British privatisations (excluding the secondary offering of BP shares which coincided with the 1987 crash), BE saw its opening share price fall, by about 5 per cent on a fully paid basis, to 192p. CEO Bob Hawley bought 45,000 shares on his own account, followed by John Robb and Mike Kirwan buying undisclosed amounts (Reuters, 1996). But the selling was in the millions. In stock market terms, the issue was a flop.

This was especially embarrassing for BZW because it was conventional for the government minister responsible for the privatisation to be present in the investment bank dealing room on the morning of the opening of the new shares. Ian Lang, Trade and Industry Secretary, and Tim Eggar, Minister for Energy, duly turned up at BZW's concrete office block on the Thames and were shown the dealing desks with their computer screens, charts and flashing lights. The BZW trader in charge of BE shares faced the unenviable task of trying to keep the share price from falling while the Ministers were actually looking at the screen. Mr. Lang, like many politicians, may not have been particularly expert in the ways of stock trading but even he could tell a red light from a green one.

The original selling from the disgruntled US institution was bad enough but other investors, sensing that something was not right, decided they too would sell, while anybody looking to buy felt it was safe to hold back and wait. As a cascade of selling hit the market, BZW was the only buyer in town. Buying shares that nobody else wants to hold might not sound like a smart way to make money. But BZW wasn't actually using its own money; under a standard agreement with the client, BZW had scope to stabilise the market through buying and selling. Ordinarily stabilisation means evening out minor peaks and troughs in demand and supply. In this case it meant buying back a significant part of the shares in issue on behalf of the government that had just sold them. It was only in mid-August that it was revealed that the government, having intended to sell 100 per cent of its shares in British Energy, had in fact retained 11.5 per cent of them. Luckily, by the time the government sold this residual holding in December 1996, the shares had appreciated and the taxpayer was actually better off by some £33m than if they had been sold as planned in July.

The first week of trading saw little improvement, as the share price rose modestly to 195p, still below the 203p issue price. This was both embarrassing for BZW, whose investor clients were far from happy that they had made an instant loss, and a problem for the government which had just advertised these shares to the general public. Retail investors were used to getting a good deal on privatisation shares, although there was the consolation that at least they had paid less than the so-called professional investors. Critics of the privatisation were delighted, though some were clearly confused about the transaction. Labour's shadow energy minister John Battle put out a press release saying that "British

Energy is increasingly looking like a bad deal for the shareholders as well as short-changing the taxpayer" (*The Times*, 1996c). Quite how the share sale had made both the seller *and* the buyer worse off wasn't revealed. The same day Friends of the Earth's senior energy campaigner Patrick Green told an interviewer: "The temptation to say we told you so is overwhelming" (*Independent*, 1996b).

Hardly anybody noticed that during the first week of trading BE shares, both of the reactors that had been controversially closed in the middle of the offering were given a clean bill of health and restarted.

Conclusion

In late July 1996 British Energy was associated in most people's minds with the least successful privatisation in British history, with millions of people having, on paper, lost money by investing in it. But at least it was in the private sector. The nuclear industry had overcome the humiliation of 1989 and transformed itself into a viable company which had passed the stringent test of a stock market flotation.

The AGRs had been through a renaissance. Under the focused management of NE and SNL, these descendants of the early British atomic bomb programme had at last shown they could produce power on a commercial basis. The hopes of the management and of the new shareholders rested on this performance transformation having further to go, and on there being no immediate fall in power prices.

BE and the advisers to the flotation had also shown sceptics that the nuclear liabilities could be dealt with to the satisfaction of the private sector. Decommissioning liabilities were being funded though the segregated fund and fuel reprocessing liabilities were largely fixed by long term contracts with BNFL. The goal of the BE management was now to show a somewhat disenchanted shareholder base that they had, after all, made a good investment.

8   Hubris (1997–1999)

Introduction

Although the privatisation had gone badly for BZW and for the government (but they did get their money), BE management were in high spirits in the summer of 1996. They had got their commercial freedom and the shares had been priced on a pessimistic outlook which would make it easier for the management to beat expectations. In briefings to the City in October ahead of its first private sector results presentations, the company announced a cut of 1,460 jobs, more than 20 per cent of the total, which would lead to annual savings of £50 million (*The Times*, 1996b). It also confirmed that the company was on course for annual output of 80 TWh, equivalent to a load factor of 80 per cent (compared with only 71 per cent the year before and BZW's much derided medium term forecast of 82.5 per cent).

The *Financial Times* caught the change in the wind. In a column titled "Poor old BE" the anonymous Lex columnist argued in characteristically double negative fashion that: "It is difficult ... to believe the share price is not underrating the company's formidable cashflow." Future dividend growth potential looked "far greater than management has led investors to expect" (*Financial Times*, 1996b). The share price crept up to 205p, just above the flotation price. Investors were back in the black.

Suddenly the management seemed to be on the front foot. The interim (six months) results in November showed that the company was still delivering improvements – operating profit was £81 million up from just £3 million a year before, although the company still made a loss after financial charges (British Energy, 1996). It also announced an innovative long term power contract deal with Southern Electric, which appeared to hedge some 15 per cent of the company's output for up to 15 years. The *Financial Times* headline the next day was "Darling of the utilities". The shares reached 233p, some 14 per cent above their privatisation level. Even in the supposedly professional financial markets, people would rather buy a share when everyone else is buying it – this herd-like behaviour is known as "momentum" investing.

BE's great share rally had begun. Over the next two and a half years BE shares were to rise almost in a straight line, as profits and cashflow steadily grew and investors came to love this strange machine for dividend growth.

The operational gearing benefits that BZW had pointed to drove steadily higher profits and cashflows. Output rose, costs fell and, crucially, wholesale power prices remained buoyant. And the cash came pouring in.

The board and chief executives

The company presented its first set of full year results as British Energy on 4 June 1997. It was the first of a series of increasingly triumphant annual presentations. Pretax profit had swung from a pro-forma loss of £155 million the year before to £61 million. Net debt had fallen from £679 million at privatisation to £262 million, confirming the company's cashflow strength. The dividend of 13.7p was as forecast in the privatisation prospectus. Chairman John Robb restated his discomfort that the dividend was uncovered (i.e. was less than the company's accounting profit, equivalent to 5.1p a share). But the cashflow was prodigious: free cashflow was £459 million. Admittedly this figure was boosted by some £108 million of non-recurring items (and the fact that the company had not yet paid any tax). But that still left an underlying free cashflow of £361 million, or 51.9p a share (see Figure 8.1). The company also announced a new £1.5 billion ten year contract with BNFL covering AGR fuel fabrication services. This new deal would raise annual profits by a further £10 million from next year.

The huge difference between accounting profit and cashflow was a distinctive feature of BE which made conventional stock market valuation methods potentially unreliable (see Chapter 11). The market liked the results. The shares rose by 9p on the day, to reach 251p. The *Financial Times* sounded a note of caution, suggesting that "with BE vulnerable to cuts in pool [wholesale electricity] prices, the shares look fully valued" (*Financial Times*, 1997a). But a leading broker, HSBC James Capel published a new valuation for the shares of 340p,

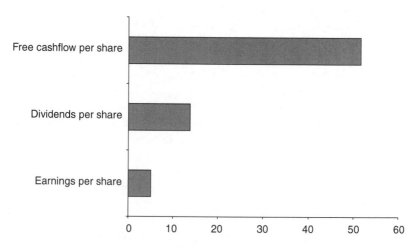

Figure 8.1 Key results for year ending 31 March 1997 (pence per share) (source: British Energy Annual Report 1996–1997, pp. 16–17).

arguing that the shares were currently trading on a prospective EV (enterprise value) to EBITDA (earnings before interest, tax, depreciation and amortisation) multiple of only 3.2 times (HSBC James Capel, 1997). Although HSBC had used a discounted cashflow valuation too, the use of the EV/EBITDA ratio was to become routine over the next few years, despite its unsuitability for a company whose core operations had a limited life (see Chapter 11).

A year after its fraught privatisation, British Energy seemed to have been fully rehabilitated. A week later Bob Hawley received a CBE in the Queen's birthday honours list. Then, three days after the honours news, a company press release announced tersely that Hawley was leaving British Energy "to expand his career in other directions". A confused stock market was told that Hawley (aged 60) had been told he was not in line to succeed John Robb as chairman and had therefore decided to quit. Robb (aged 61) told the press that the company needed a chief executive to lead for ten years and that with Hawley and himself being about the same age, he couldn't allow a situation where they both left the company at about the same time. Robb would run the company for up to six months while they searched for a new chief executive (British Energy, 1997b).

The lack of a successor made it obvious that Hawley's exit was unplanned. Nobody believed age was the real cause. The press and investor speculation turned to the "did he jump or was he pushed?" debate. If Hawley had been fired, why get rid of the man that a BZW research note described as "the main architect of Nuclear Electric and British Energy's improved performance in the last few years" (BZW Research, 1997)? Chief executives normally leave when companies are doing badly, not when they're beating the market's profit expectations. Why would Hawley want to leave so successful a position, and so abruptly?

The real problem was that Robb and Hawley didn't get on and were competing for power. Both were strong and sometimes inflexible men, who expected to give orders, not receive them. The division of labour between a chairman and chief executive is formally clear; the chief executive is appointed to execute the strategy agreed by the board and the chairman leads the board in monitoring the chief executive. Robb, a former chief executive himself, appeared to expect the chief executive to show more deference to the chairman. Senior executives who saw the men working together were not surprised when the relationship broke down. As *The Scotsman* put it, "Robb has proved beyond doubt yet again that there can be only one chairman, and he has enlisted the non-exec powerbrokers of the board – in the persons of Sir Robin Biggam and Peter Stevenson – to prove it. In such a politically sensitive company, the Anglo-Scottish status of these three could prove crucial" (*The Scotsman*, 1997).

The stock market seemed relatively relaxed at the prospect of a six month search for a new chief executive. Hawley, who left with £450,000 compensation, was much admired for his executive skills, but had not built much of a fan club in the City. He was too often abrasive and impatient with investors whose backgrounds were more likely to be in classics than engineering. Some investors thought he was too keen on diversification and were concerned by the announcement just before Hawley's resignation that BE would take a minority equity stake in a gas-fired power station on the River Humber being developed by the French oil company Elf. Although BE also signed a power contract with Elf, there was no operational benefit to the company in the capital investment. Investors had told the board that they would prefer to see any surplus cash safely returned to them. The *Financial Times* Lex column saw Hawley's departure as a "golden opportunity to press the company to focus its ambitions", i.e. pay back cash to shareholders (*Financial Times*, 1997c). The pressure was building that would lead to the disastrous "return of value" in the summer of 1999.

Many investors also took comfort in the view that the company had two excellent internal candidates for the job of chief executive: Robin Jeffrey, the head of Scottish Nuclear; and Peter Warry, the boss of Nuclear Electric. But sensitivities over Anglo-Scottish rivalries meant that neither candidate could be appointed for fear of upsetting the balance of power. The nationalist rivalry was to deny the company access to well qualified leadership and to cost the departure of the highly regarded Warry.

But Hawley's departure didn't seem to dent the company's momentum. The company pulled a rabbit out of its hat in September 1997 when it revealed that the renegotiations with BNFL mentioned in the June results meeting had been even more valuable then expected. The new contracts with BNFL meant that nuclear fuel costs had turned out to be some £400 million less than before, leading to £30 million higher annual profits through to 2004, not the £10 million originally announced. Second, the contracts would mean that some 82 per cent of future fuel reprocessing costs were now covered by fixed price, index linked contracts, up from 62 per cent previously (British Energy, 1997c). Higher profits and lower risk, all in one package. The shares rallied by 13 per cent in a day.

The BNFL contracts in fact remained opaque to investors. What had happened was the result of a long negotiation between the two companies, led by Peter Warry, who had used the negotiating strategy successfully applied before by Scottish Nuclear. This was to threaten to abandon reprocessing of spent fuel and opt for dry storage instead, which would be cheaper for BE and would deprive BNFL of one of its two domestic customers (the other being Magnox Electric, which had become part of BNFL on the creation of British Energy). BNFL were not sure that BE were serious and there would have been serious planning permission problems, just as there had been in Scotland. But the upshot was a deal which both extended the contract coverage of BE's future back end liabilities (thus transferring the risk of cost increases to BNFL) and delivered an overall cut in costs of about £1 billion. Most of these cost savings fell far into the future so the net present value was around £400 million, still a sizeable improvement in value for a company with a market value of about £2 billion. BE's team tried to get the annual costs linked to the price of power but BNFL were not prepared to take the extra risk this entailed (private interviews).

The BE board had a happy choice to make on the £400 million present value of the contract benefit. It could take it gradually over time, in the form of several years of higher cashflows. But instead, and fatefully, the board decided to take the full benefit up front, envisaging a special repayment to shareholders. Thus the City priority on returning cash displaced the chance to build up protection against future power price weakness.

From 1997 through to 1999, it appears from interviews with former executives that the board rejected any notion that power prices might become a problem. In the first half of 1997 Warry's commercial team submitted to the board price forecasts that assumed deteriorating prices, including a "low" scenario in which prices fell to the new entry cost of gas power stations, which was then about £17–£18/MWh. With excess capacity, the price would likely fall further, to marginal cost. The logic was that BE needed to produce power at a cash cost of £16/MWh to be confident that it could survive the low scenarios. Even on the central case the power price was expected to fall steadily. The job of a board is not to forecast the future but ensure that the company has made prudent provision for reasonably foreseeable risks. Nobody in 1997 could pretend to "know" that power prices would fall – and in fact they stayed remarkably high for the next two years, at great benefit to BE shareholders.

But, of all the generating companies, BE was the most exposed to the threat of lower prices, as had been emphasised by the directors themselves in the privatisation prospectus of June 1996. Yet the board seem not to have been worried. Former senior managers report that the message repeatedly came back that they were too pessimistic about prices and in any case it was the job of the managers to keep prices high. Yet the point about a pure commodity power producer like BE is that it has no pricing power. Wholesale electricity prices for most of the 1990s were set almost entirely by the duopoly of National Power and PowerGen (and partially by Eastern Energy). And if the duopoly was either regulated or competed away, the price would be set by a competitive market, one that looked increasingly as if it had too much capacity.

Investors weren't worrying much about power prices in 1997 either. Investment bank Morgan Stanley published an influential report that argued that the company was possibly 30 per cent undervalued relative to its peers. The valuation was based again on the EV/EBITDA ratio approach. The analyst pointed to the likelihood of five year life extensions for two power stations, which they estimated would add £300 million to the company's value (*Financial Times*, 1997b), a much larger figure than government advisor BZW had estimated a year before (BZW Research, 1996a p. 59). The company's shares continued their climb through the late summer and early autumn of 1997, helped by the news that the electricity regulator, Stephen Littlechild, was moving away from the threat of price controls on the fossil generators, National Power and Power-Gen (Reuters, 1997). Any such controls designed to restrain the duopoly's profits would have hit British Energy's too.

Further good news came in September when British Energy announced the formation of a 50/50 joint venture with the American nuclear power utility PECO, to be called AmerGen. This was the first step towards building a new business in the US, buying up stakes in nuclear power stations and making them more valuable though consolidation and improved operations (see later in this chapter). Although shareholders were keen that BE didn't waste its cash on diversification into areas it had no competitive advantage in, the market could see that AmerGen was a well thought-out scheme with good profit potential.

Then in November BE announced what looked like a sensible deal to build small peak load power stations in association with regional electricity company Southern Electric. Peak power prices were very high and such power stations could be very profitable. Plus it meant that British Energy was diluting its exposure to the off-peak prices that determined most of its revenue. By the time of the interim profits announcement in November 1997, BE was on a roll. It had survived the loss of its chief executive, revealed two sensible strategic moves (the US and the peak plants), delivered a £400 million benefit from the BNFL contract and kept output running at a high level. Power prices still showed no signs of falling. The company made a small profit for the first half of 1997/1998, compared with a loss of £53 million the previous year (British Energy, 1997a). The shares were now trading around £4, up from £2.50 in the summer. And then on 28 November 1997 the company finally found a new chief executive.

Peter Hollins could hardly have been more different from his predecessor. A calm, easygoing figure, ready to listen and exuding a quiet confidence and determination, he quickly made a good impression on investors. A former senior manager at the iconic British chemicals company ICI, he brought with him two things that should have helped him manage BE effectively. The first was ICI's consensual style of problem solving, based on a willingness to get round a table and figure out the right actions. The second was an awareness of the tough realities of commodity prices. Hollins had been responsible for a division of ICI's PVC business, an industry notorious for a cycle of high prices and profits followed by over-capacity, low prices and huge losses. PVC had much in common with electricity; it was a capital intensive commodity manufacturing activity in which the tendency for herd behaviour into over-investment constantly threatened to destroy shareholder returns.

But these two advantages didn't help in practice. Hollins' friendly style was appreciated by many of his staff but failed with the board. Now that Hawley had gone, the non-executive directors (including Chairman John Robb) seemed to square up for constant fights with the executives. Former executive directors recall Hollins being treated with open contempt right from his first meeting. Hollins appeared to be completely unprepared for this, admittedly unusual behaviour. Right up until his departure in June 2001 Hollins was liked and respected in the City but he seems never to have commanded the authority of his own board (private interviews).

When Hollins took the chief executive job he ended the uneasy period after Hawley's departure during which Robin Jeffrey and Peter Warry could pretend to still have serious executive roles at the company. Warry left BE, depriving it of one of the few people who seemed to understand the future power price risk. Robin Jeffrey became head of the new North American operation, which was to be a great success over the next four years. He would fly back to Scotland for monthly board meetings. But his role in North America meant that the only board member with direct, engineering experience of nuclear power stations was mostly absent abroad.

Investing in North America

The logic of investing in North American nuclear power was compelling. British Energy reckoned it had two strengths. First, it had five years of experience of world class operations of nuclear power stations, having taken the AGRs from world's worst to best load factors and with an excellent first year at Sizewell B. Second, it understood the complex issues in privatising a nuclear power company in a deregulated industry – it had safely and profitably operated nuclear plant in a (somewhat) competitive market. The first of these strengths turned out to be transient – the world's best practice was constantly improving and soon overtook BE to leave it back in the second division again. But the overall story was compelling at the time. So BE decided they should look at the US and Canadian nuclear markets, which were both ripe for investment.

In the US, deregulation was happening in a piecemeal fashion, reflecting the state-based regulatory system. Several states were ending the right of utilities to captive customers, which increased the risk to those with high cost generation. Nuclear plant was widely seen as very high cost. It was hard to improve nuclear performance because many stations were jointly owned by several utilities, so there was no clear control. Many of these utilities wanted to get rid of their nuclear assets and the transition to competition provided a financial cushion in the form of compensation from regulators for the introduction of competition. Utilities were therefore happy to sell their nuclear assets for relatively little money.

Even before Bob Hawley's departure, BE had identified an opportunity to buy individual nuclear stations and consolidate them into a single company, achieving the benefits of focused management that they gained when NE and SNL were set up after the rest of British power generation was privatised. But they needed a US partner: electricity is a highly political industry in the US and a foreign company would find it hard to do business. BE identified the Pennsylvania-based US electricity company PECO, which had already begun a plan to build a larger nuclear business but lacked cash. BE had cash, and a growing reputation for turning around underperforming nuclear stations. PECO Nuclear's president and chief nuclear officer Dickinson M. Smith was a former Rear Admiral, part of the wave of former US navy personnel whose discipline and thoroughness were revolutionising the American nuclear industry in the 1990s. Robin Jeffrey had led the first meetings with PECO and developed a good working relationship. In September 1997 the two companies set up a joint 50–50 venture called AmerGen to invest in US nuclear power plants.

The other part of BE's North American plan was Canada. With roots going back to research during the Second World War, Canada had a major domestic nuclear programme based on the CANDU (CANadian Deuterium Uranium), heavy water-moderated reactor. But Ontario Hydro, the provincial utility, had recently been performing poorly. Half the reactors were shut down and the Minister of Energy wanted advice on what to do. BE's predecessor Nuclear Electric had contacts with Ontario Hydro – Bob Hawley and Mike Kirwan had visited the company in early 1995 (Nuclear Electric, 1995b). In late 1997 Robin Jeffrey presented BE's story to the Ministry and realised that the profit from giving advice would be small compared with the possible returns from ownership. In January 1998 Jeffrey chose Toronto as his North American base, which was convenient for the north-eastern US and allowed him to keep a close eye on the political developments that would determine whether the Ontario provincial government would allow privatisation of the nuclear stations to a foreign company. To the company's frustration the Ontario privatisation had to be suspended in August 1998 owing to political difficulties connected with the planned introduction of competition to Ontario's electricity markets. By the time talks on privatisation were restarted BE was in a much weaker financial state.

In July 1998 AmerGen announced its first investment – at Three Mile Island, Pennsylvania. It shows how much investor credibility BE had built up by this point that it was able to tell City investors that it was buying a sister plant (TMI 1) to the famously damaged (TMI 2) plant for some US$100 million, with only a slight frisson of nervousness in the stock market. The BE board were apparently initially hostile to the idea but were persuaded to support the deal.

Corporate strategy and the attempt to vertically integrate

On 4 March 1998 the largest UK generator National Power, announced a serious and poorly handled profit warning to the stock market. The ending of the government-sponsored coal supply contracts revealed how much profit the fossil generators had been receiving in exchange for helping to bail out the coal industry since 1993. As National Power's shares tumbled, British Energy was able to distance itself from the fossil generators. BE gave new guidance to investors that current year profits (1997/1998) would be around £160 million, which was some £35 million–£40 million above brokers' previous expectations (*Dow Jones International News*, 1998). BE's shares reached £5.75 and were now the best performing of the FTSE 100 largest companies over the previous 12 months. They had risen 185 per cent over the two years since privatisation.

One of Peter Hollins's main goals was to end the long standing absurdity of, in effect, having three head offices. This he achieved when in June 1998 the company confirmed a total merger of the Nuclear Electric and Scottish Nuclear subsidiaries, with an annual saving of £5 million–£10 million (British Energy, 1998b). Analysts had always been puzzled why this completion of the original merger had taken so long but the reason was outside the company's control. The rules of the industry safety regulator, the Nuclear Installations Inspectorate, stated that the nuclear operating licences that NE and SNL separately held could not be simply transferred along with a change of ownership. A full re-licensing process was needed, which prevented full integration of NE and SNL for over two years.

With the additional cost savings from the NE/SNL merger, the company had implemented most of what it had promised at privatisation. It had continued to cut costs; it had driven output up further and it had set up a promising new North American business. Its next goal was vertical integration in the UK.

The logic of vertical integration was threefold. First, buying a "downstream" business – meaning a retail electricity supply company – would provide a partial hedge against the volatility of wholesale power prices. Retail power prices were fully deregulated in 1999 when all customers were free to shop around for power. Retail prices would probably fluctuate broadly in line with wholesale prices, but there would probably be some lag between them which would mean that to some extent profits in the "upstream" (generation) and "downstream" businesses would be uncorrelated, so that ownership of both would mean a more stable overall profit stream.

The second argument was strategic. British Energy's core UK assets were ageing nuclear power stations. Although their lives might be extended by five or ten years, they must eventually close. So, unlike most manufacturing businesses, BE's core business would shrink, unless there was a dramatic change in the economics and politics of new nuclear power stations. With an increasingly saturated non-nuclear generation industry, there was little reason to invest in other generation assets (other than the peak load stations agreed with Southern Electric). This left two alternatives: accept gradual extinction of the company, while paying back cash to shareholders; or invest the cash surplus in other electricity assets that the board could persuade investors were near enough to generation that they didn't count as diversification. Buying a regional electricity company (REC) might just pass this test, particularly as the two non-nuclear generators had tried to do the same thing.

The twelve RECs consisted of two separate businesses, which could in principle be separated once the regulator agreed. Distribution was the capital intensive, regulated natural monopoly of carrying power from the national transmission grid to individual customers. Often known as the "wires" business, it made relatively stable profits, had limited growth prospects and employed lots of engineers. The main risk arose from the still new system of regulation. It was quite different operationally from the business of running generation, which was a competitive, cyclical manufacturing business with considerable commercial risk.

The second REC business was known as "supply", a name that frequently caused confusion with distribution. Supply meant the commercial buying and selling of power, together with billing and payments collection. Supply required little capital and very few assets. It was a combination of mass transaction processing (reading millions of meters, sending out bills and collecting of accounts) and electricity purchasing. Since the dominant cost in electricity purchasing was the wholesale cost of electricity, there was a potential commercial value in a generating company owning a supply business.

But the purchase of distribution needed more justification, which came in the third reason for BE to buy a REC: the need to provide a means of investing cashflows to pay for long term liabilities that would fall due in the future. BE's liabilities for decommissioning power stations were dealt with by investing in a separate financial fund – the pension fund for retired power stations. But the other liabilities, most of which involved decades of payments to BNFL, would have to come from operating cashflows because there was no separate fund of investments to cover these. As the power stations closed, it would be necessary (or at least desirable) that there was some new source of operating cashflows to meet these outgoings, preferably one with stable, relatively predictable earnings and little risk of obsolescence. Regional electricity distribution fitted this rather well. Arguably an even better solution would have been simply to set up another segregated fund, investing in a portfolio of equities. But, unless BE one day built new nuclear stations, that would have deprived the management of any long term career options.

The deal that got away: Southern Electric

From the middle of 1997 until early 1999, it was known that BE was trying to buy a REC. But what has not previously been in the public domain is that in mid-1997, BE very nearly pulled off a merger with probably the best managed and most successful REC, Southern Electric plc. This merger would have produced the largest electricity company in the UK and one that might have been big and strong enough to take part in the future consolidation of the European power industry, which in early 2007 was dominated by two German companies (E.ON and RWE), two French (EDF and Suez) and one Italian company (ENEL). A BE-Southern combination would have provided a resilient supply of profit and cashflow that might have carried the generation side through the trough in prices in 2001–2003 without the crisis that forced BE shareholders to lose their investment. So the failure to consummate the merger was of great significance to shareholders – but they never knew about it.

Southern Electric during 1996 and 1997 enjoyed a reputation for vigorous cost cutting under its chief executive, Jim Forbes, who hailed from Scotland and was known in some quarters as the "jockweiler". Forbes had an impressive management team and the company was well regarded by investors, save for one thing. The company refused to do what so many other RECs had done and take on far more debt on its balance sheet, allowing it then to pay out a large special dividend to shareholders. Southern wanted to keep its balance sheet strong in case it could find a good acquisition or merger opportunity. It was widely expected that eventually the larger and stronger RECs would be allowed to buy the smaller ones, with substantial cost saving potential. As the leading cost cutter, Southern expected to benefit from this trend when it was allowed.

But Southern's board was mindful of the risk that a takeover might entail paying such a large premium to the owners of the acquired REC that there would be little benefit for Southern's shareholders. So Southern's directors had settled on a search for a "nil-premium" merger, in which the benefits of future efficiency gains would be shared between the two companies' shareholders. This stance was far from popular in the City at the time because it conflicted with the conventional wisdom of returning surplus cash. But Southern's excellent operational success and the quality of the management gave the company enough of a supporters club that it could withstand the pressure for a time.

Somehow, the exact details are not clear, the close working relationship between Southern and BE led to the idea of a merger between them; it would provide Southern with automatic power hedging and BE with a partial hedge for its power price risk. Partial, because Southern's total electricity needs were about 28 TWh, a long way short of BE's total output of 67 TWh. It would create a powerful integrated company that would be well positioned for consolidation of the RECs. And it would provide Jim Forbes with a new area to put his cost cutting skills to use. Discussions started between Forbes and Hawley, who both liked the idea. The market equity values of the companies were about £1.9 billion (BE) and £2.7 billion (Southern) in mid-1997 so that although Southern was the larger company, a nil-premium merger of equals was broadly plausible.

The talks stopped when Hawley left BE. Some former BE executives believe that part of the reason Hawley left was that the BE board – and chairman John Robb in particular – felt that the Southern talks had been kept back from them. Some have speculated that Hawley hoped that the new BE–Southern combination would have seen Hawley elevated to chairman and Robb pushed out. Whatever the truth of this, the speculation indicates just how bad the rivalry between Robb and Hawley appeared to their colleagues. Some time after Hawley's departure, the talks with Southern were resumed, suggesting that the BE board shared Hawley's view that a deal could work.

Events then moved quickly to the point that in August 1997 the two companies were set to merge. Robb would become chairman of the combined company and Forbes the chief executive. The boards of both companies went to the office of lawyers Clifford Chance in London. The advisors had the press releases ready and expected that the deal would be signed and announced imminently. There was a joint meeting between both boards and then each retired to separate meetings. The Southern board were waiting, confident that the deal was done. Then something strange happened. The board of British Energy, after a heated discussion, voted to reject the merger. A group of non-executive directors, including the chairman, apparently expressed doubts that this was the right deal and that Forbes was the right man. The executive directors, shocked that an excellent deal was about to be lost, argued for it. But the vote went against them.

As time went by, the waiting Southern directors were at first puzzled, then concerned and then annoyed at the delay. Two former BE board members recall that the non-executive directors, having voted against the deal, then urged the chairman to tell Jim Forbes personally that the deal was off. But it was the company secretary (the chief lawyer of the company) Robert Armour who had to tell the Southern directors that regretfully the BE board had decided not to proceed. No explanation was given and the Southern directors were left furious and perplexed (private interviews). Companies fail to merge for all sorts of reasons but they seldom get so close to agreement before breaking up.

Exactly what happened at the BE meeting is hard to reconstruct from diverse and increasingly unreliable personal memories. But it appears that the chairman, John Robb, changed his mind on the deal. Robb had met his prospective new colleague Jim Forbes for dinner the night before, although this was not the first time they had met. Did the forceful Forbes remind Robb rather too much of Bob Hawley? Forbes would not strike anyone as anything other than his own boss. The official reasons given in the minutes of the board meeting of that day are not very convincing:

> The board considered management cultures and the individuals proposed for the [merged company] board membership. Forbes had a forceful reputation for cost cutting but his experience in business development and international investment was unproven. This applied to the rest of the [Southern] team. The issue of investment was critical as the merger would increase the cashflows available and would also allow for the options of some return of cash to share-holders. Mr. Forbes' commitment to move to Scotland was less than whole-hearted and there were concerns it would not be implemented post merger.
>
> (British Energy board minutes 4 August 1997, provided to author)

Note that the issue of Forbes' willingness to move (back) to Scotland was regarded as important, even though Forbes was actually (and famously in the electricity industry) Scottish.

Other RECs

It is too much to say that the failure of this deal alone destroyed the hope of BE surviving through the later power price collapse but it is one of the British electricity industry's great might-have-beens. Whatever the reasons for the board's decision to block the deal, they cannot have realised at the time that this would be the best chance they would get of buying a REC. BE and its financial advisors continued to search for targets. In September 1997 BE's name was linked in the financial press to that of the REC Yorkshire Electricity (*Sunday Times*, 1998). BE made no comment and Yorkshire was subsequently sold to another company. Not knowing anything of the abortive Southern talks, investors continued to push the share price up.

Over the course of 1998 BE talked at various stages to pretty much all the RECs that were potentially up for sale (private interviews). Some had already been bought by US companies, which added an extra barrier to BE because consolidation among those US companies complicated the disposal of their assets. BE was perhaps unlucky, but it also had a reputation among some corporate financiers as a "serial under-bidder" (private interviews).

In November 1998, as BE's share price soared to £6.19 (three times the privatisation price), the company made a bid for London Electricity, another REC.

Unfortunately the market for RECs had by now become highly contested. In the case of London Electricity the other bidder was the French electricity giant, EDF, ironically the world's largest nuclear power producer and at that time still wholly owned by the French government. EDF was something of a legend in financial markets for always being willing to pay more than anybody else for acquisitions. Bitter rivals would point to the company as having, in effect, state subsidised finance since it could borrow at barely a higher rate than the French government.

Nor did EDF seem constrained by the normal rules of shareholder value. Both EDF and BE put in cash bids around £2 billion. On 23 November EDF not only raised its bid further but, very unusually, made the bid "unconditional". This was a potentially reckless move because it committed EDF to paying out even if there were regulatory or other barriers to the sale, in which case EDF could be liable for substantial costs. British Energy could not match such tactics and EDF added London to its growing international portfolio.

BE tried to get the British government to block EDF on the grounds that it was impossible for foreign companies to buy into EDF's protected and monopolistic market (private interview). But the DTI's view on mergers was that the market ruled. It had already been very relaxed about US acquisitions of RECs so it decided not to block what became the first of several European acquisitions.

By early December 1998, BE's share price was nudging £6.50. Having been frustrated in their attempt to buy a REC, BE's management despaired of finding a major investment opportunity in the UK. It wanted to buy one or both of the two large 2,000 MW coal stations being sold by PowerGen as part of a deal for regulatory approval to buy the REC East Midlands Electricity. But the DTI made it clear that it was opposed to the sale of the stations to BE, even though it had no other price-setting generation plant (*Guardian*, 1999). The stations were sold – at what soon looked like a very high price – to the American company Edison Mission Energy.

The "return of value"

The blocking of its attempt to buy coal power stations seemed to remove the last option for investing BE's apparently endlessly growing cashflow. In meetings with investors ahead of the close of its financial year in March 1999, the finance director and investor relations team indicated that the company accepted the logic that if it had no other use for surplus funds then they should be returned to shareholders. This was in one sense obviously true: basic shareholder value logic dictates that companies must not simply pointlessly sit on cash in the bank. The question was, how much truly surplus cash was there and what sort of payment to shareholders would be sensible?

There were also voices inside the company arguing that there was a need for investment inside BE, to improve the reliability of its plant. The improvement in AGR load factor had stopped and output in 1998/1999 was to prove the peak. The case for investment was that the stations could be made to produce more, adding revenues, and do it more consistently. More reliable output would reduce the risk that the company would contract to sell power to a customer then find it couldn't deliver it and have to buy it in from the market at possibly great cost. One internal study suggested that output could be raised by some 6 TWh by investing £35 million–£40 million annually over four to five years. So for a total investment of the order of £200 million the company might raise annual revenues by around £120 million (at a price of £20/MWh). Assuming a profit margin of, say, 25 per cent this would provide a pretax return of around 15 per cent, plus the benefits of greater reliability (private interviews).

The board turned down the proposal. At the end of March 1999 the company's balance sheet showed net cash of £176 million or *negative* gearing of about 10 per cent of net assets. BE had been keeping its financial position strong in case of a major acquisition that would lead to taking on a lot of debt. But having failed to do a deal, it seemed indefensible to keep the balance sheet debt free. Or at least it would be if the company could be confident that it would continue to generate surplus cash in future. In the financial year 1998/1999 the company created some £514 million of operating cashflow after tax. Of this, £109 million went on various investments and a tiny amount of debt interest, leaving £405 million of "free" cashflow. In other words, if BE's managers believed they could generate a similar amount of cashflow next year and if they could see no other investment use for the cash then they could distribute around £400 million to shareholders as dividends or share buybacks and still have no increase in debt on the balance sheet.

Both board and investors could see this logic very clearly. BE must pay back cash – the only question was how much. The annual results meeting on 13 May 1999 was probably the highpoint in British Energy's corporate history. The tone of the meeting was little short of triumphant. British Energy was the largest UK power generator and was now worth £4 billion. Peter Hollins was happy to tell the assembled shareholders and analysts that the company had increased profits by 56 per cent to £298 million. The Torness and Heysham power stations were confirmed as having received five year life extensions, adding around £500 million to the company's value. The ordinary dividend was raised 9 per cent to 16p a share. And, in recognition of the company's strong cash position and the lack of major acquisition opportunities, the board was proposing a "return of value" of £432 million to shareholders, equivalent to 60p a share (British Energy, 1999d). Anybody who had bought the shares at privatisation for £2.03 would have received back a total of £1.14 of dividends (including the return of value) and still have shares worth over £5.

There is something paradoxical about companies returning equity to shareholders; it can be seen as a mark of failure because it shows a lack of investment opportunities. But during the 1990s the British utility sector had turned into a cash machine, with a variety of share buybacks, special dividends and enhanced dividends. For the true utilities, companies with stable, predictable monopoly businesses like electricity distribution and water supply, distributing cash shouldn't be too risky because the company could rebuild reserves in the future.

For a manufacturing company like BE, facing the possibility of much weaker revenues in future, the risk was greater.

And it was quite reasonable to think that British Energy's best days were already behind it. The electricity markets were preparing for a major change in the way power was traded – the New Electricity Trading Arrangements (NETA). NETA, scheduled to start in early 2001 was intended to make the power market more competitive (see Chapter 13). The electricity regulator OFFER (which became OFGEM when it merged with the gas regulator in 1999) and the DTI had become utterly frustrated at persistently high wholesale electricity prices. They attributed the high prices to the continuing lack of competition in the generation market. NETA was intended to bring about more aggressive pricing by altering the way in which prices were actually set. Nobody could be quite sure what NETA would bring. But it was obvious that regulatory and government policy was now to get power prices down. An analyst from Salomon Smith Barney told the *Financial Times* in April 1999, power prices "fell by about 5 per cent in real terms last year and are only going one way. The question is how quickly" (*Financial Times*, 1999c).

In no area of life than the stock market is it more true to say that it is better to travel hopefully than to arrive, or as market lore has it, "buy on the rumour and sell on the fact". BE's shares fell on the day of the announcement from £6.17 to £5.97. But this was because most of the news of the day was expected or "priced in". Some investors correctly believed that this was as good as it gets. The shares had actually peaked in January 1999 at £7.33. But in May the general mood was far from pessimistic. The *Financial Times* commented a few days after the results that the shares were "worth buying purely on cashflow valuations" (*Financial Times*, 1999a). Nobody would have believed that just one year later the company would be *cutting* its dividend.

The return of value ("value" being a polite word for cash that is preferred in institutional investor circles) happened in June. The company reduced its equity base by £432 million and consolidated its shares in issue, so that although the value of the company had shrunk by 10 per cent, the number of shares in issue had fallen too, leaving the average share value unchanged, at about £5.50. This was a cosmetic result that made life easier for financial analysts, who didn't need to re-jig their models.

In a break with tradition the front cover of the 1998/1999 annual report was adorned with a blue and mauve image of a ceramic sculpture by Jane Blackman, part of a series sponsored by British Energy. The report was titled "The Art of Energy". Inside the front cover investors were told that BE had commissioned artists in Glasgow and Scotland to "produce a piece of work that conveyed a sense of innovation, creativity and vitality as well as expressing energy in the environment and how it touches our everyday lives" (British Energy, 1999a p. 1). It is a cliché of insolvency practitioners that an early warning signal of companies heading for financial trouble is a tendency to place expensive art in the head office. Was BE unintentionally signalling that dark times lay ahead? The company's senior managers can hardly be blamed for feeling pleased.

The chairman looked uncharacteristically cheerful in his annual report photograph. The chief executive appeared relaxed and confident in his. But both referred in their statements to the likelihood of lower power prices ahead.

The report also reaffirmed that, despite the failure to buy London Electricity, the company was still seeking an electricity supply business. It was also in the market for flexible generation, meaning a coal power station. And only a few days after the annual report came out, BE finally pulled off a UK acquisition, albeit a relatively small one in financial terms. On 24 June 1999 BE announced that it had bought the electricity supply business (but not the distribution business) of the small Welsh electricity company SWALEC (from South Wales Electricity Company), which since 1996 had been part of the combined Welsh utility Hyder. For £107 million BE was getting a business that supplied electricity to about 870,000 commercial and domestic customers, and gas to about 310,000 customers, mostly in Wales.

SWALEC was a minnow. Its total supply volume was about 8 TWh, compared with BE's total output of around 69 TWh. British Energy's own electricity retailing business had achieved a market share of between 3 per cent and 4 per cent, made up of large industrial and commercial customers. SWALEC mainly domestic retailing business brought the total to about 6 per cent of the total electricity market (Competition Commission, 2001 para. 6.10).

In the previous year, SWALEC supply business had made pre-tax profits of £23.6 million but this included a one off credit of £7.3 million. So the underlying profit was £16.3 million. Assuming a tax charge of 30 per cent, the net profit would be some £11 million, which would imply that BE were paying 9.4 times earnings, a price that seemed reasonable for the supply business alone.

Unfortunately that was not all that BE bought. SWALEC had a long term contract to buy 20 per cent of the power produced by the Teesside Power CCGT power station owned predominantly by Enron – about 2.5 TWh a year. The price of the power on this contract was confidential but it was known to be high relative to prevailing power prices. SWALEC had signed the contract to help underpin its equity stake in the plant, an arrangement typical of the deals signed by most RECs at the time of privatisation and later approved by the regulator. SWALEC was now selling the "out of the money" power contract but retaining the profitable equity stake. The cost of the contract had to be added to the cash cost of £107 million that BE was paying.

The price of the power in the Teesside contracts was widely rumoured to be in the region of 3p/kWh, high at the time of the contract and increasingly so as the market price of power fell. With a wholesale market price of 2.4p/kWh the annual loss to the contract would be around £14 million pre-tax. But when later the wholesale price fell to below 2p/kWh the loss would balloon to around £24 million pre-tax. The future value of this contract was evidently negative and significantly so. BE did not get a bargain when it bought SWALEC's supply business.

Not only was SWALEC the smallest supplier in Britain, it had no useful brand name outside southern Wales. The operational side of the business – billing, cash collection and so on – would be run by SWALEC's previous owner, Hyder, under a five year contract. BE had no similar business so there were no efficiency gains from integration. BE later told the Competition Commission that it had intended to build up a national electricity supply business and that buying an existing one, even a small one, was cheaper and much quicker than trying to build one from scratch (Competition Commission, 2001 para. 6.10).

The stockmarket was indifferent, BE shares falling two and a half pence to 517p, now nearly 30 per cent off their peak. Press comment was muted; nobody yet saw the problems with the Teesside contract. There was no sense of crisis. Over the next month the shares rallied to £5.86. But they would not reach that level again.

The day after announcing the SWALEC purchase, BE's American joint venture AmerGen announced it had agreed to buy two Boiling Water Reactors near Syracuse owned by Niagara Mohawk and NY State Electric and Gas Corporation. BE's share of the investment was £57.5 million. BE had now invested £165 million in expansion since the return of value, but the biggest investment of the financial year was yet to come.

At the interim results on 10 November, profits still seemed to be growing. First half pretax profits had risen to £55 million from £46 million (on an underlying basis) despite a "temporary reduction in output arising from abnormal technical problems" (British Energy, 1999b p. 1). AmerGen's US investments yielded their first operating profit contribution, albeit of only £6 million, but with potential for "substantial" contribution in future. AmerGen had agreed in principle to buy five more nuclear stations (British Energy, 1999b p. 2).

Chief Executive Peter Hollins said his team had identified a further £25 million of cost savings to come, involving a further 250 cut in staff. The company was targeting a power station average load factor of 85 per cent within three years, up from the 81 per cent achieved the previous year. Unit costs were just over 2.0p/kWh. And "we are confident that the initiatives we already have underway and the others planned will enable us to reduce our unit operating costs at least as fast as any likely fall in selling prices" (British Energy, 1999b p. 3). Net debt at 30 September had risen to £137 million from a net cash position of £176 million a year before, a swing of £209 million. But this had included the return of value of £432 million so the underlying cash generation was evidently still strong. In fact Hollins felt confident enough to tell investors that the company had balance sheet strength to buy several non-nuclear UK power stations *and* another British supply business, *and* a large part of Ontario Hydro nuclear assets *and* more US generation (*Financial Times*, 1999b).

Buying coal power

Hollins was hinting at a UK power station acquisition and a week later BE revealed it was buying the 2,000 MW Eggborough coal power station in Yorkshire from National Power for £615 million. Why buy a coal station? First, under the new electricity trading arrangements (NETA), there was a potentially severe financial penalty for failing to deliver power that had been contracted with a customer. Nuclear stations were prone to sudden unplanned shutdowns that meant that BE faced a high risk in contracting its power. Owning Eggborough, which would typically be run some way below full capacity, provided a source of standby power to back the nuclear contracts.

Second, and more controversially, Eggborough would allow BE to sell contracts that were "shaped", meaning they would provide more power at some times of the day than others, in contrast with the normal base load (continuous output) contracts that the company had traditionally sold. It had been restricted from competing in the higher priced shaped contracts market because nuclear stations naturally run at full load. Eggborough could be flexed up or down to meet customer demand and thereby provide physical backing for the more valuable shaped load contracts.

All of this was reasonable – the problem was the price. National Power had been receiving the value of Eggborough's output flexibility which presumably would be reflected in the selling price. In other words BE would indeed be able to enter the shaped contract market but it wasn't clear that it would make any money out of it. The price in any case looked high. BE's defence was that the price looked reasonable compared with other transactions such as the purchase by the experienced US generator AES of the giant Drax coal plant and the previous year's acquisitions by another US company Edison Mission. This is an argument used by investors in any speculative bubble. BE expected Eggborough to enhance earnings per share in the first full year of ownership. But this is not a reliable test of project returns, as it means only that the profits will exceed the (tax-deductible) interest on the debt raised to fund the acquisition, not that they will cover the investment risk.

Credit rating agency Standard & Poor's (S&P) reaffirmed the company's A– long term rating a couple of days after the deal and noted that the company's financial position remained strong. But it also pointed out that BE would "remain vulnerable to the anticipated downturn in U.K. pool [wholesale power] prices" (Standard & Poor's, 1999). It also put the company's debt on negative outlook, implying that the next change in credit rating would probably be downwards. The other major credit rating agency, Moodys, was more sanguine and reaffirmed its rating with a stable outlook.

Having been so keen to diversify away from nuclear power stations for so long, BE's management evidently gave little thought as to why National Power was now so happy to sell its coal stations. PowerGen, the other main fossil fuel generator, was also divesting much of its coal plant. The duopoly seemed to be liquidating its assets. Internally, the management at National Power and PowerGen were astonished at what other companies were willing to pay for these stations (private interviews). They were selling because they couldn't see these stations being profitable if power prices continued to fall.

Conclusion

The two years since flotation had seen British Energy become one of the most highly regarded companies in the London stock market. Its value had tripled, the management had built a reputation for steadily improving profits and the board had honoured stock market principles by returning £432 million of cash to shareholders. It had made strategic progress too: the North American investment strategy was building momentum; the company finally had acquired a toehold in the supply business; and it had at last diversified into coal power stations. The balance sheet was still reasonably strong, even after buying back 10 per cent of the company's shares, plus a supply business and the acquisition of Eggborough power station. So why were the shares falling?

9 Nemesis (1999–2001)

Introduction

By 1999 British Energy, having travelled hopefully, had arrived. The company had raised profits, returned cash to shareholders and was executing a credible investment strategy in North America while building a vertically integrated business in the UK. But there was one thing outside management's control which would ultimately wreck their reputations and consume the great majority of shareholders' money: the price of power. At privatisation, the chief executive and finance director had endlessly pointed out to prospective shareholders how vulnerable the company was to price weakness. But in the three years since privatisation the wholesale price of power had stayed flat (in nominal terms), and investors seemed to have forgotten about the risks. But a long running war between the regulator and the electricity generating duopoly was about to enter a new phase with British Energy the main casualty.

The cascade of bad news

When chief executive Peter Hollins stood up to make his statement at the interim results on 11 November 1999 BE's shares had fallen by 45 per cent from their peak of £7.33 in January. The reason was market concern over a coming change in the wholesale power market. This was NETA, the New Electricity Trading Arrangements. NETA's purpose was to increase competition in the power market, to reduce prices.

Of all the companies in the UK electricity market, BE was the most exposed to lower power prices because it was a producer of a commodity, namely electricity. Like all nuclear generators it had a large fixed cost base so any change in revenues led to a disproportionate change in profits, which is known as operational gearing (or, in the US, operating leverage). With the large rise in output that BE's managers had achieved in recent years the operational gearing had worked in investors' favour, causing a strong increase in profitability. Now those investors were worrying that the process might go into reverse and drag down profits.

BE had repeatedly played down the likely impact of NETA on power prices and on its own financial prospects. But by November 1999 even BE was forced to recognise a deteriorating outlook. Hollins told investors that the company saw prices falling 10–20 per cent over the next two to three years and that although it would hurt, the company would be able to cope (British Energy, 1999b). The tumbling share price suggested investors didn't agree.

BE investors had got used to rising profits, output and cashflow. The first break in this trend went relatively unnoticed, when in the first half of 1999/2000 output fell by 4 per cent. The company, ascribing the fall to one-off technical factors, reaffirmed its target of a continuing upward trend (British Energy, 1999b). The shares fell 5 per cent over the next two days, to £3.79. Then BE brought forward its monthly output statement for November to announce on 29 November 1999 that its output for the whole year was likely to be below expectations at about 8 per cent below the previous year, owing to unexpectedly long power station outages. This knocked about £40 million–£50 million off analysts' profit expectations for the company. The shares, which had been drifting down since the interim results two weeks before, fell only a further 5 per cent to £3.49, implying that investors thought the bad news was confined to a single year. The company remained "confident that its plans for increased output in the medium term remain unaffected" (British Energy, 1999c). Power prices might be at risk but the company seemed to have retained most of its operational credibility.

The shares rallied a little in early 2000, to just short of £4, still a long way down on the peak of £7.33 a year before, but not yet disastrous. After any pronounced share price fall there are brokers who argue something like the "froth has been blown off", meaning that the stock market had now reappraised the company's value in line with falling power prices. This view turned out to be radically premature. In the month to 8 February the shares fell to £2.37, a further fall of about 40 per cent. By the beginning of March they had fallen to £2, below the original privatisation price.

Stock markets are meant to be forward looking and in this case they certainly were. It was the rapidly deteriorating outlook for power prices that was damaging BE's value. Ironically 1999 had ended with the industry regulator OFGEM (the new name for the merged combination of the electricity and gas regulators) investigating unusually *high* power prices in the summer of 1999. OFGEM attributed these prices to tactical capacity reductions by the coal-fired generators (i.e. nothing to do with British Energy).

It accused the coal generators of manipulating prices and decided that the changes in power trading due to start in 2001 were not enough to discipline the generators. In December 1999 it announced a "good behaviour" regulatory amendment to the licenses of the seven largest power generators. Between February and early April 2000 five of these generators accepted the new condition but two rejected it: British Energy and AES, the US generator which had just bought the giant Drax coal-fired power station from National Power. The companies were therefore referred to the Competition Commission.

Investors were worried by two things. First was the fact that in 1999 a new electricity regulator was appointed. Callum McCarthy, a former investment banker (ironically from BZW), gave the impression that he was going to get much tougher with the generators. The second was the uncertainty entailed by British Energy's referral to the Competition Commission. Aside from the possible harm from getting on the wrong side of the regulator, there was the open-endedness of the process – nobody could be sure what the Commission would recommend. This uncertainty, combined with the perceived hostility of the regulator, reinforced the pressure on BE's shares.

The fall in power prices

The pricing of electricity was far from transparent. Although the pool offered a daily spot price, most power was sold on contracts, the price of which might differ from the spot price. Power prices also vary seasonally, reflecting higher demand in the colder months (in the UK; in countries with lots of air conditioning demand peak prices can be in the summer). Contract prices had until 2000 typically been at a small premium to the average spot price. British Energy had achieved an average price of 2.57p/kWh for the financial year 1999/2000, 12 per cent above the actual time-weighted average pool price (Competition Commission, 2001 para. 7.137). Two things started going wrong in the run up to the contract sales round for 2000/2001: the contract price premium disappeared; and the underlying price of power began to fall.

Although the details were not yet clear, the financial markets began to get wind of significantly lower power price expectations for the new financial year 2000/2001. The trade magazine *Utility Week* reported in April 2000 that the price of new electricity contracts was coming in around 14 per cent lower than a year before, much worse than previously expected (Competition Commission, 2001 para. 7.157). This would have stark implications for BE's future profitability.

In the run up to the firm's annual results announcement for the financial year 1999/2000, analysts were expecting a significant drop in profits, because of the shortfall in output announced in November. The power prices reflected in the 1999/2000 revenues had been set in contract negotiations a year before. It was the following year, 2000/2001 that would see the damage to profits from falling prices. The fall in the shares since the beginning of the calendar year had priced in low expectations for next year's profits and there were plenty of analysts who saw the shares as still a buy. Morgan Stanley, the most consistently bullish supporter of BE shares, still had a "strong buy" recommendation on the shares (Chapter 11).

BE published its full year results on the morning of 10 May 2000. It was something of a nightmare day for shareholders. Things started badly when the company had to announce that the previous year's profits were down by 18 per cent, caused mainly by the unplanned shutdowns at Dungeness B and Heysham 2 power stations and falling power prices. This was broadly as expected since the company published monthly output figures. But there was much worse to follow. The company announced it was cutting the annual dividend by 50 per cent and warned that the current year (2000/2001) might even see the company make a loss. The Torness reactor in Scotland had also unexpectedly shut down the morning of the results. But the problem was no longer just output, it was prices. Forward electricity prices for six months ahead had fallen by 15 per cent in one year, compared with the company's earlier forecast for a similar fall over two to three years. Each 0.1p fall in prices wiped about £70 million off pre-tax profit so the fall of about 0.4p/kWh was already pointing to about £280 million less profit for the next year. Hollins told the shocked investors that: "In November, we said we expected prices to fall within a range of 10–20 per cent in the next two to three years. It now seems likely they will fall more rapidly" (British Energy, 2000b).

The management weren't giving up without a fight. The output losses at Heysham had been partly covered by £23 million from BE's business interruption insurance. BE was also in negotiations with Siemens, who had supplied the generator rotor motors (and later paid undisclosed compensation payments). BE was returning to the fight with BNFL over the contract payments and suggested that "substantial" savings in the £300 million annual payments might be feasible if reprocessing was replaced by storage. Finance director Mike Kirwan told the *Independent* newspaper that "reprocessing is an economic nonsense and should stop straight away" (*Independent*, 2000). BNFL put out a statement that it would be willing to look at the contracts again but the truth was that the contracts had been drawn up very carefully and BNFL saw no reason why it should bail out BE from problems of its own making (see Chapter 10).

By the time the markets closed on 10 May the shares had fallen more than 20 per cent to £1.32. They were now some 80 per cent off their peak of 15 months before and were trading at one-third below the flotation price. Chief Executive Peter Hollins, asked about his own position, told the *Financial Times*, "It would be absurd to claim that investors are not disappointed but there has been nothing to suggest that shareholders have been anything but supportive of management." The Dungeness B and Heysham 2 shutdowns that had cost £113 million of lost profit were "beyond the company's control" (*Financial Times*, 2000b).

When companies report bad news there is sometimes a double negative effect on the share price. The news itself cuts the company's value, as analysts revise their share price targets. But there is often a second order effect which is the damage done to the management's credibility. After three years of consistently good news, the market was alarmed at the sudden impression that the BE management seemed to have lost their ability to manage the stations reliably. And they had clearly underestimated the fall in power prices.

They had also showed a poor understanding of the company's share price. Since December 1999 the company had been buying its own shares in the market, under the normal authorisation granted at the Annual General Meeting (up to a maximum of 10 per cent of the total). When a company buys its own shares it is signalling that the management believes they are undervalued. BE had bought some 25 million shares during the previous few months, about 4 per cent of the total outstanding, at prices around £2.50 per share. The buying hadn't stopped the shares falling but had helped absorb selling by some large shareholders. Company share buybacks are a form of legalised insider trading which can take place only when there is no news due that would likely affect the share price. This suggests that the company was buying shares up until March with no idea that two months later it would be halving the dividend. It had bought shares for around £2.50 a share that would only a few months later be worth not much more than half that.

Unexpected dividend cuts are punished severely by the stock market. Profits and cashflow are expected to be somewhat volatile and investors look to dividends to smooth some of this volatility away. Economists are still far from sure just what drives dividend decisions but one view is that the dividend conveys the management's view of the underlying sustainable growth of free cashflow (Easterbrook, 1984). A cut in the dividend therefore indicates a serious deterioration in business prospects. Hence the 20 per cent fall in a shareprice that already reflected a lot of bad news.

It wasn't just the stock market that was reappraising the company's prospects. Standard & Poor's, the major credit rating agency, announced on 12 May that it was downgrading the company's debt rating to BBB+ from A– because cashflows in the year just reported had fallen short and because of the risks of lower electricity prices. The rating remained on negative outlook, implying that S&P were far from confident that things had hit bottom. At BBB+ BE's debt was now close to the bottom of the "investment grade" range. Debt which is rated below BBB is termed "junk" (or more politely, high yield) because many institutional investors are not allowed to invest in it. Equity analysts tend to be relaxed about credit ratings because there is a conflict of interest between equity and debt investors: a higher level of debt is generally better for equity shareholders (because of the tax deductibility of the interest payments) but worsens the value of the existing debt. But under the new electricity trading rules to be introduced in 2001, the credit rating of electricity generators would become critical. Firms with sub-investment grade credit ratings would have to post collateral against the risk that they failed to deliver the electricity they had contracted for, forcing them to buy in the short term balancing market at potentially very high prices.

BE's shares reached a low of £1.25 at the end of May. At this level many analysts believe the company was undervalued, even with the prospect of lower power prices. Influential US investment bank Merrill Lynch raised its rating from "neutral" to "buy" in early June (Reuters, 2000) and the shares were given a push up by speculation that the giant German utility RWE might be looking to takeover BE (*Daily Mail*, 2000). RWE had very deep pockets, plenty of nuclear expertise and was looking to expand in the UK energy market so the idea didn't seem far-fetched. But RWE was suffering from a wholesale price collapse in its German home power market, where at least it had some protection in the form of vertical integration. No bid appeared.

Internal discussions

For a company to go from a major return of value to cutting its dividend in just one year suggests either a dramatic change in business conditions or serious misjudgements, or both. In BE's case there can be no doubt that the board had radically changed its view of the future. Directors don't want to be associated with dividend cuts unless it is unavoidable. What had changed and should it have been foreseen?

There were two changes: one may have been temporary but the other looked more permanent. The temporary change – or so it was hoped – was that the long term improvement in the output of the old AGR power stations had stopped. Chapter 14 goes into more detail about the problems of running these unique British stations. The board had expected the load factor to keep rising, which would have meant a higher volume of power to offset at least partly the falling price (although at the margin, the higher volume would have meant more downward pressure on power prices).

Figure 9.1 shows that the AGR's dramatic operational improvement petered out after privatisation, apart from one last spurt in 2001. The timing of maintenance and statutory (safety check) outages can distort a single year's result so the three year moving average is shown too.

Figure 9.1 shows that the AGR load factor hit a peak around 1998 and then deteriorated. The data are consistent with the view of several company insiders that the company failed to invest in continued output improvements and that the relentless pressure on costs under Peter Hollins' regime may have damaged longer term output performance (private interviews) (see Chapter 14).

The second change in the company's fortunes was the falling price of power. Chapter 13 argues that a large fall in power prices was likely at some point and that BE was remiss in not planning for it. Figure 9.2 shows the path of spot power prices from the beginning of the pool through the introduction of the UKPX spot market when the new electricity trading arrangements began. Most power is sold on contract and the spot price, aside from being very volatile, is an

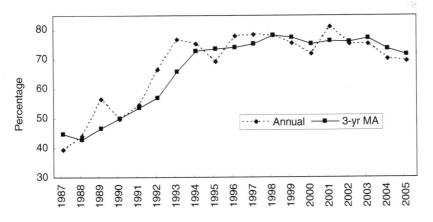

Figure 9.1 AGR load factors, 1987–2005 (source: IEAE, NE, SNL and BE company accounts, author's estimates).

Note
MA: moving average.

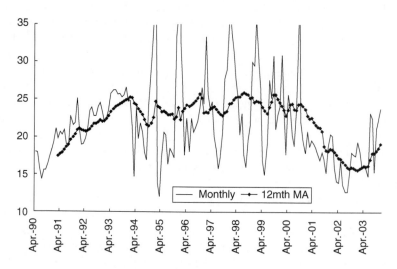

Figure 9.2 Monthly wholesale spot power prices, 1990–2003 (£/MWh) (source: UKPX, Pool, author's estimates).

Note
MA: moving average.

imperfect guide to the underlying price, but contract prices are confidential. The twelve month moving average (which smoothes out seasonal effects on price) shows no clear pattern until late 2000 and early 2001 when prices were clearly falling.

When it decided on the return of value in spring 1999 the BE board evidently believed that there was little risk of a sudden drop in prices. A year later, although spot prices were still quite high, the evidence from the forward contract market was clear: prices were falling around 15 per cent a year ahead. The introduction of NETA in spring 2001 was intended to push prices down (Helm, 2003 p. 307). Given British Energy's very high profit exposure to power prices, even a modestly worse outcome for prices implied a substantially lower level of medium term profits. This explains the board decision to halve the dividend in May 2000.

With output down and prices likely to be worse than previously expected, the board sought measures to rebuild profitability. Hollins was put under increasing pressure to cut operating costs, which he continued to do. But there was a limit to how much costs could be cut by reducing staff, not least because the nuclear safety regulator, the Nuclear Installations Inspectorate (NII), was becoming concerned at the risks of further headcount reductions. A report from the NII (which is part of the Health and Safety Executive) published in January 2000 insisted that BE halt cost cutting until it could reassure the NII that there was no risk to safety. The report said current safety was not in question but there were concerns that future job reductions would lower standards (Health and Safety Executive, 2000). The NII has the power to shut down any nuclear power station it suspects of operating unsafely and BE had to ensure it enjoyed their full confidence.

The company shifted the emphasis away from front line operations to management. In March 2000 a number of management posts were cut including the head of business development, who had only been with the company for 15 months. The following month the Edinburgh office was closed, with staff transferring to the cheaper office at Peel Park, East Kilbride. Then in May the director of generation Mike Low, a veteran from Nuclear Electric days, left the company, his responsibilities being taken over by Hollins himself. No reason was given for Low's departure but Hollins said "As we go through this transition to the New Electricity Trading Arrangements, I am keen to personally steer our core business through this period of change" (British Energy, 2000c).

Fuel costs, even for a nuclear power company, are significant. BE had been developing better fuel management policies which got more energy out of a given amount of uranium fuel. These were yielding around £25 million a year in cost savings by 2000 with several million more to come in future.

Having achieved greater fuel efficiency and cut the management team, the board turned to the other area of significant costs: the BNFL fuel reprocessing contracts. These cost some £300m annually but they had been already been renegotiated in 1997 and were legally watertight – there was no chance of simply opting out of them. Although BNFL made vaguely conciliatory noises in public, in private there were quite adamant that they had no intention of transferring value from their shareholder (the British government) to BE's shareholders (private interview).

John Robb, BE's chairman, therefore wrote directly to the Secretary of State for Trade and Industry, Stephen Byers. This correspondence was secret (but has been confirmed to the author by two senior sources). Robb told Byers in a letter in May 2000 that "The situation we face is very grave indeed." Was this a negotiating ploy, or was the board really more concerned that it had publicly let on? Robb sent another letter to Byers in July 2000. Hollins wrote to a senior civil servant in the DTI in December 2000 (private communications). Unfortunately for BE there was no evidence that the government would put any pressure on BNFL to soften its stance. The correspondence with government would continue through the next two years, with increasing frequency and urgency.

The strategic shift to North America

Inside BE, the dramatic fall in the share price and the deteriorating power price outlook led to growing pressure on Peter Hollins at the increasingly acrimonious board meetings. Former directors describe extraordinary verbal attacks on Hollins, who failed to defend himself effectively. Some directors appeared not to grasp the fundamental problems of commodity pricing and insisted that the managers go out and achieve higher selling prices. Hollins, with his petrochemicals background, presumably knew that this was moonshine – the price was dictated by the market and there was nothing BE could do about it. What he could do was to keep cutting costs, and that was what he did, with the board's approval. But some managers on the operational side began to fear that the continued cost cutting would further undermine power station reliability. Raising output and keeping it reliably higher would take investment they believed (private interviews). There was therefore tension between the operations people, who wanted to spend more money, and the board which wanted to cut it. At board level the only executive with real experience of running a nuclear power station was Robin Jeffrey, who was mostly absent in North America. But it was there that BE pulled off a real business coup.

Jeffrey and his team in Toronto had been courting the Ontario provincial government since 1998 in the hope of buying the poorly performing Ontario Hydro nuclear stations. After a series of delays, the BE team had begun to make real progress and during the spring of 2000 rumours grew that BE had won a major contract. The full deal was announced on 11 July 2000. BE's Bruce Power subsidiary in Toronto was to take a 17 year lease on eight nuclear reactors owned by Ontario Power Generators, with an option on a further 25 year lease after 2018. The deal involved a £279 million payment (later deferred) followed by annual rental payments of about £48 million. The two main unions representing workers at the Bruce power stations would take 5 per cent of the equity.

Four of the eight nuclear reactors were operating and two more were thought capable of being brought back into production. This was the attraction of the deal for BE. By applying its skills in improving the performance of nuclear power stations it could bring the operating capacity up from 3,000 MW to 4,500 MW. Peter Hollins indicated that each station should bring about £20 million of operating profit to BE (*Financial Times*, 2000c). The prospect of an extra £120 million of operating profit (offset by the interest cost of about £15 million) drove BE's shares up from £1.96 by over a quarter to £2.50 over the next two days, although the AGM on the 12 May reminded investors about the gloomy UK business outlook, pushing them back down a bit to £2.37. The deal even got the approval of the *Financial Times* Lex column, generally sceptical about any diversification investments, which judged that the deal was "a good use of British Energy's cashflow" (*Financial Times*, 2000d).

The Ontario deal had been won through steady persuasion of the provincial politicians by Jeffrey and his team, supported by detailed legal and business modelling of the various risks and scenarios involved. It drew on the operational strengths of the BE team (although those were coming into question in the UK) and its experience of dealing with governments and deregulating power markets. Combined with the growing success of the US nuclear investments, it suggested that BE's main source of profit in the next few years would be outside the UK.

Unfortunately the prospects for further profit growth in the US were now being curbed by the rising price of second-hand nuclear power stations. AmerGen had been one of the first companies to spot the potential for consolidation of the fragmented nuclear power sector. It had entered a buyers' market in which utilities were desperate to sell off their reactors. Only one other US buyer had been active, the Arkansas-based electric company Entergy. But the success of the early AmerGen and Entergy deals had attracted another entrant. Dominion Energy, a Virginia-based power company that counted George Washington and James Madison among its founders, entered the market in 2000, bidding for two nuclear stations being sold by the New York Power Authority. Dominion and AmerGen were both outbid by Entergy. But in September 2000 the US power market was amazed when Dominion pay $1.3 billion for the wonderfully named Millstone nuclear power station in Connecticut. The price of $660/kW was far higher than any previous transaction and threatened to price AmerGen out of the market.

Strategy reversal: the sale of SWALEC

The impression of a decisive shift in the company's business towards North America was confirmed on 8 August 2000 when BE called a special meeting to reveal that it had sold the SWALEC electricity supply business that it had bought in June the previous year. This appeared to reverse the strategy of the last three years to build an integrated supply business. But the company had been priced out of the race. It had failed to buy any other supply businesses, most recently having been outbid for the supply business of United Utilities (Norweb Energi) just a week before. A small, unremarkable business with no useful brand was worth very little. So the board had decided it would be worth more to somebody else, in this case Scottish and Southern Energy.

The sale raised £210 million which Hollins said would be reinvested in North America (*Financial Times*, 2000a). The company was diverting its increasingly scarce finance resources to Canada, where it had a good chance of a high return. The sale price looked attractive compared with the £107m that BE had paid for SWALEC a year before until it was realised that BE would retain the increasingly costly Teesside Power Limited purchase contracts. With the price of electricity having fallen sharply in the last year, the TPL contract – to purchase power at a fixed price that was increasingly above the current market price – was now a serious liability. BE had already made a provision of £107 million for this "onerous contract" in the previous year's accounts (after netting off some tax benefits acquired with SWALEC). Each time the market price of power fell, the liability would increase. Far from hedging the company's financial exposure to falling electricity prices, the net effect of buying and selling SWALEC had been to increase it.

The stock market shrugged off the announcement as relatively unimportant; investors had already given up hope of BE building a serious national supply business. Selling SWALEC to fund the Ontario investment seemed reasonable. Norweb Energi had been bought by the US company TXU for £500 million. This was far more than BE could afford. Its priority was to make sure it funded the highly promising Canadian project while making the best of the UK generation business through the transition to NETA.

The shares had been trading around £2.50 after the boost from the Ontario deal. After the SWALEC disposal they started drifting down again and reached £1.85 at the end of September when BE gave its pre-interims business briefings. The normally reliable investor relations machine somehow misfired and investors thought they were being told that the dividend was in jeopardy again. BE rushed out a rare intra-day statement to reaffirm the board's belief that the new dividend was "sustainable and capable of growth in future years" (British Energy, 2000d). The shares rallied, but only back to £1.75.

In the middle of these briefings, the company's hitherto strongest supporter, Morgan Stanley, downgraded its recommendation to "neutral" (*The Times*, 2000a). Folk wisdom in the markets has it that when the last "bull" gives up is when you should buy the shares (or equivalently when the last "bear" gives up you should sell). Morgan Stanley had (correctly) recommended BE shares from August 1997 up through the dramatic share price performance of late 1998 and early 1999 and then (less correctly) all the way down again to the lows of mid-2000. Switching to a neutral recommendation was a muted admission that the recommendation had been wrong for some time, since US investment banks seldom used an outright "sell" recommendation for fear of jeopardising corporate finance business. But the stock market wisdom seemed true and the shares began a new climb which would take them back over £3 over the next year before a last crescendo in September 2001.

False dawn

The new optimism was based rather prosaically on the fact that expectations for profits, output and prices had all reached levels where it would be hard for the company to disappoint. And the next set of figures, for the first half of 2000/2001, was well received. The company made an underlying pre-tax loss of £56 million (compared with £55 million profit a year before), better than many analysts had forecast. Two more power stations (Hartlepool and Heysham 1) received life extensions, which would raise the value of the business, assuming the stations were net cash generators at the new lower power prices. Hollins reaffirmed yet again the company's goal of higher output, despite the poor recent performance. And he suggested that power prices might have reached their trough, since gas prices had risen sharply, which ought to raise the costs of the gas-fired power stations that were increasingly entering the market.

All this went down well with weary investors who were relieved that there was no new bad news; the Lex column stated that the shares deserved to recover (*Financial Times*, 2000d). But Hollins's targets were increasingly questionable. The company's nuclear output target was 70 TWh, compared with the actual peak of 69 TWh in 1998/1999. Investors took this as attainable but inside the company the operational managers knew this target was increasingly at odds with the other stated target, to cut a further £150 million of operating costs (private interviews). The strain between these goals – greater output and lower costs – would only show fully several years later.

BE ended a miserable year in 2000 with one further humiliation. An annual poll in the magazine *Management Today* voted BE as one of four companies that were "least admired" (*The Times*, 2000b). But at least the shares were up, trading around £2.50, double their low point at the end of May. They were benefiting from the modest bounce in confidence in the company, now that the bad news seemed to have stopped. But they were also part of a general recovery in "defensive" shares against the backdrop of a falling equity market. The great 1990s share rally had peaked in September 2000 and the UK stockmarket was now falling. Utility shares, which had been out of favour during the technology, media and telecoms frenzy of the late 1990s, were now regarded as a relatively safe haven. British Energy lagged behind the regulated utilities like water companies but was still seen as a relatively safe port in the global financial storm.

Regime change

The team running British Energy in late 2000 had changed little since privatisation, the key exception being the chief executive, Peter Hollins. But it changed considerably during 2001. In October 2000, John Robb announced that he would be standing down as chairman in July 2001 and would be replaced by Robin Jeffrey, deputy chairman and the architect of the successful North American strategy. Investors could see that Jeffrey had a good record of achievement but few knew him personally. The long standing and highly regarded finance director Mike Kirwan stepped down at the end of August 2001 but remained on the board for the rest of the financial year as business development director. He was replaced by Keith Lough, whose background was in the upstream oil business.

Terry Brookshaw joined the company in October 2000 as the new director of power and energy trading, replacing Andy Clements, who was retiring owing to ill health. Clements was a former CEGB manager who had steered first Nuclear Electric and then British Energy through the evolving electricity market. It would fall to Brookshaw to try to cope with the onset of NETA, which had been postponed to March 2001. Brookshaw had previously worked at Centrica, the holding company for the retail supply part of British Gas. Centrica was by far the largest new entrant into the deregulated market for retail electricity, trading successfully on the well known brand name. Centrica had no power generation assets and had decided not to buy any because it expected the price of electricity to keep falling. It therefore was acquiring customers but had no power supply of its own – it was "short" the power market, in trading terms. By contrast BE had no retail customers (at the household level) since having sold SWALEC but had plenty of power generation assets – it was "long" the market. Brookshaw brought with him a strong view about the poor outlook for prices and what was needed to cope with them.

David Gilchrist joined the board in September 2001 as Managing Director of British Energy generation. Gilchrist, an engineer with significant private sector experience, had been heavily involved in the privatisation of British Energy and had then worked closely with Jeffrey to build the North American business.

Together with Jeffrey's greater involvement as chairman, Gilchrist's appointment brought more engineering and operational experience to the board. It also meant that there was a separate board member responsible for generation for the first time since Mike Low's departure in April 2000, after which the job had been done by Peter Hollins.

At the same time the increasing importance of the Canadian and US businesses was recognised by the appointment of Duncan Hawthorne as Executive Director for North American operations. Hawthorne was the chief executive officer of Bruce Power, which owned the Ontario nuclear stations, and president of AmerGen.

But the most dramatic change in the BE team was the resignation of the chief executive, Peter Hollins, in June 2001. It may seem unsurprising that the boss is forced out when performance has been poor but the timing was unexpected. Several institutional investors were shocked by the news. They had liked and respected Hollins and understood that the biggest problems facing the company were external (private interviews). His easy and frank manner had made him popular with many investors, although there were others who wondered whether he had grasped the commercial realities of the company soon enough. For example, Hollins had told Reuters in July 1999 that the new electricity trading arrangements would not hurt British Energy: "The auction room may be changing but the fundamental economics aren't." He went on to say that he thought "the downside has been heavily oversold in some cases" (Reuters, 1999). The buying and then selling of SWALEC had also cast doubt on the company's strategy. Hollins had said in January 2000 that "British Energy has a clear strategy – to develop as an integrated UK energy group" (British Energy, 2000a). Then he had sold SWALEC, the only manifestation of integration, seven months later.

There were other problems. The cost cutting strategy had run into conflict with the NII and with employees. Power station managers were voicing their concerns at the impact that further cost cuts would have on reliability. Hollins was executing the orders of the board, which had demanded he cut costs in order to offset the damage from lower revenues. But he never had a good relationship with the board, although it is far from clear that this was his fault. The *Financial Times*, reporting his departure, said that Hollins was "understood to have felt beleaguered by the attitude of some British Energy directors who claimed longer experience of the nuclear industry" (*Financial Times*, 2001b). One former director described the board meetings as like "out and out war" (private interview). This was not evidence of a smoothly functioning board and Hollins' consensus driven management style didn't fit.

Hollins' last set of results was announced in May 2001. Having warned of a loss during the year 2000/2001, the company just scraped into the black with a £10 million pre-tax profit (excluding exceptionals) compared with £241m the previous year. Contract power prices had fallen 16 per cent during the year before and the current market price was a further 10 per cent down. It was "conceivable although unlikely" that the company would make a loss in 2001/2002 (British Energy, 2001c). Hollins insisted that although output had again fallen short of planned, the current year should see a recovery closer to the 70 TWh that the company had been targeting for some time. He also talked up the prospects from North America, suggesting that Bruce and AmerGen could deliver £150 million of pre-tax profit by 2003/2004. With the shares having recovered strongly during the winter period there was no great reaction to the results, which were seen as broadly in line with expectations. The optimists pointed to the jam tomorrow across the Atlantic. The pessimists worried about the future for UK power prices. The shares closed 9p down on the day at £2.99.

In his final AGM speech to shareholders on July 17, John Robb forecast "significant profit growth in the medium-term" (British Energy, 2001a). He also publicly relished the company's victory over the regulator: the Competition Commission had ruled in BE's favour over the disputed "good behaviour" clause. But it seemed unimportant now; although the stock market had worried about the uncertainty of a Competition Commission referral the victory brought no share price benefit. The regulator, Callum McCarthy, showed no sign of backing down on his goal of making the British generation industry more competitive, which meant lower prices.

Conclusion

Between the summer of 1999 and the summer of 2001, British Energy was revealed as a commodity power producer exposed to the uncertainties of the wholesale electricity market. As Chapter 11 argues, that sort of company needs a different financial policy from a regulated utility. The collapse in BE's share price after the return of value in the spring of 1999 suggests that many investors realised that it had been a mistake. Private interviews suggest that some members of the board had reached the same conclusion by 2001.

But the position in 2001 seemed far from lost, if BE could fully exploit the profit potential in Canada. So long as UK power prices didn't deteriorate further the company would face a period of poor generation profitability but the prospect of growing overseas profits. The bounce in the shares to £3 showed that the market saw considerable value to come. But the UK power market was to become much tougher and in 2002 BE faced an increasingly desperate fight to stay afloat.

10 Crisis (2001–2002)

Introduction

When Robin Jeffrey took over as chairman and acting chief executive the fate of BE was probably sealed. From July 2001 until the crisis of September 2002 the board was in a race to keep the UK generation business afloat long enough to allow the profits from North America to come through. The price of electricity was outside Jeffrey's control but he and his team chased every other possible source of profit. Right up until early September 2002, Jeffrey and his team thought they had a chance, mainly because of the prospect of BNFL altering the fuel reprocessing contracts. But their hopes were frustrated and the government was forced to step in.

The battle to save the company

After July 2001, the board meetings were more consensual, partly because of Jeffrey's style but also because of a growing sense among directors that the company was in considerable trouble. With Gilchrist and Hawthorne joining the board, the structure in September 2001 was now five executives (Jeffrey, Gilchrist, Hawthorne, Kirwan and Lough) and four non-executives (Biggam, Hill, Stevenson and Walsh). In December 1991 Claire Spottiswoode, the former head of OFGAS (which regulated the gas industry), joined as a further non-executive.

The board composition had shifted in a subtle but important way. In 2000, the board had been made up of only three executive directors (Hollins, Jeffrey and Kirwan) plus five non-executives (Robb, Biggam, Hill, Stevenson and Walsh). Ever since privatisation there had been a sense that the role of the board was for the non-executives to hold the executive directors to account. There had been a hostile atmosphere during the period that Hollins was chief executive and, before that, lingering tensions between the English and Scottish contingents. In 2001 the board seemed finally to pull together.

The position facing the company was grave. The wholesale price of electricity was still falling and unless it recovered soon the UK generating business would be unprofitable. The company's previously strong balance sheet had deteriorated because of the return of value, the purchase of Eggborough power station and a collapse in operating cashflow. The company had abandoned any attempt at a structural hedge against power prices through vertical integration. The board considered the options. They could try to cut operating costs. They could try to raise more revenue by selling longer term power contracts. And they could try to get government help.

Figure 10.1 shows the company's shareprice from the time that Robin Jeffrey took over as chairman until the company's collapse in September 2002. It also shows the spot electricity price (on a 30 day moving average basis to smooth out some of the volatility). There is a seasonal pattern in the electricity price, reflecting higher demand in the winter than summer. But the underlying trend is downwards.

The operating costs that BE wanted to tackle were the BNFL contracts and its rates (property taxes) bill. BE had been pressing BNFL for cuts in its fuel reprocessing contracts since late 1999 but with no success. BNFL's management took BE's shrill insistence on lower contract costs to be an opportunistic attempt to reverse BE's falling share price and lacking any legal basis. The discussions had been unproductive and ill-humoured. When Jeffrey took over as BE chairman he improved the tone of the meetings by appealing to both companies' shared interest in reviving the British nuclear industry.

About the same time BNFL's management team was giving up hope of being privatised any time soon, which might have made its board more receptive to possible changes in commercial arrangements with its biggest customer (*Financial Times*, 2001a). But there was still no question of giving money away. In the

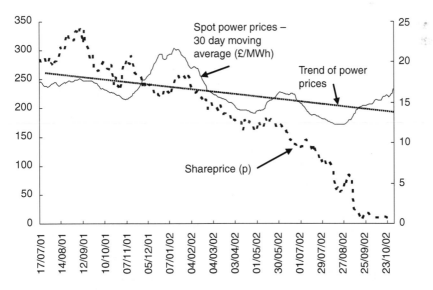

Figure 10.1 British Energy share price (p – left axis) and spot price (£/MWh) (source: Datastream, UKPX).

autumn of 2001 Jeffrey had threatened to refer the fuel reprocessing contract to the Office of Fair Trading. But BNFL didn't take this very seriously. Although BNFL was a monopoly supplier to BE, the contracts had been signed in good faith and renegotiated after privatisation. It would be hard to convince the OFT that BE had been forced into anything by abuse of monopoly power.

Through the winter of 2001/2002 the two sides stopped arguing. Instead the two companies pledged in February 2002 to work together to find cost saving solutions and to promote the long term future of nuclear power in the UK even though at current power prices new nuclear stations were obviously uneconomic. BNFL's US subsidiary Westinghouse had a promising new nuclear reactor type called the AP1000 that it wanted to promote. BE was increasingly looking to a revival of nuclear build in the UK as a long term source of profit, and a possible lever for government intervention (private interviews). But the BNFL contracts remained in place and by the spring of 2002, though talks continued, BE had not saved any money on fuel reprocessing.

The other area of possible cost cutting was the property taxes on the company's power stations, known as "rates". For historical reasons these rates were levied at a much higher rate on nuclear power stations than on coal and gas plant (£14,000 per MW of nuclear but only £9,500 per MW of coal or gas capacity and £5,000 for wind power). This amounted, BE claimed, to an unfair tax disadvantage for the company amounting to £25 million a year. Governments seldom give up tax lightly so this was bound to be a long battle but BE seemed to have a good case. But by the end of the financial year in March 2002, the government hadn't moved.

If the battle to cut costs was bearing little fruit, was there anything the company could do to boost revenues? The director of trading, Terry Brookshaw, faced an unenviable challenge. BE had eight large factories producing a commodity product, the price of which was falling. The only way to make a commodity more valuable is to sell it with a contract that adds some value, by reducing the buyer's risk in some way. This can be done either by fixing the price for a longer time ahead or by selling an option to buy more at a preset price. A risk averse electricity buyer might pay a premium over the normal one year contract price for one or both of these contracts.

The problem was that there were only two sorts of big customer and neither was in the mood to pay for long term contracts or for options. The first type was the large industrial and commercial customers who were the most price sensitive. They bought in large volume but generally only for one year at a time. This was partly because they were more worried about getting locked into an uncompetitive long term contract than they were about facing higher prices in the future. In the second case they could blame it on market conditions, but in the first case it would look like bad commercial judgement. Most of the large customers were convinced that prices would keep falling for a while in any case. (If they had bought long term contracts from BE at that stage they would of course have saved a great deal of money in 2004 and later years when power prices surged).

The other type of big customer was the retail supply businesses that sold power to households and small business. These consisted of the remaining RECs, the newly integrated generators PowerGen and Innogy (which was the UK business left after National Power divested its international operations in 2000), plus Centrica (trading as British Gas). But these companies were either deliberately going short the market (like Centrica) or had enough generation assets of their own to cover their buying needs. There was little demand for long term contracts at any price that BE found appealing.

As for selling options, they depended on a reasonably sophisticated market. Most commodity markets have evolved over time from a pure spot market to add futures and options contracts. But the process takes time. Ten years after privatisation there was still relatively little interest in the Electricity Forward Agreement market because the lack of competition in generation meant customers feared the prices could be rigged. Enron (of which more later) was one of the few companies trying to build a more sophisticated trading business in UK electricity but had decided this wasn't really feasible until the generation market became less concentrated, which had only happened since 2000. All physical power stations represent a form of option to generate power in the future and with general over-capacity the price of options available from BE was very low.

The government energy review

The third area the company was pursuing was government help. Having dropped its hostility to nuclear power in its manifesto for the 2001 general election, the Labour government set up an energy review in June 2001 under energy minister Brian Wilson to examine "the challenge of global warming while ensuring secure, diverse and reliable energy supplies at a competitive price" (*Financial Times*, 2001c). Until then, Labour had done little to move away from the previous Conservative energy policy of leaving as much as possible to the market. But Tony Blair had reportedly been concerned about Britain's ability to avoid an electricity crisis similat to the one in California, which in 2000 led to blackouts and utility bankruptcies. The California disaster had been blamed on deregulation, which was partly true, though market manipulation by Enron and other power companies had played a part. Britain had one of the most deregulated power markets in the world so perhaps it could face blackouts too. Wilson was known to be sympathetic to nuclear power, not least because the Hunterston B AGR was in his constituency, which led environmental group Greenpeace to describe the choice of chairman as "putting a fox in charge of the hen coop" (*Financial Times*, 2001c).

BE's submission to the review was published in September. It emphasised the two arguments for a continued large share of nuclear generation: i) the environmental case – avoiding carbon dioxide emissions; and ii) the energy security case – avoiding excessive import dependence on gas. These arguments implied that the government needed to do more to help the cost of new nuclear build, which was uneconomic at 2001 prices. BE estimated that new nuclear build would need an electricity price of £25–£30/MWh, compared with the then current price of £18–£20/MWh (British Energy, 2001d). BE specifically called for: i) the ending of nuclear fuel reprocessing in favour of storage (which it claimed would cut its own annual back end fuel bill from £300 million to £100 million); and ii) a carbon-free obligation scheme under which electricity suppliers must maintain a minimum proportion of carbon-free generation, thereby providing a protected market segment for nuclear.

The submission repeated the argument that former chief executive Bob Hawley had made in the early 1990s, that on current trends the UK would have only one nuclear power station running by 2025 – Sizewell B. The gap would be filled by gas power stations with an increase in carbon dioxide emissions that would wreck any chance of the UK meeting its greenhouse gas targets.

This was a long term strategy for the company; there was little that would improve the immediate outlook. But the company saw the review as a possible vehicle for government action on the rates question, on the BNFL contract costs and perhaps even on NETA. Senior executives believed that they had been given "nods and winks" that encouraged them to be optimistic (private interviews).

But the energy review was caught between strongly differing views within the government over nuclear power. Although energy minister Brian Wilson was widely believed to want to build new nuclear stations to replace those due to close, the environment minister Michael Meacher was opposed to further nuclear power. The review, when it was published on 14 February 2002, was indeed disappointing for the nuclear industry. Although it recommended keeping the nuclear option open it proposed nothing concrete that would stimulate any new station build. It recommended abolishing the climate change levy, to which British Energy's electricity was subject, in favour of a proper carbon-based levy, which would exempt nuclear power (Cabinet Office, 2002). But the document was not a guide to policy, which would have to wait for a White Paper promised in October, but rumoured to be due only in 2003. Meanwhile the months were ticking by and even October would prove to be too late.

After a few months in the job as chairman and with a strong and cohesive team around him, Jeffrey was able to report some good news in the interim results released in November 2001. Output was finally rising again (up 10 per cent), the profits from North America had reached £87 million and the company was confident about achieving a £150 million cost saving plan. So although electricity prices were still falling (10 per cent over a year before) the company had trimmed its first-half loss from £56 million to £17 million. The year as a whole should produce a modest profit. Jeffrey was combining the roles of chairman and chief executive, against the conventional wisdom on corporate governance best practice. But it was clear that finding a new chief executive for the company in its current state would be hard. What person of ability would want to join a company that faced such difficulties?

The company statement asserted that electricity prices "continued to be reduced by regulatory action" (British Energy, 2001b p. 1). BE's corporate view was now that lower power prices were the fault of the regulator, OFGEM (a view shared by the bosses of some other generators). But this only made sense if one believed that the new trading system introduced earlier in the year had somehow distorted the market so that prices were lower than they would have been under "normal" competition. As Chapter 13 argues, a number of academic experts on electricity reject that view. Power prices had fallen because of competition in the market. It was pointless to blame the regulator.

The statement also took up two other points that were being pressed privately with government. The statement recorded that "British Energy firmly believes that reprocessing is no longer the most cost effective option for spent fuel and that its shareholders should no longer be required to shoulder this burden" (British Energy, 2001b p. 4). The company compared the reprocessing cost with the US, where back-end fuel costs were paid by all nuclear generation as a levy of \$1/MWh. The government collected this money and then assumed all responsibility for subsequent spent fuel handling. BE pointed out that it would be profitable in the UK, even at the current low power prices, if it had the same system. Instead its costs amounted to nearer \$6/MWh. As a matter of arithmetic this was fine but it seemed wildly optimistic to believe that the British government would adopt the US system after all the fuss at privatisation over the company assuming responsibility for the liabilities.

BE also made clear the other concession it wanted from the government: to be freed from the liabilities for waste generated before the creation of British Energy in 1996. This issue had been bitterly fought during the pre-privatisation arguments about how much debt the company would take on. The outcome (see Chapter 7) had been that the company had won its case for assuming far less debt than the government wanted but had lost the argument over the pre-1996 liabilities. To re-open it now wasn't very persuasive, since logically the government would point out that the liabilities and the debt were broadly equivalent and the deal had been done as a whole.

BE was adopting a more publicly assertive tone, while giving the impression that the management team were getting to grips with those things under its control, chiefly output and costs. Then on 3 December 2001 the gas and electricity company Enron, one of the largest participants in the UK energy trading market, declared bankruptcy. It would be several months before it became clear that Enron's collapse would have damaging consequences for BE.

UK generation market response

In early 2002 the falling electricity price triggered a market response. A number of generators started to shut down their stations. Several power station owners had been making losses in 2001 but were still receiving enough revenue to cover their short term variable costs (mainly fuel). They weren't covering their staff costs but shedding labour would cost redundancy pay plus the cost of rehiring them in the event that prices went up again.

The US-owned utility TXU announced in January 2002, in the middle of yet another mild winter, that it was mothballing one unit each at its stations at High

Marnham and Drakelow. The remaining units of both stations would remain open but there would be some saving in property taxes and on short term maintenance as well as saving on coal. The message from this was that power prices were now too low to justify running some of the older and less efficient coal plant, which was being pushed out by the new, much more efficient gas power stations. In March, another US-owned generator, AES, mothballed its 363 MW Fifoots coal plant in South Wales. An AES spokesman told the *Financial Times* that it was cheaper to buy power in the market than run the stations (*Financial Times*, 2002a).

These reductions in capacity weren't permanent – mothballing meant putting the stations into a state where they could be brought back to service at some point, but not at short notice (the distinction mattered for paying property tax). The market was starting to operate as it is supposed to: lower prices lead to falling supply. The amount was still tiny: about 885 MW. Combined with the shutdown of the Blyth small coal plant, some old gas turbine stations and the Hinckley Point A Magnox during 2000, a total of 2,712 MW of capacity had been withdrawn from supply. Unfortunately, 3,427 MW of new CCGT capacity had been added during the same period, leaving total industry capacity higher (National Grid, 2003). The new gas power stations had been planned and financed two to three years before when they had looked profitable. Although prices had fallen, the capacity was committed and would run as long as the price covered marginal costs, which it still did.

Other capital intensive industries such as petrochemicals have shown that the supply response to low prices can take a long time and that prices can settle around marginal cost for years on end. The capital costs of the power stations were unavoidable and largely sunk, i.e. there was little value in trying to resell them. So if prices at least cover marginal costs the grim logic for the industry is that most competitors stay in the game. Nuclear power had the lowest marginal costs and so would be the last to shut down. But that was scant comfort when the price was too low to cover the fixed costs of staff, long term maintenance and corporate overheads.

BE's deteriorating financial position

BE's structural risk position ever since privatisation had been that it was "long" of the price of electricity, meaning it gained from higher prices. Buying a REC was intended to reduce this long position by adding a retail supply business that was "short" the power price, i.e. gained from lower prices. This strategy, as we have seen, failed for a combination of bad luck and an unaccountable failure to merge with Southern Electric in 1997. So BE had remained long. But then in November 1999, BE had bought the Eggborough coal power station from National Power, increasing its net long position. At that time it had been a seller's market for power stations, with American companies AES and Edison bidding up the prices of the large coal assets. And on top of buying physical assets, BE had added long term contracts for power through its temporary acquisition of SWALEC, which further increased its economic exposure to power prices.

BE announced in February 2002 that it was taking a £509 million provision against the value of Eggborough power station and of its long term power contracts. A provision is a book keeping entry that reconciles the historic cost balance sheet value of an asset acquired or built with its current value. £300 million of the provision was for Eggborough. In effect, BE was admitting that of the £636 million they had paid just two years ago, nearly half the value had vanished because of lower power prices. The remaining £209 million of the provision reflected the increasing gap between the prices the company was committed to pay for electricity and the current market price. This included the Teesside Power contract (which came via SWALEC) which was becoming more costly with every fall in the power price.

One might expect the stock market to be shocked by a half billion pound write off but investors and analysts had long since factored these costs into the share price. The fall in BE's shareprice during the previous two years reflected the market marking down the future cash generating potential of its various assets, including Eggborough. The official balance sheet numbers were largely irrelevant to any sensible valuation because they were backward looking, whereas the market (mostly) looks forward.

But the write down still damaged the company's financial credibility. The balance sheet at the end of March 2002 was seriously weakened. A company's financial health can be captured in at least two ways: balance sheet leverage (a stock measure at a point in time); and interest cover (a flow measure of leverage over a period of time, usually a year). The stock gearing or leverage is traditionally taken by comparing the company's debt (net of any spare cash or other liquid investments) with its equity. The equity represents the risk capital supplied by shareholders – in theory it could be wiped out but still leave the company able to pay its creditors. If it can't pay its creditors the company is insolvent.

At 31 March 2002 BE had net debt amounting to 137 per cent of its equity, a level which by any measure is seriously high. The figure was flattered by netting off a relatively large amount of liquid investments (£209m). But some, perhaps most of this "near-cash" should be regarded as necessary for the normal functioning of the company, i.e. it wasn't available to reduce debt. So the true gearing figure was arguably even higher. The damage was done not by taking on more debt in 2001/2002 but by the fall in the company's equity arising from the massive provisions against Eggborough and its power purchase contracts (see Table 10.1).

Balance sheet leverage is a crude measure of financial strength because the values on the balance sheet are at historic cost and may bear little relation to the current market value, assuming they could be sold. So the second measure of financial strength compares the actual cost of servicing the debt with the company's ability to do so. The measure is EBIT (earnings before interest and tax) divided by interest payments and is known as "interest cover" because it

Table 10.1 British Energy balance sheet structure (£m)

Year ending 31 March	2001	2002
Short term debt (1)	40	153
Long term debt (2)	917	915
less: Investments (3)	(227)	(209)
Net debt (1+ 2 + 3)	730	859
Total equity (4)	1,298	627
Net debt/equity (%)	56	137
EBIT (5)	226	231
Net interest payments (6)	56	66
Interest cover (5/6)	4.0	3.5
Total capital (1+ 2 + 4)	2,255	1,695
Debt/total capital (%)	42	63

Source: British Energy Annual Reports for 2000–2001 and 2001–2002.

measures how many times the interest payments made by the company are covered by operating profit. Table 10.1 shows that for BE this figure had fallen from 4 times in 2001 to 3.5 times in 2002. If profit covers interest payments by more than three times, surely there is nothing to worry about? But if profit only covered interest it would leave nothing for dividends or for any surplus to be invested for the future. And even if profit fully covers interest now, a deterioration in revenues might cut profits to the point where they no longer cover interest. This is particularly true for a company like BE with high *operational* gearing, meaning that changes in revenue affect profits disproportionately. High operational and financial gearing ("leverage") makes for a risky financial position.

The credit rating agency Standard and Poor's looks at several measures and combines them with subjective expert judgement on the company's management and strategy. But interest cover is a key variable. In 2001, those bonds rated BBB by S&P were issued by companies with an average interest cover of 3.7 times. For the next rating down, BB, the figure was 2.1 times. But BB is below investment grade, or junk. These figures imply that BE was close to the edge of investment grade status. This impression is confirmed by looking at another ratio that S&P uses, debt to total capital. Total capital is the sum of equity and debt capital (gross debt, without netting off any cash or near-cash). Table 10.1 shows that this figure for BE was a respectable 42 per cent in 2001 (equivalent to an A rating). But in 2002, with the damage from the provisions, the figure rose to 63 per cent, which is equivalent to a BB rating (S&P data, quoted in Brealey et al., 2006 table 24.2).

The significance of the credit rating for BE was that under the electricity trading system introduced in March 2001, all power was sold under contract to buyers. Any failure to deliver against the contract (for example in the event of an unplanned station outage) would force the seller to buy the power instead in the "balancing" market at whatever price ruled. So a power seller must show that it had the financial resources to buy such power, just in case – in other words that it had good credit. A deterioration in credit rating to below investment grade would mean power purchasers would only deal with a seller if it posed collateral against the risk that the power was never actually provided. If BE lost its credit rating it would face a sudden need for cash, just when it couldn't afford it.

BE also faced a different kind of financial problem. Even if a company is in principle creditworthy it doesn't want to face a situation where all of its debt falls due at once, because it would then have to raise a lot of new debt to replace it all at once. If the timing happened to coincide with some external bad news that made credit more expensive the company would face a sudden rise in its borrowing costs, or in extremis be unable to refinance its debt. In the spring of 2002 BE faced a debt structure as shown in table 10.2.

The company had some £153 million of debt due for repayment in the next year, most of which was a sterling bond that matured in March 2003. The company needed to replace the sterling bond with another source of medium or long term finance. It decided in June 2002 to raise $400 million through a sale of ten year bonds to major US institutional investors.

Unfortunately BE's timing was terrible; the collapse of Enron the previous December had destroyed investor appetite for anything connected with power generation. Finance Director Keith Lough later described it as a "perfect storm" (*Financial Times*, 2002b). After a month of failed investor meetings in the US, the company announced that "in view of current market volatility" it was not going ahead after all but would continue to "monitor market conditions" (British Energy, 2002b). BE would now have to find the money to repay the sterling bond in March 2003. There wasn't yet a crisis; the company still had undrawn bank credit facilities, meaning a predetermined borrowing agreement with a series of banks. These amounted to £615 million, comfortably more than the £110 million bond.

Desperately seeking cashflow

As 2002 progressed, the board was meeting more and more frequently, considering every option for raising profits. One idea, revealed in May, was to take over the management of the Magnox nuclear power stations owned by BNFL, in exchange for a fee. BNFL would retain ownership and of course the liabilities

Table 10.2 Term structure of BE debt, 31 March 2002 (£m)

Less than one year	153
of which: bond due 2003	110
Between one and two years	41
Between two and five years	410
Over five years	464
Total	1,068

Source: British Energy Annual Report for 2002, section 21.

but BE would generate some additional income. On paper this seemed a reasonable scheme, and had been discussed back before privatisation. BE had nuclear power station skills and could probably save some costs by managing the AGRs and Magnoxes together.

But BNFL's management were lukewarm. Having achieved a better atmosphere between the two companies after several months of rancorous talks over the reprocessing contracts the BNFL management were reluctant to dismiss the idea. But they could see serious disadvantages. There was a strong operational linkage between BNFL and the Magnoxes. The unique fuel canisters that had given the Magnoxes their name were manufactured by BNFL. And the waste fuel was reprocessed by BNFL. Unlike the AGR fuel the Magnox spent fuel had to be reprocessed because the magnesium canisters were unstable in air and gradually corroded in water. The decision on how long to continue operating the Magnoxes was closely bound up with the continuing operation of the fuel fabrication and reprocessing facilities, so having a single overall management was valuable. Hiving off operations to BE put this at risk and it wasn't at all clear that BE would be able to achieve offsetting gains. The idea gradually was abandoned (private interviews).

The Magnox proposal was made public on 6 May. Less than two weeks later the company released its financial results for the full year to 31 March 2002. This would be the last set of "normal" results the company would publish. They showed a huge loss arising from the previously announced £509 million provisions. Excluding this the company had raised underlying profit before tax by £32 million to £42 million. This broke down as shown in Table 10.3.

Table 10.3 shows that the North American operations were now the only thing keeping the company in the black. The UK business was losing even more money, neatly offset by an increased contribution from the AmerGen joint venture in the US. The increase in profit came entirely from the first contribution from the new Bruce Power venture in Canada. Thankfully this should grow significantly over the next few years. The question was therefore whether it would grow quickly enough to compensate for any further deterioration in the UK business.

Viewed this way, the company's position looked serious but not disastrous. It faced a gloomy prospect in the UK for some time but it had a strong and growing source of profit in Canada. The US business was unlikely now to grow

Table 10.3 Components of increase in British Energy pretax profit, 2001–2002 (£m)

Component of change in profit	Amount
Increased loss from UK generation	(26)
Increased contribution from AmerGen joint venture	26
Contribution from Bruce Power	42
Increased interest charges	(10)
Net change in underlying pretax profit	32

Source: British Energy Annual Report for 2002.

much because the rapid increase in the price of nuclear power stations had undermined the case for further investments. The balance sheet was stretched but still just on the right side of investment grade credit. There was a bond to pay back a year ahead but there were still undrawn bank credit facilities that would cover it. The company should be able to continue, so long as UK power prices didn't fall much further.

A controversial dividend decision

This sort of reasoning led the BE board to their last controversial decision – to pay an unchanged dividend for the year of 8p a share. A flat dividend implied that the business remained in serious difficulties but had not fundamentally deteriorated compared with the previous year. Could this be squared with the falling electricity prices and the half billion pound provision? Yes, because the bad news in the UK was counterbalanced by the improving outlook in Canada.

When companies get into difficulties it is the cashflow position that matters more than profits because cash is what pays interest and tax bills. Figure 10.2 shows the trend over BE's history, using the company's preferred measure of net cashflow after capital spending. This measure treats capital spending as a largely unavoidable cost of being in business, which is reasonable, since saving on capital spending will damage future years' cashflow. The *net* cashflow left over is available to pay for tax and interest, which are not discretionary, and then for dividends or new investment, which are discretionary, at least in the short term. From 1997 till 1999 the net cashflow was large and growing, and far in

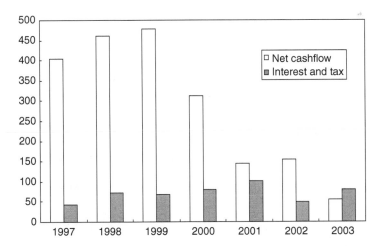

Figure 10.2 British Energy net cashflow after investment, interest and tax, financial years 1997–2003 (£m) (source: company accounts, author's calculations).

Note
Net cashflow is operating cashflow after investment but excluding acquisitions and disposals.

excess of the company's tax and interest payments. The surplus was available for large dividends to shareholders (including the return of value in 1999) and for funding new investments in North America.

The surplus shrank dramatically in 2000 and 2001, but improved a little in 2002. The board could justify maintaining the dividend on the basis of this improvement in the cashflow position. Unfortunately, as Figure 10.2 shows, the following year would see the company move into a cash deficit, where net cashflow was insufficient to pay the interest and tax. This is unsustainable and if expected to continue would imply the company is insolvent.

The dividend decision was unusually finely poised. There was a widespread view in the markets that BE would cut the dividend, to save cash at a time when the UK business was worsening. But the board were mindful of that elusive thing, confidence. The company was tottering on the edge of a junk credit rating and was about to launch its US bond issue (see above). Although a prudent view might imply that saving the final dividend payment of £31 million was the right thing to do, the shock of a further dramatic cut in the dividend might kick off a downward spiral in confidence that would make the bond fail and result in the very credit downgrade the company wanted to avoid. BE's financial advisors forcefully recommended no cut in the dividend. One independent director disagreed but was persuaded to change his mind (private interview).

The reason the decision was wrong, at least in hindsight, is that the maintained dividend did indeed send a signal, but one that would seriously undermine the company's case for government help. BNFL's management took the dividend decision to mean that BE might be in difficulty but in no sense in crisis. The continuing talks over the reprocessing contract were therefore dealt a blow; BE seemed to BNFL to be crying wolf (private interviews).

Perhaps more seriously, within the government, there was exasperation, even anger that the company which had been telling them for nearly two years that it faced serious problems, could nonetheless pay out £31m to shareholders (private interviews). Few people in the government or civil service had any experience of financial markets or the politics of dividend decisions and BE's management failed completely to explain the dividend decision. Thirty-one million pounds sounds like a lot and those in the government who were sympathetic to the case for helping BE were undermined.

It was a bad time to upset the politicians. Jeffrey's team continued to pursue three possible source of new profit: lower property taxes; scrapping the pre-privatisation nuclear liabilities; and above all renegotiating the BNFL reprocessing contract. But all of these were connected to the government.

Appealing to the government

BE chairman John Robb had first written to the government in 12 May 2000, when the company's situation was difficult but not yet disastrous. Emphasising that the board had taken the serious step of halving the dividend, he wrote "the situation we face is very grave indeed". Robb was trying to get government help on the burden of the BNFL contracts, which, he wrote, "threatens to make UK nuclear generation unviable". The correspondence accelerated in 2001. One of Robb's last acts as chairman was to write to the new Secretary of State for Trade and Industry, Patricia Hewitt, on 17 July 2001, focusing on the damage to power prices being done by NETA, which had started in March (private correspondence). But the letters seem to have been intended mainly to get ministers to put pressure on BNFL to improve the terms of the reprocessing contracts. Since the British government is not normally interested in helping private commercial enterprises in difficulty, the company had to construct an argument that made the government feel responsible. It went as follows.

- BE faced serious financial difficulties because of falling revenues.
- This was caused mainly by the fall in electricity prices.
- This in turn had been caused by the introduction of the new electricity trading arrangements (NETA) which had been driven by the government and regulator.
- BE would be able to survive even these low prices if only it didn't have the burden of fuel reprocessing contracts with BNFL.
- BNFL should renegotiate these contracts, reflecting the commercial realities of its main customer, but had refused to. The government, as BNFL's owner, should force it to act.

In summary, the government was responsible for both creating the problem (lower power prices) and for pushing BNFL to create the solution. Since it was extremely unlikely that the government would reverse NETA, BE's main hope was that it would put pressure on BNFL's management to do a deal that would bring financial relief sufficient to keep BE in business through the period of low power prices.

While Jeffrey and his team were no doubt sincere in their argument, they may have been naïve politically. The government was very unlikely to help BE out unless there was a compelling public policy reason to do so. The Blair government was very keen to distance itself from the old days of state support for ailing industries. The self consciously New Labour government would be humiliated if it was seen to bail out a "lame duck", in the cliché of the interventionist 1970s. But there was a legal obstacle too. The European Commission's rules limiting state aid had been tightened up considerably over the previous decade and the government would not want to clash with Brussels.

In any case, these obstacles would apply only if the government actually wanted to intervene. The evidence is that they didn't. The letters back from the government to BE were couched in reasonable, sympathetic but essentially negative language. In July 2001 Secretary of State for Industry Patricia Hewitt wrote back to John Robb thanking him for his letter and adding in a handwritten note that "we have a lot to resolve." The board appeared to have drawn some comfort from this, especially the use of the word "we".

But it fell far short of a specific commitment. Jeffrey wrote to Brian Wilson in January 2002 and a meeting followed in February (private communication). The BE position was that the losses were serious but not expected to worsen and that in the medium term the North American profits would push the company back into profit. What Jeffrey wanted from the government was help on the BNFL contracts, action on the unjust property tax treatment of nuclear stations, transfer of the pre-1996 liabilities back to the government and some help with the higher security costs following the 11 September 2001 attacks in the US. He offered a complete "open book" process, whereby the company would allow the government's advisors Credit Suisse First Boston (CSFB) unrestricted access to BE's internal accounts.

Some BE executives believe there were hints that there would be some help for the company in the energy review which was published in February 2002. Others recall a degree of "selective listening" to Wilson, hearing all of his sympathy but ignoring the political difficulties (private interviews). In the event the review contained nothing that directly helped the company's finances.

By April 2002 the government evidently wanted to keep the company's expectations in check. Joan MacNaughton, the Director General of the Energy section at the Department of Trade and Industry, wrote to Jeffrey, after a face to face meeting with the minister that, "You and your colleagues should not draw comfort from the contacts that we are having in relation to these issues." In effect, this said that the government was listening but wouldn't act. In July, after the dividend payment had undermined sympathy for the company's plight, the minutes to a joint meeting between the company and DTI noted that "The DTI now has a much clearer picture of BE's financing requirements" (private communication). But that was quite different from a promise to help with funding.

BNFL's management had their own point of view. BNFL was a public limited corporation, which just happened to have a single shareholder, namely Her Majesty's Government. After many years when the management had been picked largely from the civil service, with somewhat mixed results, the company was now being run in a more commercial way. The company's chief executive since March 2000 had been Norman Askew, an experienced private sector business man who had built a strong reputation as the chief executive of REC East Midlands Electricity before a stint running Virginia Power in the US. Askew had been hired to introduce some commercial discipline into BNFL, and prepare the company for privatisation. Askew and his team were not going to give away money to anybody, unless their shareholder told them to.

The early days of renegotiations in 2000 and 2001 had gone badly, partly because the BNFL side didn't see any evidence that BE was really in trouble. But by the spring of 2002 peace had broken out again and there was a real sense of constructive negotiations between the two sides. BNFL understood that it is good business sense to see if you can help out your main customer, but they were only willing to do a deal that was value neutral or positive for BNFL's shareholder. So long as privatisation remained a possibility (which in theory it did although no City investor took the idea very seriously) there was additional pressure on BNFL to make sure that any new deal would not reduce its value.

There should have been scope for a value neutral deal. The contracts were very long term and it should have been possible to provide BE with what it needed – near term cash savings – in exchange for compensating gains for BNFL – higher cash income in future. Any new contract could be written to ensure the net present value of the contracts remained the same or even higher. There was a related precedent in the long term gas contract renegotiations that Centrica had signed with its upstream gas suppliers, after its de-merger from British Gas in 1997 (Chapter 15).

But reaching a deal proved difficult. BNFL had drawn the same conclusion as the government from BE's decision to maintain the dividend in May; things weren't yet that bad (private interviews). BNFL sources insist that there was no interference from the government at any stage to push them into a deal. The upshot was that BNFL were happy to talk but required BE to give up some future gains (i.e. pay more) for any near term savings. As BE came reluctantly to accept that principle, the discussions focused on linking the price of the fuel handling contracts to the price of electricity. This would cut BE's fixed costs by making a large part of its cost structure variable in line with its revenues. And BNFL were happy to calculate that the current low electricity prices would be offset by higher prices in the longer term, so short term revenue loss would be balanced by long term revenue gain. The problem was then the exact numbers; through June and July the talks continued but without a resolution.

The Accenture electricity price forecast

By the summer, the financial outlook had deteriorated seriously. In May one of the two reactors at Torness in Scotland had to be closed because of problems with one of the giant pumps that pushed the coolant gas round. These huge electric motors operated in a ring around the reactor, inside the pressure vessel. They were subject to enormous strains because of the very high temperatures of the gas. One of them had started vibrating, suggesting failure of a component. But there was nobody left at BE who knew anything about these motors. BE was forced to contact the Clydeside-based company that made them, Howdens, who found a former employee in retirement who remembered building them (private interview). But Howdens couldn't fix the problem and BE was left struggling to repair the pump, while losing around £250,000 a day in revenue.

Then in June the US bond issue flopped and the company was on a timetable to a liquidity crisis when the existing sterling bond matured at the end of the financial year. In July BE had to accept a lower price for the power it sold to Scottish Power. Since a dispute began in April 2001 BE had been denied access to Scottish Power's payments. BE, desperate for cash, settled at a price of some tens of millions of future lost revenue (private interviews). Meanwhile electricity prices continued to drift lower. Through the summer the board was meeting almost daily. Robin Jeffrey was enormously energetic, writing detailed papers to brief all board members of the various issues: the station operating problems; finances; discussions with government and BNFL. Former colleagues talk of emails arriving at 3 a.m., making them wonder if he ever slept (private interviews).

It became clear that the company would soon be forced to draw on its £615 million credit lines with the banks. But in the post-Enron heightened sensitivity to the directors' legal responsibility, the question was raised, would it be acceptable to borrow more money if the board wasn't sure when it could pay it back? All businesses face an uncertain future but in this case there was one critical variable: the UK price of power. So the board decided to commission an independent consultant to advise it.

There are several expert consultants in the energy sector but the board's choice was a little surprising. Accenture was the former Andersen Consulting, an international and well respected consultancy that was best known for large IT projects. It was far less well known in the UK energy sector. BE had employed better known energy consultants such as Oxera and ILEX in the past but some in the management team believed that their forecasts of electricity prices had proven too high in the past (private interviews). Accenture was known to the newest independent director, Claire Spottiswoode, and they won the job of building a new detailed model.

Forecasting the price of electricity is, like any commodity forecasting, a mixture of logic and crossed fingers. Any model depends on the assumptions put into it and the idea of buying independent advice is therefore somewhat illusory. Accenture's model was reportedly a very thorough one and perhaps commanded more authority than the company's own internal forecasts, which had been pretty gloomy but had not been taken seriously enough by the board. The outcome was a set of forecasts that suggested a very pessimistic outlook for power prices. Accenture's work, combined with the company's own operating assumptions, indicated a base case of no significant improvement in power prices for three years. A lower case suggested prices falling further and getting stuck at the marginal cost of coal for years on end (private interviews).

The Accenture forecasts made it hard for any board member to remain optimistic about a future upturn in power prices. If the forecast was even broadly accurate, it meant that BE would face continuing substantial losses in its UK generating business. The future North American profits would mitigate but not offset these losses; the company would eventually run out of cash. The board's legal advice was that the directors could not authorise the drawing down of the bank credit lines if it had no realistic estimate of when the money could be paid back. This would amount to trading while insolvent and the directors would be individually liable to criminal prosecution.

On 10 August the spot price of electricity fell to £10.39/MWh, an all time low. Even allowing for the time of year, this was an alarmingly low price which seemed to confirm the dismal tone of the Accenture forecast. Only one thing stood between insolvency and survival; the prospect of a breakthrough with BNFL. Talks were continuing and Jeffrey believed that there was still a reasonable chance of a deal that would save the company enough money to allow it to draw down the bank credit and stave off a liquidity crisis.

Just as power prices hit their low, Dungeness B station had to be shut down. The station had such a dreadful operating history that investors didn't react to the unexplained outage. But then on 13 August the second reactor at Torness second unit had to be closed, because of a cracked fan blade in the same type of coolant pump that had shut the first reactor in May. The pumps had developed metal fatigue. The same design of pump had been used at the Heysham 2 station so there would be costly repairs there too.

The company made a statement explaining that there would be additional costs to fix the pump problems but that the company did not face a crisis. Even so, the shares fell 30 per cent, to just 69p, and the BE team decided to call a conference call for analysts and investors the following day, to elaborate on their statement and take questions. This was the right thing to do. Good investor relations is about providing as much information as is commercially feasible to allow investors to estimate the financial consequences of news, whether it is good or bad. British Energy had always had an excellent investor relations team and there was no attempt to bury or "spin" the news. But the investor call was to become very controversial and lead to an inquiry by the Financial Services Authority (FSA), the regulator for the British financial markets.

The analyst conference call: August 2002

Key parts of the 14 August call were reproduced in the *Financial Times* of 13 September when the FSA announced its inquiry (*Financial Times*, 2002b). The quotations below are taken from that account. On the call from BE were: Robin Jeffrey (chairman); Keith Lough (finance director); and David Gilchrist (managing director of generation). Listening were analysts, investors and anybody else who was interested – including BNFL.

Jeffrey began by saying: "I want to emphasise to you that we do not face a financial crisis and that we have a clear and well thought out way forward." He repeated the team's goals on cost cutting and their hopes for a "level playing field" for nuclear power in Britain. He refused to be drawn by questions on the likelihood of a cut in the dividend at the interim results in November, pointing out quite properly that this was for the board to decide. He was then pushed on the possibility that the earlier decision to pay a dividend might have blocked government help to the company. Jeffrey replied: "[M]y inference would be that government knows very well the importance that owners of companies place on dividends being paid and the importance of companies being in a sound financial position in order to be able to pay dividends." This inference was probably wrong, or at least politically naïve.

Jeffrey closed his introductory remarks by saying "I believe as a management, we've acted very promptly in order that you had at all times the best available information we could give you. I believe what we've outlined in the announcement is prudent and as I said at the beginning, the company continues to be on course to achieve its key objectives at the end of the year, especially the 1.6 pence per kilowatt hour [unit operating cost target], and the £150 million cost reduction programme."

Finance Director Keith Lough then spelled out the financial damage from the Torness outages. He estimated a shortfall of some 4.5 TWh in output for the year. The company saw the revenue loss at about £18.4/MWh but there would be a saving on marginal costs of £6/MWh. In other words not running the stations would save £6/MWh in terms of fuel savings and avoided fuel reprocessing costs, leaving a net financial cost of about £12.4/MWh. Multiplying this by the estimated 4.5 TWh output shortfall implied a total hit of some £56 million. The company's annual profits this year would be this much lower (excluding the cost of putting the problem right) but this should be a non-recurring cost.

Lough then talked about the company's general financial condition. "Robin has been very clear that we do not have and we are not faced with an immediate credit crisis." He said the BE team always knew that 2002/2003 was going to be a year of peak capital spending. This would amount to some £300m, being spent on improving the nuclear generation plant (about £120 million), fitting flue gas desulphurisation equipment to Eggborough power stations to cut acid rain emissions (about £30 million) and on investment in the AmerGen joint venture in the US (about £150 million). In other words, the company was facing a significant hit to profits and cashflow just when its need for cash was unusually high. Moreover, the Ontario Power financing was being reorganised to provide greater flexibility for BE in future and a lower interest rate. But this reorganisation would entail a need to repay about £100 million of lending within 180 days of completion, and the clock would probably start ticking in the coming autumn. Together with the sterling bond due at the end of March, BE faced a cash outflow of £210 million around the end of the current financial year.

But this was all still manageable, Lough insisted, because BE retained £615 million of bank credit lines. The rating agencies knew all of this and the bad news from Torness didn't fundamentally change the overall financial picture. Of the failed US bond issue he said: "We went to the US, again as you are aware, in the week beginning of 8 July, and walked into to what one of our co-leads described as a perfect storm of US market, and we came back and effectively withdrew from that possible issue. We're now reconsidering our various options to rebalance the business and that does not preclude going back into the bond market under more sensible and settled conditions. So hopefully that gives you an overview as to where we are in terms of financial structuring."

Lough told investors that both the company pension fund and the decommissioning fund (the "pension fund" for retired nuclear power stations) had recently been reviewed and there was no need for additional company funding for either. In further questions, David Gilchrist confirmed the calculation of the financial cost of the Torness closures. The call ended.

The call was successful in conveying a number of messages:

- The company's management were aware of and managing all of the financial flows into and out of the company;
- The medium term picture of a UK nuclear business with break-even costs of £16/MWh was intact;

- The management realised their investors' need for information and were being as open and helpful as they could;
- There was no crisis or panic.

The shares closed down a further 6 per cent on the day but this wasn't a bad result in such difficult circumstances. Over the rest of August the shares remained around 60p and then drifted up to about 80p in early September. The company faced grave difficulties but the share price was not indicating any imminent collapse.

Jeffrey's confident tone and emphatic assertion that the company did not face a financial crisis were to come under question later in the year. But the sub-sequent FSA inquiry completely exonerated him from any charge of misleading investors in making these comments. The crux of the FSA argument was the Jeffrey completely believed what he said and had good reason for his belief (Financial Services Authority, 2003).

That belief, which lay behind Jeffrey's statement that he and his team had a clear and well thought out way forward, was the prospect of a deal with BNFL that would allow the company to remain financially viable until the Canadian profits came through. The negotiations between BE and BNFL had made Jeffrey confident that an acceptable deal would be done.

The exact details of the negotiations remain secret but it appears that there was a difference of perception during that August between the BE and BNFL teams. BE had provided detailed financial projections so that BNFL now knew just how much money BE needed – absolutely *needed* – to keep running. The BNFL team's acceptance of these numbers appears to have made Jeffrey and Lough confident that some sort of deal on that scale would be done. The amount at stake was about £150 million. If the annual BNFL costs could be cut by that much, then BE would be able to survive the low power prices, draw down its bank credit lines and successfully refinance the maturing sterling bond and Ontario Power loan.

But the BNFL team had not *agreed* to anything. The negotiations were close and constructive; both sides realised a lot was at stake and the old antagonisms had been replaced by a common desire to see a long term future for nuclear power in the UK. But BNFL was still bound by its need to protect its own share-holder's interests. When the BNFL managers heard the conference call on 14 August they drew the same conclusions as the investors: there were difficult times but BE was not on the edge of collapse. But the irony was that BE was not on the edge of collapse only if BNFL *believed* it really was.

Hopes spring eternal

During the last weeks of August BE's share price gyrated around rumour and counter-rumours of whether the government would help the company. On August 25 two newspapers claimed that the Department of Trade and Industry had a secret "project Blue" to save the company (*Independent on Sunday*,

2002; *Sunday Times*, 2002). The favourite scheme was to give BE the management of the BNFL Magnox reactors but even renationalisation of the company was on the cards. Energy minister Brian Wilson went on the BBC radio programme "The World This Weekend" to set the record straight. He played down the stories of company rescues but acknowledged that the government was keeping an eye on things and considering various scenarios. The DTI would be considering how NETA affected the viability of generators as part of the work for the forthcoming White Paper on energy (quoted by Reuters, 26 August 2006).

The next business day the stock price jumped nearly 30 per cent on these vague hints of support, the shares closing at 76p. Wilson's reference to the possibility that the electricity trading system was somehow responsible for low prices and therefore for BE's problems led some analysts to expect government to change the system.

This brought a strong retort from the industry regulator, Callum McCarthy, who told *The Times* that the trading system merely allowed competitive forces to operate. He argued that it was wrong to make the market uncompetitive to rescue any particular generator, avoiding any specific mention of nuclear power. The same article reported that the regulatory body OFGEM supported exemption of BE from the climate change levy, which would save the company £100 million a year, as this wouldn't interfere with the power market. A "government source" was quoted as saying that: "The one absolute certainty is that it costs more to shut them [nuclear stations] down than it does to keep them going" (*The Times*, 2002).

The following day Brian Wilson was at a North Sea operators' conference in Norway. But the press wouldn't leave him alone. He added to his analysis of BE's problems by saying "The difficulty is that some of them [power companies] are protected by having a customer base so they are able to compensate for the low wholesale price by maintaining a high retail price to domestic customers" (Reuters, 2002a). Wilson's accurate insight carried the implication that other energy suppliers were ripping off their customers by not passing through the low wholesale prices but nobody seemed to notice this implied criticism of OFGEM's laissez-faire approach. It still added up to sympathy rather than concrete action.

BE meanwhile had confirmed publicly that it was indeed in talks with BNFL about a number of issues, including a possible transfer of the Magnox management, but that this was a long way off. The real discussions were about the reprocessing contract and there was little chance of the Magnox deal happening at all, let alone soon enough to save the company's financial position.

The shares swung up and down according to whether the optimists or pessimists set the tone. The optimists pointed to Wilson's evident concern for BE's position and recognition that both NETA and the working of the climate change levy were problems. The pessimists replied that Wilson hadn't actually promised anything and we had heard these stories before.

One leading investment bank decided to upgrade their recommendation on

British Energy shares from "market perform" (i.e. hold) to "buy". On 29 August Deutsche Bank's new report argued that "all the bad news is in the price" and suggested the shares were worth £1.50 each, compared with their current price of 79p. Although Deutsche noted that the shares were "not for the faint-hearted" (Reuters, 2002b) BE's stock rose over the next few days to 85p. The idea that one should buy shares when "blood is running in the street" is usually attributed to Lord Rothschild. The logic is that when the news is truly terrible, financial assets are priced at distress levels so there will be big profits from any improvement. Sometimes this is excellent advice; the Rothschilds were supposed to have made a great fortune after the news that Napoleon had been defeated at the battle of Waterloo (although the truth is a bit more complex (Ferguson, 2001 pp. 286–287)). There are times when a broker can make a glorious reputation by daring to "call" the bottom in the face of apparent disaster, if fortune turns and the shares rally to many times their former, depressed value. But this was not such a time; Deutsche's report was thoughtful, well argued and spectacularly wrong.

Away from the press speculation and stock market fever, the company's fate depended on a single question: could a better deal be done with BNFL? After two years, the negotiations reached a climax at the beginning of September. The BE team clearly thought over the previous weeks they had reached agreement in principle for a contract cost cut large enough to save BE. But nothing had been yet put in writing. The words finally came in the form of a term sheet (draft contract) delivered to Jeffrey's hotel room in London at about midnight on 3 September. Former colleagues talk of how tough a job Jeffrey had had over the previous year. As both chairman and chief executive he carried the full weight of responsibility for the company. It must have been very lonely. Those colleagues pay tribute to his energy, leadership and analytical intelligence. As 3 September turned into 4 September, Jeffrey was about to find out if it had all paid off.

According to the *Independent* BE needed £150 million in immediate savings to keep the company afloat. Jeffrey believed that BNFL had agreed orally to that amount. The figure in the term sheet was £120 million but £50 million of this would be retained by BNFL against future costs, leaving only £70 million of actual cash savings (*Independent*, 2002). This was far less than Jeffrey had expected. It would not be enough to keep the company afloat. Jeffrey's hopes of a BNFL deal to save the company had been wrecked.

Recollections of negotiations are problematic and unreliable. The FSA inquiry, which included interviews with all of the people involved and examination of key documents, concluded that Jeffrey had good reason to believe when he made his 14 August statement that the BNFL deal would be materially larger than the one actually proposed. The FSA "found no evidence to suggest that BE's financial condition or the Company's expectations as to its performance changed materially in the period from 14 August until 5 September" (Financial Services Authority, 2003). The only change was in the size of the expected BNFL deal. How to explain the gap between Jeffrey's belief and the actual

BNFL offer? Sources at BNFL accept that Jeffrey "had reason to form his belief" (private interviews) but that no actual deal was ever explicitly offered of the size he wanted. The actual offer was far too little and therefore came as a bitter surprise to Jeffrey and his colleagues.

The fatal board meeting

The BE board met at 7 a.m. on the morning of 5 September 2002. They faced some grim logic. The BNFL deal "fell far short" of the cut in UK generating costs they had hoped for (Financial Services Authority, 2003). The Accenture forecasts for power prices suggested that the British nuclear business would be unprofitable for the foreseeable future. Their legal advice was that they could not draw on the £615 million bank credit lines that would be necessary to pay back the sterling bond and keep the company running. Any hopes for other cost savings such as rates relief or exemption of nuclear electricity from the climate change levy were still speculative. The board had spent months explaining its position to the government, who surely knew what the true state of affairs was. They had negotiated as much as they could with BNFL, but with only partial success. The company's credit rating was on the edge of junk status, which would require yet more cash to be found to provide trading collateral. There seemed no escape. The company had run out of cash and needed emergency funding or it would have to cease operations.

After the stock market had closed on 5 September 2002, BE put out a statement. It said that the company faced insolvency if it did not get immediate financial assistance. It had agreed to meet the government for discussions about financial support "and to enable a longer-term restructuring to take place.... If these discussions are not successful, the company may be unable to meet its financial obligations as they fall due and, therefore, the company may have to take appropriate insolvency proceedings. The board has reasonable grounds for believing that these discussions will be successful but there can be no certainty that this will preserve value for investors" (British Energy, 2002b). In other words the power stations might keep going but the shareholders would lose their money. The shares were suspended, having closed at 80p. When they resumed trading on 9 September they fell to 28p.

There is an old stock market joke which runs: how does a company's share price fall by 90 per cent? Answer: it falls by 80 per cent then halves. Anybody who bought BE's shares at privatisation for £2.03 or later at up to £7.33 might have considered that a fall of 53p was painful but small beer. But some investors must have bought the shares at around 80p, just before their suspension. They immediately lost two thirds of their money. But there was still a long way to go. BE's shares resumed trading after investors had been told that insolvency was now a serious possibility. Equities are a form of call option; as long as there is some chance of a recovery the shares have value, although that value may be hard to estimate. Speculation about various rescue plans kept some value in the shares. But eventually it became clear that the company was either going into administration (meaning no value for shareholders) or faced a very serious financial restructuring in which creditors would get most of the company. The shares at 28p still had another 82 per cent to fall. They closed at the end of December at just 5p.

It is very hard for anybody not present at the board meeting to appreciate fully the pressures the directors were under. The board of a company doesn't lightly put itself into the hands of the government. Some of the assumptions the directors had made were at least arguable, especially the long term power prices forecasts, which turned out to be seriously wrong. But at a time when the Enron bankruptcy the previous year had forcefully reminded all company directors of their responsibilities, it would be very hard to blame the directors for their decision.

The financial story of 2002

The interim (six monthly) figures published later in the year showed the deterioration in profits and cashflow that would have been apparent to the board when they took their decision. They are shown in Table 10.4 with the previous year's interims for comparison.

Table 10.4 shows that operating profit fell into loss and net operating cashflow fell to only £76 million. After paying interest, tax and capital spending cashflow was already negative and became more so after paying the dividend declared for the previous year. Overall net cashflow was a negative £121 million, compared with negative £54 million the year before. The figures show that a surge in capital spending was as much to blame as the fall in profit. But this capital spending was largely unavoidable. The previous year's negative cashflow was after spending £129 million on acquisitions, meaning the business

Table 10.4 British Energy interim cashflow figures for 2001 and 2002 (£m)

Six months ending 30 September	2001	2002
Operating profit (before exceptionals)	72	(26)
Depreciation	142	143
Net liabilities payments (including decommissioning fund)	(91)	(51)
Change in working capital	1	10
Net operating cashflow	124	76
Net interest	(3)	(20)
Tax	9	6
Net capital spending	(25)	(147)
Acquisitions and disposals	(129)	(2)
Dividends	(30)	(34)
Overall net cashflow	(54)	(121)
Memorandum items:		
Nuclear output (TWh)	32.7	30.3
Average unit cost (p/kWh)	1.74	1.85

Source: British Energy Interim results statements for 2001–2002 and 2002–2003.

Table 10.5 Components of fall in interim operating profit, 2002–2003 over 2001–2002
(£m)

UK:	(86)
lower prices	(42)
lower output	(49)
higher costs	5
Bruce (Canada)	(8)
AmerGen (US)	(4)
Total change in operating profit	(98)

Source: British Energy Interim results statements for 2001–2002 and 2002–2003.

was cash positive before investing in new businesses. But the first half of 2002/2003 cash deficit came from the business operations alone. Without improvement, the company would sink further into debt.

Table 10.5 shows the causes of the fall in operating profit, most of which was in the UK business. The two main components were lower electricity prices and lower output. The board might have hoped for a recovery in output in the medium term but the Accenture forecast made them doubt that there would be any early rise in power prices. In the event, output deteriorated further in the next couple of years, although power prices bottomed out in 2003.

Conclusion

For Jeffrey it was a personal tragedy. A man who had given so much of his career to the British nuclear power industry had been unlucky enough to be in the driving seat when the car went off the road. By 2001 it is hard to see how Jeffrey or anybody else could have made much of a difference to the company's fate given the twin facts of low power prices and an intransigent BNFL. It is not even clear that the BNFL deal could have saved the company. The company's output was actually lower three years later than in the crisis year and the restructured BE announced in 2006 that it would be spending £250 million a year for the next few years to get the plant reliability up to an acceptable level. The cost cutting and underinvestment since privatisation had undermined the company's ability to produce power reliably. But the saddest irony is that the price of power reached its nadir almost exactly as BE ran out of money. The spot price of electricity oscillated around the £16/MWh target break even price for the rest of 2002 and through 2003. But in late 2003 it started to rise and never fell back below that level again. In 2006 it was trading at over £50/MWh, three times the level at which BE hoped to break even.

Part IV

Analysis

The causes of the crisis

11 Financial strategy

Introduction

In September 2002, BE ran out of money. It is tempting to assume that financial policy must have been to blame. This is unfair; if a company cannot generate a cash surplus then no financial policy can save it from insolvency. But the board's decision in 1999 to return £432 million of capital to shareholders contributed critically to putting the company at risk ahead of the collapse in electricity prices that began in 2000. That decision, combined with the £775 million of investment just a few months later, turned a very strong balance sheet into a dangerously stretched one.

This chapter analyses the decision to gear up the company. It argues that the board was under enormous pressure from investors to take on more debt, reinforced by a surging share price that indicated stock market approval of that widely anticipated policy. The share price rise then reversed with a vengeance. It is argued below that the share price became seriously overvalued in 1998 because of a mixture of faulty valuation by financial analysts and widespread investor misunderstanding of the company's financial workings. In pursuing shareholder value, as they were supposed to, the company's directors made a strategic error that fatally weakened it just when it needed great reserves of financial strength. The directors were at fault in not realising the risk the company faced from lower power prices (Chapter 13) and in making some questionable investment decisions (Chapter 12). But they were encouraged greatly in their errors by the stock market.

The road to the return of value

We first describe what BE did with its money, before analysing why. Table 11.1 shows how BE disposed of its cashflows. Resources start with operating cashflow after normal capital expenditure ("capex"). Remaining cash is then available for paying tax, servicing capital (interest and dividends) and acquisitions.

Table 11.1 shows that net operating cashflow grew relatively little from £404 million in financial year 1997 to £479 million in 1999 but then fell steadily to just £54 million in 2003, by which time the company was, in effect, insolvent. For the

Table 11.1. Summary of cashflows and other financial measures, 1997–2003 (£m)

Year ending 31 March	1997	1998	1999	2000	2001	2002	2003
Operating cashflow net of capex	404	461	479	313	144	155	54
Net interest, tax and other	(53)	(91)	(74)	(71)	(95)	(11)	(81)
Ordinary dividends	(32)	(98)	(104)	(108)	(29)	(46)	(31)
Strategic (acquisitions)/disposals:	0	0	0	(775)	179	(129)	262
Eggborough power station	–	–	–	*(636)*	–	–	–
Swalec supply business	–	–	–	*(107)*	210	–	–
North America	–	–	–	*(32)*	*(31)*	*(129)*	*262*
Net free cashflow (1)	319	272	301	(641)	199	(31)	204
Special dividends and share buybacks (2)	–	–	(69)	(471)	–	–	–
Balance of cashflow (1–2)	319	272	232	(1,112)	199	(31)	204
Net debt/equity (%)	17	(1)	(10)	71	56	137	n.a.
Interest cover (x)	6.1	19.9	473	61.1	4.0	3.5	2.0

Source: British Energy annual reports; author's calculations.

first three years there was ample cash remaining to fund ordinary dividends after paying interest and tax. In addition, in 1999 shareholders received a special dividend of £69 million following the renegotiation of contracts with BNFL.

Undistributed free cashflow leads to falling debt. BE's balance sheet gearing, measured by the year end stock of net debt to equity fell from 17 per cent in March 1997 to −1 per cent in March 1998, i.e. the company had net cash on the balance sheet. The following year the net cash reached 10 per cent of book equity. At the end of March 1999 then, BE had a very strong balance sheet, with £176 million of cash and liquid assets and no debt. It did of course have the nuclear liabilities but these are not captured in the conventional measures of gearing, which refer only to interest-bearing liabilities.

BE's managers had built up this cash pile only because they had been frustrated in their ability to find suitable acquisitions. If the company had been successful in its bid for London Electricity in late 1998, for example, it would have faced a cash outlay of £2 billion, which would have increased gearing considerably, even after consolidating London's assets. Having failed to buy London or any other REC, and blocked at that stage from buying a coal power station, BE faced very strong pressure to gear up the company by returning what investors regarded as "surplus" capital.

The year ending March 2000 was a turning point. Operating cashflow net of capital spending was actually some £166 million lower than in 1999, a fall caused roughly equally by a fall in operating profit (owing to a fall in output) and a rise in capital spending. But this was the year that the company returned some 10 per cent of its equity to shareholders as well as share buybacks that brought the exceptional equity payment to £471 million, i.e. on top of £108 million of ordinary dividends.

If that had been all, the company would have seen a net cash outflow of £337 million (operating cashflow of £313 million, less £71 million of tax and interest, £108 million of ordinary dividends and £471 million of exceptional equity payments). Having started the year with net cash of £176 million this would have left the company with net debt of £161 million, compared with about £1.3 billion of equity, for gearing of around 12 per cent. This would have been a modest gearing up of the company that left room for some financial flexibility in the light of an uncertain future as power price reform proceeded.

Unfortunately the company spent £775 million on acquisitions in 2000. Most of this was for the Eggborough coal power station with the balance for the SWALEC electricity supply business and for investment in North America. The effect of this sudden wave of investments, coming just months after the return of value, was to push gearing up to 71 per cent in March 2000, a fairly high level for a stable utility and a very high level for what was actually a commodity manufacturing company.

Measuring the strength of the balance sheet

The traditional measure of balance sheet strength is the "stock" measure: the ratio of net debt to shareholder equity defined at a particular date. But this measure is sensitive to the accounting policies that determine the value of the equity. The more reliable alternative is the "flow" measure of gearing, interest cover, which is the ratio of operating profit to net interest payments over a year. BE's interest cover was a comfortable 6.1 times in 1996/1997 and climbed to an exceptionally high 473 times in 1998/1999, when net interest paid was only £1 million. It remained high at 61 times in 1999/2000 because most of the debt wasn't taken on until very late in the financial year.

But in 2000/2001, with a full year's cost of the higher debt and falling operating profit, interest cover fell to just four times, a level that was barely compatible with an investment grade credit rating (Brealey *et al.*, 2006 p. 657). By 2002/2003 interest cover had fallen to only two times, which implies severe financial stretch and is inconsistent with an investment grade credit rating. There is no net debt to equity gearing figure for 2002/2003 because the company had negative equity after writing down its power stations.

BE's financial position was even worse then, when measured by interest cover than measured by balance sheet gearing.

Comparison with other generators

The two companies most financially similar to BE were National Power (until it de-merged its overseas assets in 2000) and PowerGen (until it bought East Midlands Electricity in 1999). Both were predominantly UK generating companies, though each had significant foreign investments by 1999. Table 11.2 shows the last comparable figures for these two generators next to the figures for gearing (at 31 March 2000) and interest cover (year ending March 2001) for BE.

Table 11.2 shows that BE had a weaker financial position after 2000 than

Table 11.2 Gearing and interest cover for British generating companies (%)

Company	Net debt/equity	Interest cover (x)
National Power (1999)[1]	52	5.8
PowerGen (1998)	28	12.0
British Energy (2000 and 2001)	71[2]	4.0[3]

Notes
1 Excluding non-recourse debt.
2 Financial year 2000.
3 Financial year 2001.

National Power and PowerGen had before they changed into different types of company. Yet British Energy also had the highest exposure to any fall in electricity prices, which meant it needed a *stronger* position than the other two going into a period when prices were likely to fall.

The most direct precedent for BE's return of value was National Power's return of some £1.2 billion of cash to its shareholders in 1996/1997. Table 11.3 shows that this raised its gearing from 13 per cent at March 1996 to 77 per cent at March 1999, slightly higher than BE's 71 per cent in March 2000. But National Power's interest cover remained strong, at 11.8 times. National Power was capitalising some interest in construction which reduced its net interest charge so the year 1998 is more representative. But even then interest cover remained at 6.8 times while book gearing was 71 per cent. BE, a company with greater financial exposure to UK power prices than National Power, had interest cover of only four times the year after its return of value.

In sum, BE's financial decisions in the year 1999/2000 left it with a financial position that was far weaker than its fossil fuel competitors, even though it was intrinsically a riskier company. This was despite the growing risk that future profits might be hit severely by lower power prices. The next section of this chapter explains why the board chose to do this.

The pressure to return cash to shareholders

BE's board was under great pressure to return any surplus cash to shareholders. It is probable that this pressure led the board to make the return of value larger

Table 11.3 National Power's financial ratios, year ending March 1996–1998 (£m)

Year ending March	1996	1997	1998
Net debt/equity (%)	13	77	71
Interest cover (x)	n.a	11.8	6.8

Source: National Power Annual Report; figures as restated in 1999 following accounting changes.

Notes
National Power had net interest income in 1996.
n.a. not applicable.

than it would have otherwise wished to. The board debated the scale and timing of the return of the value and some directors were concerned that it might leave the company short of cash. Others argued for a delay of a year, to see the effect of NETA on the outlook for power prices and the company's financial position. But the majority opinion was swayed by the message from shareholders that they expected the company to make a significant return of capital because they could see no likely alternative use for it (private interviews).

The rest of this chapter explains how the stock market contributed to what was, with hindsight, a serious financial mistake. The ingredients in this poisonous cocktail are:

- the conventional wisdom in the late 1990s on the need for utilities to pay back surplus capital;
- the mis-classification by investors of BE as a utility leading to inappropriate valuation techniques;
- a poor understanding by some analysts of the relationship between profits and cashflows;
- a likely underestimation of the nuclear liabilities; and consequently
- an overvalued share price that provided false reassurance to the board.

City conventional wisdom on utilities and surplus capital

The climate of City opinion on the return of value was influenced by two things. First, from the late 1970s, it became the conventional wisdom that mature, cash rich companies had a tendency to waste their excess capital either on projects or acquisitions that benefited management, not shareholders (Jensen and Meckling, 1976; Jensen, 1986). The utility sector in several countries illustrated these risks. In continental Europe mature utilities in the electricity and water sectors in Germany and France had built up empires of unrelated investments with no apparent regard for shareholder value. Companies such as the French Compagnie Générale des Eaux and the German electricity-based holding company RWE offered depressing examples of what corporate management would do with shareholders' money if they faced no threat of takeover. The US offered lessons too; in 1990, FPL Group, the parent company of Florida Power and Light Co., had to make a $689m charge for losses arising from a failed attempt to diversify into cable television, insurance and citrus fruit production. Investors in the UK learnt the lesson that cash rich utilities needed to be kept under pressure to return the cash.

Second, the unexpectedly high cash generation of British privatised electricity companies had led investors to expect special dividends and share buybacks. The regional electricity companies (RECs) in particular proved far more cash generative than expected at privatisation in 1990. This became clear in December 1994 when the company Trafalgar House made a hostile bid for Northern Electric plc, the Newcastle-based REC. Northern had been privatised in 1990 at £2.40 a share; Trafalgar House's opening bid was £11. Northern successfully defended itself by pledging to pay a special dividend to shareholders of £5 a share, financed by borrowing (Helm, 2003 p. 215). This led investors to put pressure on the other electricity companies to use their balance sheets to finance special dividends and share buybacks. National Power's capital return of £1.2 billion in 1996/1997 was a response to this pressure.

When BE's balance sheet became debt free in 1997/1998 it was inevitable that some shareholders would see this is as inconsistent with the maximisation of shareholder value. BE was shopping for a REC throughout 1997 and 1998 (see Chapter 8) but the understanding grew that, if BE failed to find a suitable investment, then it would return capital to shareholders. Chairman John Robb stated in June 1998 that "we will continue to review [the capital structure] in the light of our cashflow and our long-term reinvestment plans" (British Energy, 1998a p. 4). This was not very coded language for saying that there would be a cash payout if the company failed to buy a REC. In private meetings with senior management, investors sought and got a more explicit commitment (private interviews).

Analysts thought BE was a utility

The utility sector was new to the British stockmarket because until privatisation it had overwhelmingly been in the public sector. In forming a view of what utilities are like and how they should be valued, investors were heavily influenced by US experience. Investors and analysts use sector and industrial categories to organise their thoughts about individual companies. For each sector there are rules of thumb about their financial characteristics, e.g. that food retailers are relatively defensive (resilient to economic downturns) and that banks are sensitive to short term interest rates. These rules of thumb are useful for summarising information. But they can obscure individual variations within sectors.

The US stereotype of a utility stock had most or all of the following features:

- it faced little or no competition, i.e. it was a de facto monopoly;
- it therefore faced some degree of regulation;
- it experienced low long term demand growth;
- demand was fairly insensitive to fluctuations in GDP i.e. it was non-cyclical; and
- there was little risk from technological innovation.

These business features implied a particular financial policy: a high level of leverage (gearing) meaning the ratio of debt to equity; and a high payout ratio (i.e. a low level of dividend cover), meaning the majority of earnings were distributed in the form of dividends.

These characteristics logically fit together. A company with stable demand, little risk from new entry and regulated operations can support a higher level of debt than one facing more cyclical or unstable demand or at risk of losing market share to innovating firms. And a mature company with little need to reinvest its earnings would naturally return the surplus to shareholders.

The stereotypical US utility therefore was a highly levered (debt/equity over 50 per cent), stable and predictable company with a high payout ratio (over 75 per cent – a dividend cover below 1.3 in UK terms). The perceived low risk of interruptions to the dividend underpinned the idea that utility shares were suitable for "widows and orphans", investors who were very risk averse and depended on the dividends for income. (This perception was shattered by the dramatic dividend cut by Florida Power and Light in 1994 (Soter *et al.*, 2001)).

But the UK was different

The US experience was potentially misleading because the typical US electric utility was vertically integrated: it generated, distributed and supplied its power to a captive customer base. But the privatisation of the British electricity industry led to dis-integration (in England and Wales) and the creation of two new private generating companies, National Power and PowerGen that owned no distribution or transmission assets. When British Energy was privatised in 1996 it joined these two to form a sub-sector within the broader electricity sector.

The different segments of the electricity industry which are bundled together in the typical vertically integrated US utility have very different industrial and financial characteristics. In particular, generation is a potentially very competitive manufacturing industry with volatile profits and the threat of new entry. The stereotypical features of the US electric utilities – high debt, high dividend payout and low risk – would apply to distribution and transmission companies but not to generators, which could face a lot of commercial risk.

Investors appreciated that a competitive generation company was unlike a monopoly REC. National Power and PowerGen faced the threat of a loss of market share to new entrants and the possibility of volatile and falling profits from competition. But the UK power market in the first half of the 1990s was far from competitive. The electricity price was set mainly by those two companies, National Power and PowerGen, which managed to avoid any significant fall in prices even as they lost market share to nuclear power and to the growing entry by new gas-fired power stations. The lack of competition meant that the generating sector remained de facto regulated to a greater degree than other, truly competitive industries.

From an investor point of view the generators therefore looked surprisingly similar to the RECs until the later 1990s: they were quasi-regulated; they generated reliable (and for a while rapidly growing) profits; and they seemed to face little commercial risk. Although new entry was growing, it had very little effect on the market price of power until 2000 onwards (see Chapter 13). When BE was privatised it evidently had some additional risks compared with the other electricity companies, chiefly the liabilities. But investors still tended to treat electric companies as different breeds of the same animal. Instead of comparing BE with companies that had similar exposure to commodity prices, such as steel, bulk chemicals or copper miners, investors lumped it in with the utilities and applied similar – and inappropriate – financial criteria.

The problem of valuing the company

US utilities were typically valued on dividends. The government's financial advisor BZW believed a dividend-based valuation was likely to undervalue BE, which was not really a utility. The BZW analysts tried to get investors to use a different valuation technique which took into account the two distinctive features of the company's finances: the fact that accounting profit was a poor guide to its cashflows; and the very long time scales over which the cashflows occurred. This technique was discounted cashflows (DCF).

DCF use in stock market analysis was relatively rare in the mid-1990s, for two reasons. First, it is moderately technically demanding and requires judgements about parameters such as the beta of a stock (its individual risk) and the equity risk premium (the riskiness of the whole stockmarket). Second, it is not a technique which lends itself to quick and easy communication between broker and client, especially over the phone.

BZW therefore faced a sceptical audience. But their argument for using DCF valuation was sound. There were two good reasons for using DCF: first, the fact that accounting profit was a poor guide to the company's cashflows; and second the unusual time path of the company's future cashflows.

Divergences between cashflow and profits

For any company, cashflows may diverge considerably in any one year from accounting profits because the latter are designed to make each year's result comparable with other years. But there is a long term, systematic gap for companies like BE which have large and lumpy investments in long lived fixed assets, such as power stations. This is because the depreciation charge in the profit and loss account may bear little relation to the annual cash spent on investment.

BE also had very long term liabilities. This is much less common, though not unknown in areas such as extractive industries (where there may be a need to restore the landscape when mining has ceased) and in polluting industries, including those with long term health claims (e.g. asbestosis). In all these cases the profit and loss account must be adjusted to reflect costs which may not fall due in cash terms for very many years. Accounting profits may therefore differ considerably from annual cashflows.

Figure 11.1 shows the difference between accounting profit and cashflows for BE at the operating profit level. It shows that net operating cashflow in 1997 was £97m higher than operating profit, about half of this being the result of a one off benefit to working capital from uranium stocks. But over time the gap narrowed and then reversed so that after 2000 operating cashflows were significantly below accounting profit.

The main reason for the cash/profit divergence was that the depreciation charge was trending down because of a lack of any major investments. Moreover, whenever a nuclear station received an operating life extension it meant

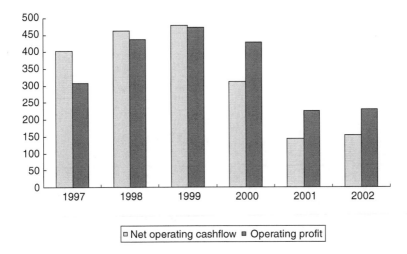

Figure 11.1 British Energy operating profit and operating cashflow, financial years 1997–2002 (£m) (source: company reports; author's calculations).

that the capital costs would be amortised over a longer period, cutting the annual depreciation charge. But cash capital spending, though erratic, was trending upwards, with a jump of £59 million in 1999/2000. So actual cash investment was growing but the accounting charge for fixed asset use was flat throughout the period (see Figure 11.2). Valuing the company on accounting profit would overvalue it.

The same message comes through at the level of total profit. Figure 11.3 compares net income – the accounting bottom line for a company – with the net cashflow available for dividends or strategic investments. In 1997 net cash generated was £325 million higher than net income. This was the gap that BZW

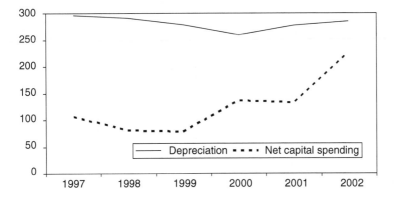

Figure 11.2 Depreciation and net capital spending, financial years 1997–2002 (£m) (source: company reports; author's calculations).

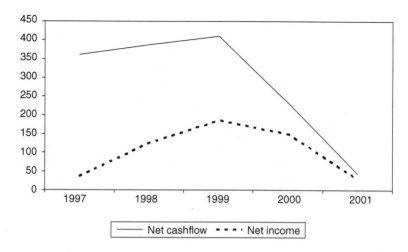

Figure 11.3 British Energy net cashflow and net income, financial years 1997–2001 (£m) (source: company reports; author's calculations).

Note
Net cashflow is operating cashflow after capital spending, tax and interest but before dividends.

had emphasised in its research (BZW Research, 1996a). But the gap gradually shrank to almost nothing in 2001.

Net cashflow fell by far more than accounting profit did over the period. Any valuation method that focused only on accounting profit would therefore fail to capture the dramatic deterioration in the company's true financial position.

The importance of time in British Energy's cashflows

The second reason to use DCF was the unusual time path of BE's cashflows. Most currently successful companies expect to have a long term future (although obviously not all do). Analysts typically model them as having a stream of profits and cashflows into the indefinite future. All ratio-based valuation measures such as P/E (price to earnings), EV (enterprise value) to EBITDA (earnings before interest, tax, depreciation and amortisation), and dividend yield implicitly assume a long term growth rate of the earnings, cashflows or dividends. They therefore collapse a multi-year forecast into a single average growth rate (Barker, 2001 ch. 4).

This may be a reasonable simplification in the case of companies that can be expected to continue operating into the long term future. But it was an unwarranted assumption when BE's eight nuclear power stations were all destined to close and, as of the early 2000s, none was likely to be replaced. BE *might* diversify into new areas or non-nuclear generation, but to value the company on the assumption that it did so successfully was a step ahead of valuing the company in its original form.

The point is illustrated in Figure 11.4 which shows BZW's base case forecast for BE's net cashflows throughout its entire future operations. The time scale is exceptionally long, because the company's assets were all forecast to cease operating by 2040 but the company's liabilities continued well beyond that, including a contribution to the decommissioning of BNFL's THORP fuel reprocessing plant around 2074.

Many investors were bemused and some were incredulous; how could anybody take seriously an 80 year forecast? But the point was the pattern or *shape* of the cashflow, not the precise numbers for 20 or 30 years hence. Figure 11.4 shows that the company had several years of gradually falling positive cashflows followed by a much longer period of negative cashflows. The valuation problem comes down to estimating the relative size of these two items, discounted to the present. Collapsing these cashflows into a single long term growth rate would be hopelessly inaccurate and misleading. So conventional valuation ratios, by implicitly assuming future growth where there wasn't likely to be any, were likely to overvalue BE.

After privatisation, BE's corporate strategy was to build a new stream of earnings that would replace those lost as the nuclear stations gradually closed (see Chapter 12). If successful that would provide the basis for a more normal, long term growth-based valuation approach. But even then it would make more sense to value the core nuclear business explicitly in terms of its decaying cashflow profile and value any new investments on their merits.

Several other equity analysts used DCF valuation. Influential investment banks such as HSBC James Capel, Salomon Brothers (later Citigroup) and UBS Warburg all showed DCF valuations for BE in their research. But these other DCF valuations mostly used the common approach of taking a number of years

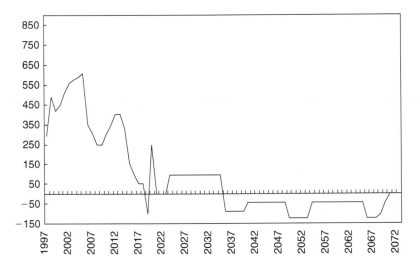

Figure 11.4 BZW forecast of net free cashflows, 1997–2074 (£m) (source: BZW (1996); author's estimates).

of explicit forecasts (typically 10) then using a terminal value to capture future years' cashflows using a perpetuity formula.

For example, HSBC James Capel wrote that "Our preferred valuation method in the electricity sector is discounted cashflow (DCF) analysis" (HSBC James Capel, 1996 p. 16). HSBC James Capel's valuation was made up of a ten year DCF plus a terminal value based on a retention rate of 50 per cent (equivalent to a reinvestment rate of 50 per cent of net profits) and a long term growth rate of cashflows of 1.5 per cent real. This gave a value in 1996 for the terminal value (called exit value in the research report) of £1.13 billion, compared with a value of £1.33 billion for the free cashflows from 1997 to 2007, for a total enterprise value of £2.4 billion (HSBC James Capel, 1996 p. 86).

HSBC's analysis assumed BE could find investment opportunities sufficient to absorb half of its net profits and that those investments could yield a future flow of cashflows growing at 1.5 per cent in real terms into the indefinite future. While these were not impossible assumptions they amounted to assuming nearly half of the value of the company lay in new investments that might never exist. This approach also took no account of the time path of nuclear liabilities, because it assumed they were a fixed annual cost into the indefinite future. HSBC is used as an example here only because their research was one of the few that specified the valuation assumptions explicitly. Other brokers appeared to make similar assumptions but it is impossible to tell from their publications.

Figure 11.5 superimposes HSBC's cashflow projections on BZW's. The two diverge completely from the point where HSBC assume perpetual growth. HSBC's lower figures in the earlier years appear to result from deducting cash for the future liabilities. The perpetual growth approach, typical of the broking research on BE, produces an implausible view of the future.

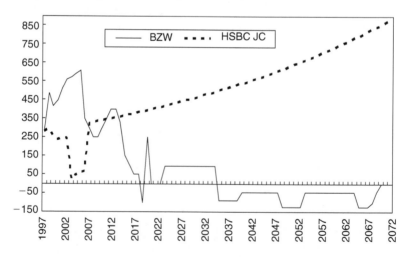

Figure 11.5 BZW and HSBC James Capel forecasts of net free cashflow, 1997–2074, 1996 prices (£m) (source: BZW (1996), HSBC (1996); author's estimates).

The use of EV/EBITDA to value the company

The problem of using a terminal value applies even more forcefully to the use of valuation ratios such as P/E, EV/EBITDA or dividend yield. Valuing BE in 1996 or 1999 using these measures collapsed the complex path of future cash-flows shown in Figure 11.4 into a single long term growth rate assumption. But what these ratios lose in accuracy they gain in familiarity. By 1998 it was commonplace to value BE on the basis of a single valuation ratio, EV/EBITDA.

EV/EBITDA was a relative newcomer to British investors in the mid-1990s. The enterprise value is the market value of the company's equity and of its debt plus the value of any other claims on the company's cashflows. EBITDA is earnings before interest, tax, depreciation and amortisation, a sort of gross operating profit measure that is sometimes identified with cashflow (incorrectly because it omits working capital and divergences between operating profit and operating cashflow).

An influential proponent of the use of EV/EBITDA in valuing BE was the US investment bank Morgan Stanley. As one of the most respected investment banks Morgan Stanley's views both reflected and encouraged the growing optimism about BE's prospects. In a report of 27 August 1996 MS's analysts stated that "We have used enterprise value to EBITDA as our valuation methodology [sic] for British Energy and have applied a multiple of 5.7 times in our valuation, which is near the average for the sector. This is our primary valuation tool" (Morgan Stanley Dean Witter, 1997 p. 1).

On page 10 of the report Table 5 shows Morgan Stanley's estimates of the prospective EV/EBITDA multiples for the electricity sector, consisting of five RECS (East Midlands, London, Northern, Southern and Yorkshire), the two other generators National Power and PowerGen, and the integrated company Scottish Power. Morgan Stanley, like other brokers, thought electricity companies should trade at broadly similar multiples, despite their very different business characteristics.

The widespread use of this misleading valuation technique offers one explanation for the dramatic rise in BE's share price in the period 1997–1999. Figure 11.6 shows the share price for this period, together with the dates of some key MS analyst reports.

Figure 11.6 shows the trebling of BE's shares from their post-privatisation level of around £2 to a peak of over £7 in early 1999. No individual broker can single-handedly push up a share price for a long period. The research published by MS both captured the market optimism and gave it intellectual justification (in the view of former BE managers – private interviews). It is impossible to tell exactly why a share price rises or falls: explanations can only be circumstantial, based on a combination of the information available and a view of how investors take decisions. Investors' own accounts are not reliable, especially after the event. Anecdotally there was a mood of optimism around BE shares during 1998 which was fed by the stream of good news about rising profits and cashflows, power station life extensions and encouraging news from the North American operations.

Figure 11.6 British Energy share price 1996–1999 (£); timing of Morgan Stanley research reports (source: Datasteam; Morgan Stanley).

Morgan Stanley and other brokers made it respectable to buy BE shares by providing an argument for why the shares were still undervalued. Until early 1999 this argument proved correct: the shares kept rising and brokers kept raising their target prices. A sceptical observer of Figure 11.6 might equally conclude that Morgan Stanley were simply lucky for a while, since the research failed to predict the reversal of the shares through 1999. This suffices to show that Morgan Stanley could not influence the market for long in the face of contradictory evidence. The long deflation of BE's shares from their peak of £7.33 to a low of £1.25 in May 2000 was driven by a growing pessimism about the future price of power and its effect on BE's finances. The market correctly anticipated the collapse in power prices in 2000–2002. But by then the damage had been done; BE had geared up its balance sheet and left itself exposed to a sharp fall in profits.

Attempting to explain the share price rise

Could the share price rise have been justified by fundamentals? If the market is rational, then the share price should have reflected a consensus of forecasts about the future that could have explained the equity value. The subsequent fall in the shares would then be explained by new information that altered those forecasts. One way to see if the peak valuation could ever have been plausibly explained using a DCF valuation is to return to the BZW forecasts published in March 1996 (BZW Research, 1996a pp. 53–57). BZW's analysts, working for the government, had every incentive to find the highest plausible valuations for

BE and were criticised by the company's management for alleged over-optimism about future electricity prices and station output. BZW's "optimistic" research provides a benchmark against which to assess the market value of the company at its peak.

Figure 11.7 shows BZW's base case (using a cost of equity of 10 per cent real) for the enterprise value of BE (i.e. excluding any debt – the balance sheet structure was not known at the time of publication) of £2.6 billion. The company's flotation enterprise value was only £1.9 billion so this is already an optimistic valuation. It then adds to it: BZW's calculations of the value of a long term improvement in station load factors of 85 per cent (the actual AGR load factor peaked at 81 per cent in 2001 and then fell); and five year life extensions for all seven AGR stations, worth £0.7 billion. It then deducts the £0.7 billion debt BE took on at privatisation to give an "optimistic" equity valuation equity of £3 billion, or £4.17 a share.

BZW didn't know about the £0.4 billion fall in the value of the nuclear liabilities owing to the BNFL contract renegotiations revealed in 1997, so this should be added. And by early 1999 BE had paid some £200 million in dividends back to shareholders, which must be deducted. These adjustments give an overall figure of £3.2 billion, or £4.44 a share. Three years later the share price of £7.33 valued the company at £5.3 billion, leaving some £2.1 billion of additional value to be explained.

Just as it is impossible to know why investors bought the shares, it is impossible to know what the market was discounting in the share price of £7.33. The easiest way to "explain" the price is to attribute a lower cost of capital to the shares than BZW was using. Using BZW's sensitivity analysis even a three percentage point fall in the cost of capital would raise the value by only around

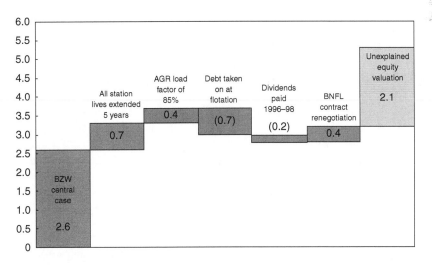

Figure 11.7 Reconciliation of BZW valuation with peak company valuation (£bn) (source: BZW (1996); author's estimates).

£0.7 billion (BZW Research, 1996a p. 57). Even a dramatic (and unexplained) cost of capital would not explain the valuation gap.

The only other source of value not included by BZW was the value of new business investments made since privatisation, mainly in North America. But BE and its US partner Peco only announced their first investment in July 1998, a total of $100m between them. BE's contribution was about £30m. It would take a very optimistic forecast to value the admittedly promising US business at many hundreds of millions of pounds.

To repeat, nothing can be proven but even an optimistic version of BZW's detailed DCF valuations leaves over a third of the peak BE market value unexplained. Private conversations with former senior BE executives confirm that they believed the stock market was overvaluing the company but they were at a loss to explain it. But since it is the duty of directors to maximise shareholder value they felt obliged to keep their doubts private, so long as the company information that investors were working on was accurate.

The possible undervaluation of liabilities

The use of multiples to value a company with declining long term cashflows is liable to mislead. But even a DCF analysis can be wrong if it underestimates the value of the long term nuclear liabilities by discounting them at too high a rate.

BZW's famous 80 year DCF model took the conventional approach of netting all cashflows into and out of the company to produce an overall estimate for each year of "free" cashflows to the firm. These cashflows were discounted to the present (which was then 1996) at the weighted average cost of capital of the company, which BZW took as the cost of equity because there was no decision at that time on the capital structure.

This approach treats all cashflows the same. It means that future cashflows arising from the nuclear liabilities are discounted at a cost of capital which BZW estimated at around 10 per cent real. But the company discounted the liabilities for its balance sheet at only 3 per cent real. The higher the discount rate, the lower in today's money are the nuclear liabilities, and the higher is the equity value of the company.

Why such a difference and who is right? There was little discussion of this point at the time of privatisation, let alone during the period of stock market euphoria about BE. One broker correctly identified the issue in a research report ahead of privatisation by pointing out that the historic liabilities (those already incurred by the company) should "be discounted at a rate more closely aligned with the cost of debt than average cost of capital" (ABN Amro Hoare Govett, 1996 p.16). But after the privatisation the question of how to value the liabilities became subordinated to the news about falling operating costs and station performance.

But the debate several years later about the correct treatment of pension fund liabilities suggests that those nuclear liabilities which are unavoidable, i.e. have been already incurred as a result of past operations, should be discounted at a lower rate than other cashflows. These liabilities are fixed commitments akin to debt, but not interest bearing. Future payments that only arise from operations that have not yet happened should be discounted at the higher, weighted average cost of capital. This means that the BZW approach and that of most other brokers using DCF valuation understated the liabilities and overvalued the company.

The scale of the liabilities was very significant. Figure 11.8 shows BE's balance sheet reorganised to show how the company's assets were financed. A typical company's capital is dominated by equity and debt – National Power is shown for comparison. But BE's main source of capital was its nuclear liabilities. In effect, the company's assets – its power stations – were substantially financed by a promise to pay for future nuclear clean up costs.

These liabilities were discounted on the balance sheet at a rate of 3 per cent real, which was the return on inflation-linked government bonds, which is the closest thing to a risk-free real rate of return. If an equivalent amount of cash had been invested in such bonds then it would in theory have grown, risk-free, to match the future cash costs that the liabilities represented. But the company didn't invest cash in such bonds; other than for the decommissioning liabilities (invested by a separate fund manager, mostly in equities) it invested no cash at all against the liabilities. Instead it invested in the real assets of the company, its power stations and new projects such as the North American operations, intending to generate a return far higher than the risk free rate, which would eventually allow the liabilities to be serviced and leave a return for shareholders as well.

The analogy with pension liabilities

Corporate pension schemes give rise to a liability similar to nuclear liabilities (except that pensions carry longevity risk). Employees annually accrue a right to

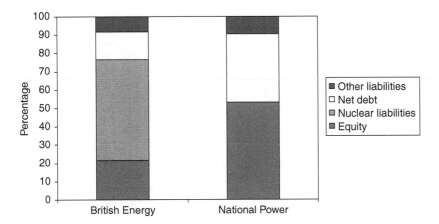

Figure 11.8 Structure of capital and liabilities, British Energy and National Power (source: British Energy Annual Report 1999/2000; National Power Annual Report 1998/1999).

a future income – a form of deferred pay. The employer incurs an obligation to pay a pension at some future point. The liability may be offset or even fully covered by a separate pool of assets called a pension fund, but that is not guaranteed.

On 30 November 2000 the British Accounting Standards Board (ASB) published a new Financial Reporting Standard for dealing with corporate pensions, FRS17, replacing the previous Statement of Standard Accounting Practice (SSAP) 24 (Accounting Standards Board). FRS17 adopted broadly the same discount rate for valuing the liabilities as used in US pension accounting (Financial Accounting Standard 87) and under International Accounting Standard 19. This is the interest rate on AA–rated investment grade corporate bonds.

FRS17, which became fully effective in 2005, was controversial because it led to many companies being forced to recognise on their balance sheet a significant gap between their pension fund assets and the present value of the pension liabilities. The economic reality was unchanged by the accounting but the new standard led to greater transparency, as was intended, and in some cases to share price falls (see for example Accountancy Age, 2001).

This led in turn to the question of how investors should value companies with net pension deficits (i.e. where the liabilities exceed the assets). There are no official rules for valuation because there is no monopoly professional body to which investors and analysts need to belong. But it quickly became a de facto standard among equity analysts to use the FRS17 valuation of pension liabilities in company valuations, treating them as net debt (Bader, 2003).

Returning to BE, the question then arises, should not nuclear liabilities also be discounted at AA corporate bond rates? Compared with the widespread practice of using the weighted average cost of capital to discount all cashflows, using a lower discount rate for the liabilities would materially cut the value of the company.

The BZW discount rate applied to all BE's future cashflows, including those corresponding to the nuclear liabilities, was 10 per cent in real terms. Using the AA corporate bond rate would have meant discounting the cashflows associated with the liabilities (but not the other cashflows) at about 5 per cent in real terms. But this is too conservative; the liabilities need to be split into those that are committed (and therefore debt-like) and those which have not yet arisen, so remain more like ordinary future uncertain cashflows. Table 11.4 shows the split for BE's liabilities.

Table 11.4 Classification of BE nuclear liabilities, 31 March 1998 (£bn)

Total projected nuclear liabilities	13.3
Discounted at 3 per cent	5.3
Accrued by company at 31 March 1998	3.8
of which: decommissioning	0.9
back end fuel costs	2.9

Source: British Energy Annual report 1997–1998 section 21.

Table 11.4 shows that the total committed (accrued) liabilities amounted to £3.8 billion when discounted at 3 per cent. But the decommissioning liabilities were expected to be covered by the segregated fund, so can be deducted (somewhat optimistically). This leaves only the accrued back end fuel costs; the company's valuation was £2.9 billion; the question is what they would amount to if treated like pension liabilities?

Table 11.5 estimates the effect of different discount rates on the present value of the committed liabilities. BE's annual report shows the undiscounted cash-flows for all projected liabilities, excluding those expected to be covered by the segregated decommissioning fund. That left £9,566 million of future cash out-flows in undiscounted terms (column1). The present value of all these liabilities was £4,981 million using the company's 3 per cent discount rate (column 3). But for valuation purposes, we are interested only in the accrued liabilities, the discounted value of which is £2.9 billion (Table 11.4). Assuming that these liabilities have the same distribution over time as the total liabilities, Table 11.5 shows the implied accrued liability payments in undiscounted terms (column 2). These are then discounted at the BZW rate of 10 per cent (column 5) and the AA bond rate of 5 per cent (column 4) to get estimates of the value.

The result is that whereas the company balance sheet has the committed liabilities at £2.9 billion, the DCF approach of using the weighted average cost of capital cuts the figure to £1.4 billion. All else being equal this raises the estimated value of the company's equity by £1.5 billion. Taking instead the pension fund approach and using the AA bond rate of 5 per cent gives a figure of £2.2 billion, some £0.8 billion higher than the BZW figure.

So if the pension fund analogy is correct, the use of a DCF approach to the liabilities potentially overvalued the company by the order of £0.8 billion, or about £1.14 a share. It is therefore quite possible that investors, even those using the "correct" DCF approach, materially undervalued the liabilities, contributing to the misleadingly high share price.

Conclusion – the stockmarket misled BE's managers

Our explanation for why BE deliberately weakened its balance sheet just before it faced a radical worsening of its trading prospects is as follows. BE was a very unusual company financially because of its long term nuclear liabilities and the variation between its accounting profit and its cashflows. It seems likely that investors and analysts misunderstood the nature of the company and so applied inappropriate valuation techniques.

The widespread use of standard valuation ratios such as EV/EBITDA was liable to overvalue a company with a core business that would eventually shut down because such ratios attributed perpetual growth rates to the company. These growth rates could only have been achieved by a substantial programme of reinvestment in new assets; valuing such a programme in advance of its successful execution was at best optimistic. Even analysts who used the theoretically superior DCF valuation may have underestimated the liabilities because

Table 11.5 Net present value of long term nuclear liabilities at different discount rates (£m)

Discount period	Total (1)	Accrued (2)	Midpoint in years	Discount rate	Accrued only		
				3 per cent (3)	3 per cent	5 per cent (4)	10 per cent (5)
Within 5 years	1,613	939	2.5	1,498	872	831	740
6–10 years	1,295	754	8	1,022	595	510	352
11–25 years	2,857	1,663	18	1,678	977	691	299
26–50 years	884	515	38	287	167	81	14
51 years and over	2,917	1,698	60	495	288	91	6
Total	9,566	–	–	4,981	2,900	2,204	1,410

Source: British Energy annual report 1997–1998 section 21; author's estimates.

they either discounted the liabilities at the same rate as operating cashflow or failed explicitly to value them at all by using a terminal value to capture long term cashflows – another form of perpetual growth valuation.

These valuation errors, combined with what might have been irrational exuberance over the company's sequence of improving profits, led to an overvalued share price. It is hard to justify the share value near its peak of £7.33 on the basis of any plausible assumptions about the company's prospects or its cost of capital.

The high and rising share price reinforced the widespread investor view that cash-rich utilities must return capital. BE's management responded to intense pressure to distribute cash by returning some £471 million to shareholders in the year 1999/2000. But in the same financial year the company took the risk of substantial investments at same time, leaving a much weaker balance sheet. The board's agreement to return the capital and to invest £775 million in fixed assets suggests a poor level of risk management, in as much as the company failed to consider what would happen if power prices fell sharply (Chapter 13). On top of this the investments were poorly conceived: the single largest investment (Eggborough coal power station) led to a £300 million write down two years later.

The gearing up might not have been so fatal if BE had been a conventional electric utility. But it was more accurately thought of as a commodity manufacturer with grave exposure to the fluctuating electricity price. It would have been more appropriate to follow a financial strategy like companies in the steel, bulk chemicals or extractive sectors. In these industries a strong balance sheet is needed to cope with the financial pressures of the periodic slumps that lead to substantial losses. If investors had understood that BE was such a company it might have been under less pressure to distribute cash, and would have had a much lower share price to reflect the riskiness of the business. But it is not at all clear that the board realised the true nature of the company either.

12 Corporate strategy

Introduction

This chapter analyses BE's key decisions on corporate strategy. The company made four investments – in the US, Canada, the Eggborough coal station and the SWALEC supply business – and one important non-investment – the failure to buy a REC. The analysis below considers the merits of each of these and whether they contributed to the company's financial failure.

The questions raised are: first, what did British Energy actually do with its spare cash; second, were those decisions sensible; and third, was the execution of the investments effective? Lastly there is the important question of what might have been; could BE have done anything very different that would have improved its prospects?

Options for BE at birth

BE's decisions were bound to be influenced by a number of points of general agreement among shareholders in the mid-1990s:

*   diversification, especially by utilities, was regarded with great suspicion because of the record of other European and US companies (see Chapter 11);
*   the UK generation market was already looking over-supplied owing to a wave of new gas stations being built by new entrants (see Chapter 13); and
*   nobody expected new nuclear power stations to be economically viable for the foreseeable future.

BE was likely to generate a lot of free cashflow; one option was simply to return it all to shareholders and make no new investments beyond what was necessary to keep the station running efficiently. This was rejected by John Robb, Chairman, when he stated that the management would seek growth rather than preside over an orderly liquidation (Chapter 7). Instead the company wanted to find investments that would generate long term earnings growth, more than compensating for the closure of the nuclear stations. This left two options: building a broader energy business in the UK, and investment abroad.

Figure 12.1 shows BE's use of its free cashflow, other than for paying down debt, from 1997 to 2002. It includes the amounts returned to shareholders in 1999/2000 which were a strategic use of capital that the company had not been able to invest (this excludes ordinary dividends). The chart makes clear that most of what BE did manage to invest went into coal generation, which turned out to be a very poor investment. The North American businesses, far more successful investments, received relatively little, partly because by the time the Canadian Bruce Power project was ready the company had little financial room and had to structure the transaction as a lease. The investment in electricity supply was reversed within a year and had little impact on the company's situation in 2002. The relatively large scale of the return of cash to shareholders reflects the company's failure to buy a REC.

Investing in UK generation assets

Investing in new nuclear generation was uneconomic under any plausible circumstances without state subsidy (see Chapter 5). But the company could argue it had competitive strengths in non-nuclear generation. Much of the equipment in a nuclear power station is common to a conventional station, because the nuclear reactor is simply a different source of heat. The turbines and alternators, switch gear and related plant are essentially the same. BE clearly knew a lot about running this plant. But it was open to question whether BE had any competitive advantage in running it, particularly as the company faced two competitors, National Power and PowerGen, who had been privatised earlier and had also improved their productivity.

Moving sideways into gas generation

In the 1990s, a combination of technical progress in gas turbine technology and the lower pollution of gas compared with coal meant that any new plant built in

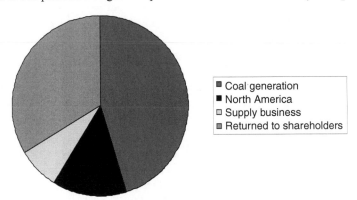

Figure 12.1 British Energy's strategic investments, financial years 1997–2002 (source: British Energy annual reports).

the UK would be a combined cycle gas turbine (CCGT). National Power and PowerGen, British Energy's main competitors, had emerged from the CEGB with practically all of their plant being coal or oil burning. Facing new entry from independent generators using CCGTs, National Power and PowerGen had started to build new CCGT plant too. If they could "diversify" from coal to gas, then surely BE could justify a sideways move from nuclear to gas too?

Unfortunately for BE, whatever the merit of investing in gas in principle, by the mid-1990s it was clear that there was quite enough gas plant under construction by other generators, including a growing independent sector backed by the electricity distributors, by oil and gas companies and by foreign electric utilities. The prospective return to British Energy on adding to what looked like a future over-supply was poor. British Energy had plans to build a CCGT power station at Heysham in Lancashire, next to its existing AGR nuclear station, which would save on site costs. But the board concluded that the profitability would be questionable and the project was abandoned in 1997.

Shareholders would probably have supported the Heysham CCGT if it had looked profitable. But they were less impressed by the company's decision to buy a passive, minority equity stake in another CCGT station under construction at Humber Bank on the Wash in 1997. The *Financial Times* Lex column summed up the conventional wisdom that British Energy risked turning into an investment trust, a holding company for purely financial investments (*Financial Times*, 1997c). BE had no competitive advantage in passive financial investing and investors believed that the cash should instead be paid back to shareholders, who could make their own, better informed decisions about how to invest.

The case for buying a coal station

Investing in new coal generation was quite uneconomic too. But BE could make a case for buying existing coal plant, if it were available. BE was a base load generator, meaning its nuclear stations operated more or less continuously, subject only to refuelling, maintenance and statutory safety outages. Aside from maintenance shutdowns in the summer (when prices were lowest and the revenue loss minimised) the stations ran, as nuclear stations generally do, whatever the weather and whatever the fluctuating level of demand.

Base load power is therefore the most commodity-like type of power. By contrast, the ability to supply power when demand is greatest – the evening and morning spikes on a cold winter day for example – has greater economic value. This higher value demand was met mostly by coal stations (except for the extreme peaks which are supplied by open cycle gas turbines and pumped storage hydroelectricity). If BE could have bought a coal station it could have taken a share of the higher demand, higher value power market.

The economics of such a move were not compelling though. The value of a coal station would reflect its ability to meet the high price demand, so any purchaser of the station would pay the full price, leaving no value creation for the shareholder. British Energy argued that it would add value because it would be able to sell "shaped" contracts to customers that combined its commodity, low price base load power, with the flexible, higher value peak power. For this to be true, the contract market would have to be inefficient, meaning that customers could not simply buy a base load contract from British Energy and a peak contract from somebody else (National Power and PowerGen at first, and later Eastern Energy) and combine them, for the same total price as buying a combined contract from one source. Although the power market was still relatively new and customers and suppliers alike were learning, it is not clear that the market was so inefficient that it would justify British Energy buying a coal station. There was little strategic justification then for British Energy's attempt to buy coal stations from PowerGen in 1998, which were in any event blocked by the regulator.

The company made a slightly different justification for buying the 2,000 MW Eggborough coal station from National Power in late 1999. By then the details of the new electricity trading arrangements (NETA) were clear. One of the features of NETA was the "balancing market", which would ensure that physical demand and supply were matched by forcing generators to meet precisely their supply obligations. Any shortfall in supply would require the potentially very costly purchase of balancing output. This was a risk to all generators but a particular problem for inflexible nuclear plant. If BE contracted to sell the output of a whole nuclear station and then the station had to be closed suddenly, it would face possibly large balancing market costs to cover its supply obligations.

Eggborough was a former CEGB heavyweight coal station, built to run on base load but by 1999 displaced to mid-merit, meaning its marginal costs were higher than the gas and nuclear plants that now met base load supply. Eggborough would run at a load factor of about 40–50 per cent. BE could use Eggborough's spare, flexible capacity to make up for any sudden shortfall in nuclear output. Having this extra reliability meant the company could sell its nuclear power at fixed contract prices, which were slightly higher than the spot, uncontracted wholesale rate.

This was a reasonable argument (and one which pointed to a weakness in the new market system). It meant that Eggborough was possibly worth slightly more to British Energy than any other, non-nuclear generator. But it is hard to quantify that extra value, which would need to be compared with an alternative strategy of buying contract cover directly from one of the other generators which owned flexible coal plant.

Assessment of the Eggborough purchase

The theoretical benefits for buying Eggborough were in practice overwhelmed by the price paid. BE bought the station close to the top of an over-excited generation market and paid £665 million. Two years later, when over-capacity in British generation had become obvious and the price of power had collapsed, the station value was written down by £300 million.

It was scant comfort for shareholders that two other coal station purchases went badly wrong. A subsidiary of the Californian utility company Edison International bought two coal stations with total capacity of 4,000 MW from PowerGen in 1999 for a total of £1.3 billion. It sold them to American Electric Power (AEP) in December 2001 for £650 million. AEP then sold them on to the British utility Scottish and Southern Electricity in July 2004 for £250 million, a total drop in value of £1 billion from the original sale by PowerGen.

Another major US electricity company, AES, bought the giant 4,000 MW Drax coal station from National Power in August 1999 for £1.87 billion, which was newer than the PowerGen stations and was fitted with flue gas desulphurization equipment. The AES subsidiary that owned Drax then signed a contract to sell about 60 per cent of the station's output to TXU Europe, the British utility subsidiary of another US company, TXU (formerly Texas Utilities). TXU Europe went into receivership in 2002 and Drax took a write-down of around £500 million. Drax's parent company AES then abandoned the subsidiary to its creditors in 2003 (AES Corp., 2003 p. 91). On the brink of bankruptcy, Drax was saved and eventually listed on the stock exchange in 2005. On the back of dramatically higher power prices it has made millionaires of its directors, proving that timing is everything (*Financial Times*, 2006b). Note that National Power and PowerGen sold 8,000 MW of coal plant for over £3 billion in 1999–2000 at the top of the market.

If BE had not bought Eggborough in 1999, it would have had to pay additional costs for contract cover from other generators, reducing its profit margin from 2000 when NETA began. But it would have had a far stronger balance sheet, having saved £665 million, enough to give it a realistic chance of surviving the period of low power prices. The only mitigating argument here is that BE put the power station into a separate subsidiary and raised a non-recourse project loan against it. This meant that in principle BE could have copied AES and walked away from the station and its debt, albeit at some reputational cost. Conceivably that might have been part of a strategy of surviving the power price collapse. But overall the purchase of Eggborough was almost as damaging a mistake for the viability of the company as the return of value to shareholders in the same year.

Investing in nuclear assets in North America

The company could claim one area of expertise which was potentially of competitive value, at least outside the UK. It had an impressive record of improving the performance of poorly performing nuclear power stations. It had inherited a very poor set of assets in the AGRs but had driven them to world class performance (for a time). It had done this in the setting of a deregulated (although initially far from competitive) power market. In principle, a management team that could do it in the UK could do it elsewhere.

There was a good reason, then, for British Energy to look abroad for underperforming, cheap nuclear power stations. The investments in the AmerGen joint venture with PECO Energy in the US, and in Bruce Power in Canada, combined three attractive features:

- each represented a market opportunity that BE was competitively well placed to respond to;
- each involved an investment in broadly similar assets to those of BE's core business (the Canadian reactors were somewhat different but the gap was less than moving into coal or gas generation); and
- each had acceptable country risk (at a time when National Power was experiencing difficulties with its investment in Pakistan).

The market opportunity in the US was that in the mid-1990s nuclear power was highly unfashionable and transitional deregulation arrangements made it attractive for many US utilities to sell their interests. This created a buyer's market that unfortunately only lasted a few years as other US utilities spotted the same opportunity, bidding up prices (see Chapter 9).

In Canada, BE took advantage of the privatisation process by building the confidence of provincial politicians that selling Ontario Power's underperforming nuclear stations would yield financial and political benefits without jeopardising safety. This was a great success for BE's negotiations and management of the complex process of deregulation and privatisation, using its UK experience.

Assessment of the North American investments

Both the AmerGen US investment and the Bruce Power Canadian investments were successful for BE shareholders. By 2001/02 British Energy's group pretax profit depended entirely on its North American businesses. Table 12.1 shows that BE's share of the AmerGen joint venture profit was £37 million and the first year's income from Canada was £42 million, for a total of £79 million. The UK business generated £189 million of operating profit the same year but against that must be set most of the interest and all of the revalorization charge of £226 million. In other words, the UK generating business was loss making by 2002 and the company only made a profit because of its North American investments.

The tragedy for the company was one of timing. BE's chief executive Peter Hollins forecast in May 2001 that North America could deliver £150 million of

Table 12.1 Components of pretax profit, £m

Year ending 31 March	2001	2002
UK	226	189
Canada	0	42
AmerGen JV share	13	37
Less: interest and revalorisation	(229)	(226)
Pretax profit	10	42

Source: British Energy Annual Report 2001/2002 (2001 figures as restated).

operating profit by 2003/2004 (British Energy, 2001c). In May 2002 the company forecast from Canada "profit contribution to rise to £25 million for each of the six reactors", i.e. £150 million from Canada alone in 2003/2004 (British Energy, 2002a p. 6). The contribution from the US reached £43 million in 2002/03; assuming this had remained flat it would have yielded a total prospective operating profit of £193 million. Set against this would be the interest payable on some £154 million of US and Canadian dollar debt, about £9 million, leaving a pretax profit of £184 million.

That level of contribution from North America might just have carried the company through a period of losses in UK generation. But the crisis came in September 2002, a year too early for the full benefit of the Canadian investments to show. Both investments were sold as part of the financial restructuring of the company. As is typically the case in a forced sale, the proceeds fell far short of what they might have fetched in a normal sale. Bruce was sold for £275 million after costs in February 2003, compared with the £410 million the company had invested (much of it in deferred payment). The asset had been valued at between £390 million and £487 million by investment bank Credit Suisse First Boston (National Audit Office, 2006 p. 24). BE's 50 per cent AmerGen stake was sold for £148 million in December 2003.

Vertical integration in the UK

Economists distinguish between horizontal integration (building market share in the same activity) and vertical integration (acquiring an economic interest in activities upstream and/or downstream of the existing business. Horizontal integration is typically motivated by the search for economies of scale and, to the extent that the law permits, market power. In commodity industries both of these arguments typically have some force.

Vertical integration is more complex. Traditionally electric utilities in many countries were vertically integrated, regional monopolies. Being monopolies, the companies lacked any incentive to investigate other structures. The England and Wales electricity industry was broken up (the smaller Scottish system remained vertically integrated) because politicians believed it was the only way to introduce competition into generation. The new structure was something of an experiment because there were very few precedents on which to draw. Several countries had a small wholesale trading market but only as an adjunct to a largely vertically integrated, regional system (e.g. Germany, Spain and the US).

Vertical integration had three possible meanings in the UK electricity context:

- combining generation with supply;
- combining generation with distribution; and
- combining generation with ownership of fuel supplies.

The first type of integration came closest to following the oil industry analogy of combining "upstream" (generation) with "downstream" (supply). Supply means the process of marketing to, contracting with and collecting payment from the end customers. It is essentially a *commercial* activity. Conceptually there is no reason why the supplier need actually own the generation. The main new entrant to the deregulated UK electricity market was Centrica (part of the former British Gas). Centrica didn't then own any power stations but was able to buy power from the market and then sell it to its existing gas customers.

The second form of vertical integration was to merge generation (and probably supply too), with distribution, which is the *physical* delivery of power to the customer. Distribution is a capital intensive and regulated natural monopoly business. Supply is a low capital intensity, competitive and normally unregulated business. Investors and customers often confused them in the early 1990s simply because the distinction had been obscured in the previous public sector monopoly structure.

The third variant of vertical integration is when a generator owns its fuel supplies. Both National Power and PowerGen dabbled in the gas exploration and development market in the early days of their privatisation (partly because they employed former oil and gas executives who doubtless thought they knew what they were doing). They also looked at buying coal pits but never bought them (private interviews). The equivalent for British Energy would be to invest in a uranium mine and possibly an enrichment facility. None of these fuel-based integration efforts lasted long because all of the markets were reasonably competitive and there was nothing to be gained from putting shareholders' money into them.

Business logic of vertical integration

Distribution had no operational fit with generation. Those companies which combined the two activities, such as PowerGen, argued that there were indirect benefits such as providing relevant skills for overseas investments, which often came in a vertically integrated form.

The more interesting combination was generation and supply, because one was the customer of the other. But if supply industry was competitive, the benefit of acquiring a supply business would be minimal. A generator would pay the market value of the business, which would continue to buy its power at competitive rates and sell at competitive rates. There would be no economic benefit from combining it with generation. If the generator tried to sell its power at a premium to its supply business it would either charge end customers too much and lose business, or reduce the profits of the supply business, which would face a cost penalty relative to its customers.

The key question was therefore whether supply was really competitive or not. Electricity supply in the UK had been deregulated in stages, beginning with the very largest customers (over 1 MW demand) at privatisation in 1990, then adding medium-sized customers in 1994 and all customers in 1999. By spring 1999, any retail customer was free to shop around for their electricity, instead of relying on their local regional electricity company. As increasing numbers of customers took that choice and actually switched supplier, the regulator withdrew the previous 1 per cent return on sales cap on supply profits.

But there were two reasons why this supply might not be a competitive industry. The first is that customers may not be price sensitive enough to bother to move supplier, even when there are price differences. This is what happens in many retail financial services, where many customers can't be bothered to shop around for the best deal. The second is that there were significant economies of scale and reputation risk which created barriers to entry in the newly deregulated supply business.

The economies of scale came first from the need to set up a client relationship management system that would keep track of millions of customers. Building such a system would cost several million pounds, whether there was one customer or five million.

Second, there were economies in marketing and advertising. Customers proved reluctant to buy an important resource like electricity from companies they had never heard of. Large companies like National Power, PowerGen and ScottishPower were able to pay for sponsorship of activities such as national cricket and TV weather and for mass advertising, to build their brand names. The advertising and sponsorship were intended to create a sense of familiarity and trust around the brand names and so to erect barriers to entry to those with less recognised and trusted names (such as the US company Amerada Hess).

The reputation risk came from the fact that most customers had little understanding of the difference between supply – the commercial process of selling power and billing them for it – and distribution – the physical supply of watts to their house. Physical disruption arising from say accidental digging up of power lines by contractors working for a cable TV company was therefore likely to be blamed on the supply company, which had nothing to do with it. This reputational risk seems to have been the main reasons that there was so little new entry into the supply business, against expectations that supermarkets and oil companies would use their brand names to compete.

The upshot was that there was only significant new entrant to the supply business – Centrica, trading on its extremely well known brand name British Gas. Gas was also a pure commodity, and had been deregulated a couple of years before electricity. Faced with the prospect of losing its core gas market, Centrica naturally looked to recoup some of its revenue losses by invading the electricity market. The main competitors in turn for Centrica were the electricity companies which were now free to sell gas as well as power.

It became accepted wisdom in the mid-1990s (not least among investment bankers seeking merger advisory fees) that the market would only support five or six large profitable supply companies (a fairly accurate description of the industry by late 2001). The forces of economies of scale, limited new entry and price-insensitive customers all pointed towards supply becoming an oligopolistic industry, similar to retail banking. But if supply was going to become an oligopoly, then there might be economic logic in a generation business buying into supply.

The benign form of the argument, for public consumption, ran as follows. Generation (wholesale or upstream) prices were bound to fluctuate as the fuel commodity prices vary (chiefly gas, which in turn is heavily linked still to the price of oil). Supply (retail or downstream) prices by contrast would be more stable, because retail customers value price stability and will pay a risk premium to avoid excessive price fluctuations. So variations in generation profit would be partly offset by the stability of the supply profit, and shareholders would enjoy more stable earnings.

This argument didn't threaten customers. There was much talk about profit migrating up and down the "value chain", in a random but harmless way. But this argument provided no investment case because shareholders could in principle choose whatever overall profit volatility they wanted by combining investments in any number of generators and suppliers with uncorrelated earnings. For generators to pay a premium to achieve reduced profit volatility would make shareholders worse off.

But there was a more sinister case for buying a supply business. As Chapter 13 argues, the profitability of UK power generation was bound to fall eventually as power prices fell to reflect new entrants and greater competition. If supply was an oligopoly, it might be possible to absorb some of the falling generation profits by keeping retail prices steady or at worst by not passing through the full benefit of lower wholesale prices. This would indeed see profit "migrate" up the value chain, in a permanent increase in the profitability of supply, now that the regulator had taken away price protection.

It was hard for companies to make this argument explicitly without antagonising politicians and the regulator. The theory of gouging customers to offset falling generation profits would only be tested when power prices fell, as they did from 2000. Retail prices did indeed fall less than wholesale price and the average household supply profit margin (return on sales) rose from the 1 per cent regulated level in 1998/1999 to 5–8 per cent (OFGEM, 2004 para. 5.18), though some of the higher margin reflected the higher operating costs and risk in a competitive market.

British Energy, proportionately more exposed to falling wholesale electricity prices than any other company, had good reason to buy into supply to hedge its wholesale power profits. This was the strategy the company adopted, but only after a fateful delay. Unfortunately for British Energy, the dance between generation companies and supply companies began soon after privatisation of the main industry in 1990. First National Power and PowerGen, then other British utilities, and finally US and continental European buyers wanted to buy British RECs. By the time BE was privatised and had established itself in the private sector, several deals had been done.

As recounted in Chapter 8, BE's board rejected their best chance to vertically integrate when they voted against the merger with Southern Electric in 1997. Their later attempts to buy a REC failed, mainly on price. Then they bought the smallest electricity supply business, SWALEC in 1999, and sold it a year later. SWALEC was too small to be much use of its own – it sold only 8 TWh of power compared with BE's annual output of about 68 TWh. And it was a poor base for building a new national business; its brand name had no value outside South Wales and its systems weren't particularly good. On top of this it bought an out-of-the-money power purchase contract with Teesside Power that *increased* BE's exposure to future electricity prices.

Assessment of the vertical integration strategy

Had BE's board not rejected the merger with Southern Electric in 1997, might it have acquired a hedge against falling generation profits that would have saved it from crisis in 2002? For the vertical integration hedge argument to work requires that: i) the profitability of the supply business remained stable or grew, as the generation business moved into loss; ii) the supply business volume was large enough to match the volume of the generation business; and iii) the profitability per unit of supply to be similar to that of generation.

Only the first of these conditions held. The OFGEM data cited above showed that the average profitability of electricity supply did rise after deregulation in 1999, from 1 per cent return on sales to 5–8 per cent in 2003, during which time the returns on generation collapsed.

On the second condition, Figure 12.2 shows the relative scale of BE's output in 2001/2002 compared with Southern's total electricity distributed in 1996/1997. Clearly Southern alone would not have been nearly enough to provide a vertically integrated hedge. Since Southern was already BE's biggest customer, these figures overstate the benefit of a merger. The chart shows the insignificance of the SWALEC acquisition.

As the largest single UK generator, BE was too large to be able to hedge its output effectively. Even in 2006 the much expanded Scottish and Southern Energy company that is a descendant of the original Southern (and which ironically also owns SWALEC supply), supplied around 50 TWh of electricity across Great Britain, about 75 per cent of BE's total output (Scottish and Southern Energy, 2006 p. 7).

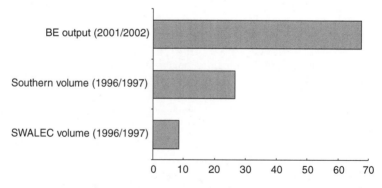

Figure 12.2 Comparison of British Energy's nuclear output with supply volumes for Southern Electric and SWALEC (TWh) (source: British Energy Annual Report 2001/2002; OFFER, 1998).

As for the third condition, supply profitability is far lower per unit of power than generation (when prices are high). Figure 12.3 shows Southern's supply operating profit in 1996/1997, the year when BE nearly merged with it. It then makes the somewhat optimistic assumption that Southern's supply profit margin would have risen from 1 per cent to 5 per cent by 2002/2003, the year of British Energy's financial crisis. For an unchanged volume this would have increased supply profits to £110 million (some of which would have represented compensation for the riskier nature of the business). But BE experienced a fall in generation and supply profit over the same period of £466 million. So even if British Energy had owned a supply business of the scale of Southern Electric's the combined group would still have suffered a fall in profits of the order of £378 million (£466 million less the increase from £22 million to £110 million).

Of course a Southern/British Energy merged company would have had a steady or rising source of profits from distribution, the regulated monopoly business that is unaffected by electricity prices. If this had been kept relatively debt free then it would have provided a base for borrowing to cover the rest of the company through the power price collapse. But most other distribution companies were geared up and it is likely that Southern/BE would have faced the same stockmarket pressure to do so. Moreover the regulator had a statutory duty to make sure that regulated business was kept financially sound and not used as a piggy-bank for unregulated businesses owned by the same company. This would have limited the scope for extracting cash from distribution to support generation.

Conclusion

BE's corporate strategy was conceptually well based but suffered from mixed execution. The US and Canadian investments were successful and, if the flow of

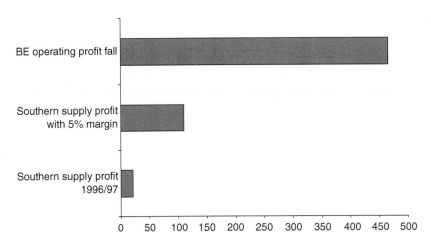

Figure 12.3 British Energy loss of UK operating profit 1999–2003 compared with hypothetical Southern Electric supply operating profit (£m) (source: British Energy Annual Report 1999/2003; OFGEM, 1998; author's estimates).

profits from Canada had come even a year earlier, might have tipped the balance towards survival. By contrast the grossly high price paid for Eggborough power station compounded the company's financial weakness after the return of value in the spring of 1999.

Vertical integration would not necessarily have saved BE. The acquisition of SWALEC didn't give a plausible base for building a national supply business and was far too small to provide a useful hedge against generation profits. But even the much larger Southern Electric supply business was too small on its own to offset much of the damage from falling power prices. Merging with Southern would have meant owning a distribution business as well but the likelihood is that any financial headroom there would have been used for a special dividend to shareholders.

13   The power price collapse

Introduction

If any one thing explains why British Energy got into financial difficulty it was the fall of electricity prices by around a third from an average of £26/MWh in 1999 to £16/MWh in 2003. For a commodity producer of electricity with a high fixed cost base, this was bound to be a huge shock to profits. This chapter analyses what caused the price fall; whether BE should have expected it; and what it might have done to prepare for it. There was nothing BE could do to stop the price falling because during the 1990s it had no influence over price setting and from 2000 onwards the generation market was both competitive and over-supplied. But it might have been better prepared for the risk of a price fall.

Explaining the power price collapse

The fall in power prices that began in late 2000 and continued to the autumn of 2002 caused financial distress to several companies, including BE. This section analyses two, not mutually exclusive, explanations for what caused the price fall. Both of the explanations imply that there were good reasons to expect significantly lower prices as early as 1999, even if the scale of the collapse wasn't then clear.

The first explanation is that the generation industry, having been highly con-centrated in the early 1990s, became much less concentrated at the end of the 1990s. Conventional economic theory predicts that highly concentrated indus-tries are more likely to set prices above the level of a competitive (i.e. unconcen-trated) industry. Specifically, the ability of National Power and PowerGen to set power prices above costs and make extra profits was reduced and then removed by their selling of large quantities of coal power capacity to other companies and by the entry of large amounts of new gas power plant into the market.

The second explanation is that the regulatory-inspired change in the electric-ity trading system, known as NETA, caused prices to move much closer to costs. The regulator, OFGEM, and the Department of Trade and Industry, argued that whatever was happening to industry concentration, the original pool mechanism for price setting was flawed and needed to be replaced.

Since both events – the increase in generator competition and the introduction of NETA – overlapped, it is hard to ascribe the cause of the power price collapse. It is possible that both contributed and that the creation of NETA, accompanied by aggressive expectations of lower prices on the part of the regulator, was a trigger for the sale of the power stations that helped bring about a more competitive market.

The path of wholesale power prices

Figure 13.1 shows the market price of electricity from the beginning of the pool in April 1990 until the end of 2003, by which time the pool had been replaced by the new electricity trading arrangements (NETA). The seasonal volatility of prices can obscure the trend, which is revealed by the 12 month moving average.

The market only started to reflect the price of power bought on contract from April 1994, by which time supply competition was opened up to the medium sized industrial and commercial customers. From 1994 to 1999 the average price oscillated gently around a price of about £24/MWh in nominal terms, implying a modest fall in real terms. The price then began to fall steadily through 2001 and 2002, reaching a trough around the autumn of 2002, just when British Energy ran out of money. At its low point the 12 month moving average was £15.65/MWh, about one-third below its level during 1994–1999.

British Energy's average selling price fell by a similar amount, from £26.6/MWh in 1998/1999 to £18.3/MWh in 2002/2003. The latter figure was flattered to some degree by the ownership of the Eggborough coal station, which was selling only at periods of higher prices. The underlying price at which the

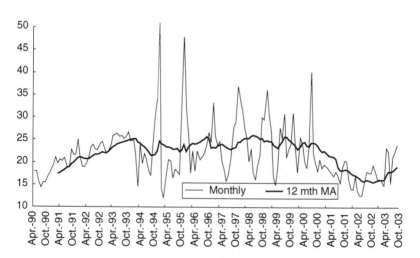

Figure 13.1 Spot wholesale electricity price 1990–2003 (£/MWh) (source: Pool; Datastream (Pool purchase price 1990–February2001; UKPX spot price March 2001–December 2003)).

nuclear output was sold therefore probably fell broadly in line with the overall power market.

The intra-year volatility of power prices was generally cancelled out by selling annual fixed price contracts. But the fall in prices from late 2000 onwards was a financial disaster, pushing the UK generation business into loss.

Explanation 1: falling concentration in the generation market

Economists believe that the level of concentration in an industry tends to have some impact on its pricing behaviour. In a very unconcentrated and competitive industry prices tend to be close to costs (including an acceptable profit margin) because if any firm sets prices higher than this it loses business to competitors. At the other extreme, a monopoly supplier can price above costs, at a level which maximises profits at the expense of consumers. Intermediate cases are in fact the most common but the starting presumption is that a more highly concentrated industry will tend to have higher prices than a less concentrated one.

The most important result of the failed attempt by the Thatcher government to privatise nuclear power was the creation of what became known as "the duopoly", the dominant ownership of price-setting coal power stations by just two companies, National Power and PowerGen. National Power had been given 60 per cent of coal capacity to make it large enough to cope with the financial cost of nuclear power. Once nuclear was withdrawn it was too late to restructure the two companies into something more competitive. So the electricity generation sector was privatised in 1990 in a highly concentrated form (Chapter 4).

Since the new electricity regulator, Stephen Littlechild, had as one of his responsibilities the creation of a competitive electricity market, there was likely to be a head-on collision. In fact the collision never quite happened. Although economists traditionally have identified industry structure as a strong influence on its performance and conduct, it was not enough to point to the concentration of ownership alone. There had to be evidence of behaviour that was damaging consumers' interests.

Littlechild's approach to the duopoly was twofold: i) encourage and eventually force the generators to sell plant; and ii) ensure there were low barriers to new entry. The market power of the generators – if it existed – would then be diluted by a combination of new gas plant and more diverse ownership of the existing coal plant.

The divesting of coal plant happened in two phases. The first was when the regulator required National Power and PowerGen to sell a total of 6,000 MW of plant. All of the plant was bought by Eastern Electricity, one of the largest RECs which had ambitions to become a broader integrated energy company. The duopoly in 1995 became a "triopoly", with little evidence of greater competition in price setting. The HHI (Herfindahl–Hirschman Index) measure of concentration of coal plant fell from over 5,000 to 3,600. Note that the US Department of Justice regards a HHI of between 1,000 and 1,800 as "moderately concentrated" and above 1,800 as "highly concentrated" (Department of Justice, 1997 para. 1.51).

It was in 1999–2000 that the ownership of coal plant became significantly less concentrated. National Power wanted to buy the supply business of Midlands Electricity and PowerGen wanted to buy the whole of East Midlands Electricity. Regulator OFGEM was willing to allow both transactions but only if the two companies sold some more of their coal stations. National Power put its 4,000 MW Drax station up for sale and when it found how strong demand was, put its 2,000 MW Eggborough station on the block too (which fatefully was bought by British Energy at the end of 1999). PowerGen sold Fiddlers Ferry and Ferrybridge, both 2,000 MW stations. In October 2000 it also sold the 2,000 MW Cottam coal station to London Electricity (owned by Eléctricité de France). In one year the former duopoly generators had sold a total of 12,000 MW out of a total stock of coal plant of about 27,000 MW (Figure 13.2). The HHI index fell to below 1,500 in 2000 and below 1,200 in 2001 (Figure 13.3).

New entry to generation by gas power stations was so dramatic that it became known as the "dash for gas". The ending of a European ban on gas use in power generation, combined with improvements in gas turbine technology and the keenness of the RECs to invest in their own generation, independent of the generators, led to a surge of gas-fired power station investment in the early 1990s (Figure 13.4).

The new gas plant largely displaced coal plant. But most of the early gas plants made little difference to the pricing power of National Power and PowerGen because they ran on base load, i.e. continuously for most of the year, like the nuclear plants. This was because they had typically signed contracts for power with the RECs (Helm, 2003 pp. 168–169). Only when their guaranteed market for power expired with the beginning of retail supply competition in 1999 did the gas stations need to fight for market share by bidding against the coal generators.

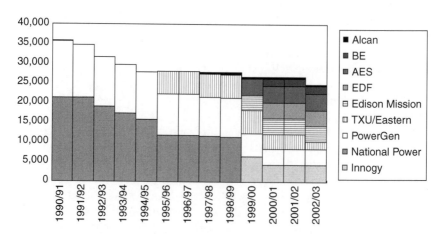

Figure 13.2 Ownership of coal power stations 1990–2003, MW (source: National Grid Company Seven Year Statements; author's estimates).

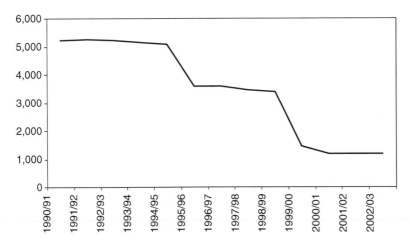

Figure 13.3 HHI measure of industry concentration for coal plant in England and Wales, 1991–2003 (source: author's estimates).

Note
HHI: Herfindahl Hirschman Index.

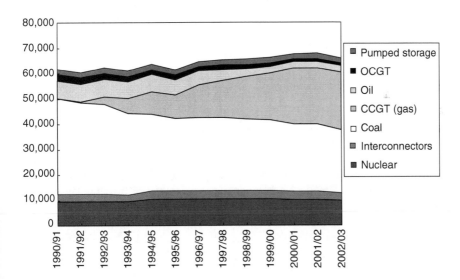

Figure 13.4 Generation capacity by type, 1991–2003 (MW) (source: National Grid Company Seven Year Statements; author's estimates).

The only benchmark for judging whether a commodity price is relatively high or low is the cost of production. Once the UK generation market was opened up to competitive entry it was to be expected that eventually the market price would be set at least partly by the cost of new entry. New entry meant a combined cycle gas-fired turbine (CCGT) station. In 1996 BZW analysts estimated the average price needed for a new CCGT to make an acceptable profit ranged from £20/MWh to £26/MWh depending on the price of gas and the thermal efficiency of the gas turbine (BZW Research, 1996b p. 14).

The same year the MMC reported a range of estimates from £21/MWh to £28/MWh, but omitted estimates based on the more advanced turbines (MMC, 1996 paras. 5.42–5.59). During the second half of the 1990s new designs of turbine were produced by General Electric, Siemens and ABB, pushing up the thermal efficiency from the existing 52 per cent–55 per cent range to the 56 per cent–60 per cent (though with some severe teething troubles along the way). Improved efficiency lowered the break even power price (for a given price of gas) meaning a lower power price consistent with new entry.

The prices quoted above include an acceptable return on capital employed. But once a station is built then it will be run as long as it covers its avoidable cash costs, which for a CCGT are not much more than the cost of fuel (assuming it doesn't have a take or pay contract in which case the gas cost is no longer avoidable). If too many CCGTs were built then the market price could fall well below the prices quoted above, to the level of short run marginal cost, which would be well under £20/MWh.

So the competition from gas-based independent power producers on the one hand and the disposal of coal power stations on the other led to a sharp fall in the pricing power of the original duopoly generators National Power and Power-Gen from 2000/2001. On this structural account of the industry, it was hardly surprising that power prices then fell to lower, more competitive levels.

Explanation 2: NETA

The second reason for the fall in power prices was the new electricity trading arrangements – NETA. NETA resulted from OFGEM's view that power prices were being kept up by flaws in the trading process itself, the pool. The pool had been introduced at privatisation and was based heavily on the previous CEGB system for scheduling the least cost generation plant. The pool built a price mechanism on top of the CEGB software and was criticised from the beginning, especially by large customers.

Table 13.1 summarises the history of NETA. Both the DTI and OFGEM saw reform of the pool mechanism as essential to getting the benefit of greater competition in generation in lower wholesale prices. It was therefore both a continuation of the efforts since privatisation to break the power of the duopoly generators, and a new scheme to make electricity trading more efficient. The DTI argued that NETA alone would cut prices by 10 per cent, whatever was also happening to competition in the generation market (Helm, 2003 p. 307).

The argument that NETA would of itself cut power prices was questioned by some leading academic economists (Green, 1999; Helm, 2003 ch. 17; Newbery, 1998). But the Competition Commission supported NETA in principle: "There are several features of NETA which suggest that both the opportunities for and the effects of the exercise of market power by generators are likely to be sub-

Table 13.1 Timetable for New Electricity Trading Arrangements

Date	Event
23 October 1997	Minister for Science, Energy and Industry asks electricity regulator to consider changes to the pool
29 July 1998	OFFER proposals for review of energy trading arrangements ('RETA')[1]
9 October 1998	Government White Paper on energy policy endorses RETA[2]
July 1999	OFGEM publishes detailed report on recommended changes ('NETA')[3]
October 2000	OFGEM postpones date for implementation from autumn 2000 to spring 2001
27 March 2001	NETA goes 'live'

Source: Competition Commission 2001 chapter 7.

Notes
1 *Review of Electricity Trading Arrangements: Proposals*, OFFER, 1998.
2 *Conclusions of the Review of Energy Sources for Power Generation*, DTI, Cm 4071, October 1998.
3 *The New Electricity Trading Arrangements*, Volumes 1 and 2, OFGEM, July 1999.

stantially less than they have been under the Pool" (Competition Commission, 2001 para. 1.6).

NETA consisted of replacing the pool, in which generators all received the market clearing system marginal price, with a new market in which generators negotiated a price at which they sold their power. OFGEM described NETA: "The new, more market-based, trading arrangements are based on bilateral trading between generators, suppliers, traders and customers. They operate as far as possible like other commodity markets whilst, at the same time, making provision for the electricity system to be kept in physical balance at all times to maintain security and quality of supplies" (OFGEM, 2002 para. 2.21). Generators could sell their power directly to a customer, or via a broker or anonymously through an exchange.

All physical flows of power had still to be mediated by the National Grid Company acting as system operator (since power cannot be stored, physical demand and supply must balance exactly). A balancing mechanism ensured that generators and suppliers were penalised for any mismatch between their planned and actual sales to and purchases from the system. Buyers and sellers of power were free to contract with each other on whatever terms they chose, and it was hoped that a range of futures and forwards markets would develop as they have in other commodity markets.

In its review of the first year of NETA, published in July 2002, OFGEM was happy to conclude that NETA had been successful, not least because wholesale spot power prices had fallen 40 per cent in real terms from 1997/1998, when NETA was first mooted, to 2001/2002 (OFGEM, 2002 para. 4.11). It also noted that although most of the spot price fall had taken place in 2000–2002, forward prices for power began falling about the time NETA was first proposed and continued falling into the first year of NETA operation (OFGEM, 2002 para. 4.12). Although prices had risen again from March 2002 to July 2002 this was probably explained by the withdrawal from supply of 2,700 MW of power station capacity, combined with a sharp rise in the market price of gas (OFGEM, 2002 para. 4.21).

A synthesis of the two causes

It is impossible to be certain what caused power prices to fall. OFGEM concluded that NETA had been the cause of the fall in power prices, allowing the more competitive generation market to be reflected in trading, in a way that the flawed pool might not have achieved.

But some leading academic researchers into electricity markets are not convinced. Professor David Newbery of Cambridge University concludes that "NETA probably delivers similar outcomes as the Pool from existing generation" (Newbery, 2005 p. 26). In other words the fall in prices was a result of increased competition in generation and would probably have happened without the trading changes. Joanne Evans (University of Surrey) and Richard Green (University of Birmingham) found that electricity prices could be explained by fuel prices and the degree of concentration in generation, both before and after the introduction of NETA. They conclude that their "results should be taken as evidence that NETA did not have a direct impact upon market prices for electrical energy" (Evans and Green, 2005 p. 19). Dieter Helm of Oxford argues that the deregulation of supply and the onset of vertical integration led to the end of the contractual framework which had kept the market stable before 1999, noting that Germany experienced a collapse in prices after liberalising supply, which had neither a pool nor NETA. He concludes that the market mechanism cannot wholly explain the price fall (Helm, 2003 p. 236).

The two explanations for lower power prices – generation competition and NETA – are not mutually exclusive. Even if NETA didn't directly lower prices by improving the trading mechanism, the prospect of a combined government and regulatory assault on power prices almost certainly influenced the decisions of National Power and PowerGen to sell coal power stations in 1999 and 2000. The companies had arguably played a very effective game in controlling prices after privatisation. They both knew that at some point the game would end and it would be better to be a seller of power stations at that point rather than a buyer (private interviews). Even if they doubted whether NETA would really affect prices, it was a clear signal that the period of high pricing was over. NETA may therefore have succeeded by a different route from that intended.

BE's approach to power prices

BE had a greater sensitivity to power prices than any other generator because it was a nuclear generator and therefore had high fixed costs relative to a fossil generator. On top of this it had high financial costs by 1999/2000 because of the purchase of Eggborough power station and the return of value to shareholders. As power prices began to fall the company had net debt to equity of 71 per cent and its interest cover was falling towards four times (see Chapter 11).

Figure 13.5 shows how falling electricity prices led to the collapse of BE's UK generation profits. The average selling price fell by 31 per cent from 1999 to 2003 but profits fell by 90 per cent, an operating leverage of three times.

Table 13.2 shows the burden of interest payments and revalorisation on overall pretax profits. These two items were, in effect, fixed financial charges that the company had to cover before making an overall profit. The figures in the table exclude as far as possible the impact of the US and Canadian operations. They show that BE's UK business was barely profitable in the year to March 2001, when power prices had only just started falling. As falling prices reduced UK operating profit almost to zero in 2003, the company was unable to meet its

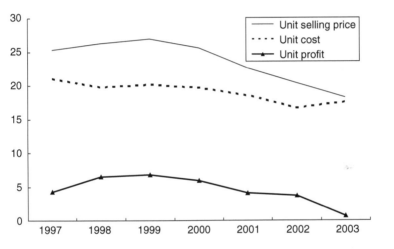

Figure 13.5 British Energy average selling price, cost and profit in UK generation, financial years 1997–2003 (£/MWh) (source: British Energy annual report).

Note
Includes Eggborough coal station for 2001–2003.

Table 13.2 Components of UK generation pretax profit 1997–2003 (£m)

	1997	1998	1999	2000	2001	2002	2003
Operating profit	307	437	473	428	226	189	7
Interest payment	(50)	(22)	(1)	(7)	(56)	(66)	(72)
Revalorization	(196)	(224)	(138)	(189)	(168)	(164)	(209)
Pretax profit	61	191	334	232	2	(41)	(274)

Source: British Energy annual reports; author's estimate.

interest payments and revalorisation charge from UK operations and was totally dependent on its North American ventures to make a profit.

There was no secret about BE's sensitivity to lower power prices; it had been the biggest talking point of the privatisation process and had been noted in the prospectus (Chapter 7). One might therefore have expected the company to be cautious about its debt levels in 1999/2000, when NETA was known to be coming and when it was increasingly clear that the concentration of price setting plant in the generation market was rapidly falling.

BE, despite being the company with most to lose if power prices fell, seems to have failed to see the risks from the increasingly competitive generation market and from the coming of NETA. The fall in BE's share price from its peak in February 1999 was mainly driven by fears about the power price. Yet BE compounded its exposure by buying SWALEC supply with its expensive power purchase contracts with Teeside Power (see Chapter 8) in June 1999 and Eggborough power station in November 1999. Chief Executive Peter Hollins forecast in November 1999 a fall of 10–20 per cent in power prices then in May 2000 accepted it might be much more. On the BE board, internal forecasts of lower power prices were rejected as too pessimistic (private interviews).

Conclusion

BE management's behaviour during the period 1999–2000 is baffling. Against a widespread view in the industry and among equity analysts that NETA and the unravelling of the National Power/PowerGen duopoly would lead to falling power prices, the company most at risk geared up its balance sheet and made a very large investment in additional power generation assets. Unaccountably these decisions were led by the one person on the board who might have been expected to understand commodity pricing, chief executive and former head of a PVC operation, Peter Hollins.

While forecasting commodity prices is all but impossible to do accurately, it is a reasonable expectation to make of the board of a company that it has a form of risk management policy. This appears to have been inadequate at BE.

14 The British reactor legacy

Introduction

BE had to cope with an unusual asset base. Seven of its eight power stations were based on the unique British AGR design, and not all of these were alike. This chapter analyses whether that legacy contributed significantly to the company's financial crisis. Certainly the outage at the Torness station in the summer of 2002 damaged cashflow and investor confidence at a critical time. The fall in output reliability from 1999 undermined the board's expectations of future profits. But the evidence of the subsequent years is that the company's own under-investment in the power stations contributed to the poor station performance. It is even arguable that the company was (inadvertently) distributing cash to shareholders that should have been kept for station maintenance.

The AGR output record

It was one of Nuclear Electric's and Scottish Nuclear's finest achievements that the AGRs became the most successful reactor type in the world in 1994–1995 (Chapter 5). But the output improvement stopped in 1999 and the record since has been poor. Figure 14.1 shows the annual level of AGR output, plus the level of annual capital spending (as far as possible excluding spending on other items). The rise in station outages in the years since 1999 may be explained partly by the low level of capital spending in the period after privatisation.

The problem facing BE can be illustrated using a standard engineering concept called the "bathtub" curve, which shows projected fault or failure rates in equipment over time. Figure 14.2 shows a typical generic bathtub profile. When first installed, most equipment has some faults arising from design or installation, which are corrected over time, giving rise to a stable period of low faults. Eventually, as the equipment ages it starts to suffer age-related faults, which increase until the plant is retired. Along the way there are random faults that inevitably occur in all equipment.

The problem with the AGRs was that their design-related faults were still being sorted out when the age-related faults began to appear. Figure 14.3

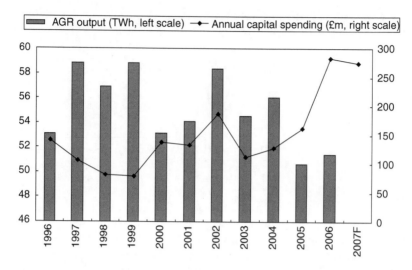

Figure 14.1 AGR output (TWh) and BE's annual capital spending (£million), financial years 1996–2007 (£/MWh) (source: British Energy annual reports; British Energy Prospectus 2005; British Energy presentation to investors ahead of re-listing 12 December 2004).

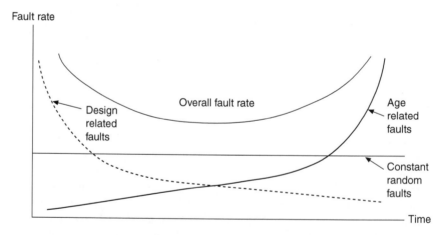

Figure 14.2 Indicative time paths of faults in long lived industrial plant (source: US Army document retrieved 19/3/2007 from commons.wikimedia.org/wiki/ Image:bathtub_curve.jpg).

shows the problem schematically; the period of low faults in the middle period of the equipment's life never arrived at the AGRs. Even in 2007 the plant remains subject to design related problems (private interviews). The age related faults have been worsened by under-investment and lack of maintenance of key plant.

The reasons for the operating unreliability lie in the fact that the AGRs are a unique reactor type with no comparator anywhere in the world. They aren't even

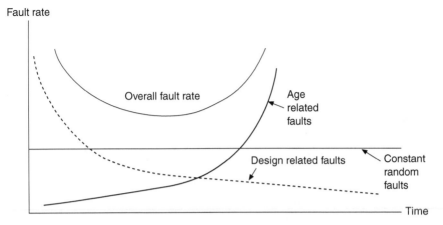

Figure 14.3 Indicative time paths of faults in AGR power stations (source: author, based on private interviews).

identical, having been built mostly in pairs with different specifications. With such a small population (seven in total) there is a tiny statistical history to draw on, compared with the hundreds of years of operating history of the standard PWR. On top of this, the engineers who designed and built the stations have largely left the industry through retirement or redundancy. The institutional memory has been depleted, and the documentary record of construction is inadequate (private interviews).

The WANO reports

The Managing Director of UK Generation, David Gilchrist, who joined the board in September 2001, was instrumental in involving WANO (the World Association of Nuclear Operators) in an appraisal of BE's nuclear operations. WANO led a team of experts to do the first ever WANO corporate review in July 2001 with a follow up in June 2003 (i.e. after the financial crisis). The report is not public but the main conclusions were discussed by Gilchrist in a frank presentation to a WANO conference in October 2003 and later detailed in the prospectus for the re-listing of British Energy Group in November 2004.

The 2001 WANO report identified five areas for improvement:

- the condition and equipment performance of BE's nuclear power stations needed significant improvement as it was damaging the reliability of those stations;
- BE needed to develop a "strong operational focus to ensure sufficient attention was given to the problems and priorities that affect safe and reliable performance" of its nuclear power stations;

- the company needed to establish clear lines of authority and accountability internally to improve overall performance;
- the company needed to make much better use of operating experience information to prevent problems recurring; and
- "an unambiguous message regarding the overriding importance of nuclear safety needed to be provided throughout the organization" (British Energy Group, 2004 p. 79).

Gilchrist told the WANO audience that BE was fourth quartile on most performance measures. The only indicator that BE excelled at was employee radiation dose, mainly because of the inherently low radiation of the AGR design. After the turn around in AGR performance in the early 1990s, BE had stood still while the world's best benchmark had continued to improve, especially in the US. The 2001 review revealed that the areas that needed improvement were "just about everything" (Varley, 2004).

The company set up a Performance Improvement Programme (PIP) to get to the world class standards. It formed a partnership with other companies with proven expertise in running their plant well, including the consulting engineers Arup, the UK water services company Severn Trent and the US electric utility Entergy. Entergy estimated that it would take £500 million to put the operations on a proper basis and that BE needed to hire 500 new people, especially in the area of project management and in plant maintenance. Having "delayered" the company in the run up to privatisation, BE was now told to introduce a new plant manager role. The simpler structure was fine for very good power stations but quite inadequate for turning around poorly performing plant (private interviews).

But the 2003 follow up WANO visit showed that progress on the five measures was "unacceptably slow" (Varley, 2004). In August 2004 a further WANO team follow up acknowledged greater progress and agreed that PIP would eventually resolve the problems but still advised that "additional emphasis should be placed on improving our reliability and safety culture" (British Energy Group, 2004 p. 79).

Problems with the equipment

British Energy Group's 2004 prospectus listed the equipment failures which had caused loss of output during the years from 2000 onwards: refuelling equipment and processes; turbine-generators; tendons; boilers; boiler feed pumps; gas circulators (which are used to pump carbon dioxide coolant gas around the reactor core); and the seawater coolant system. The prospectus recorded that:

We believe that the loss of output arising from these outages is indicative of a deterioration in the material condition of our plant over time, caused by:
(i) inadequate investment when compared with international benchmarks for

spending at nuclear power stations; (ii) a failure to perform required maintenance on a timely basis; and (iii) human errors in the operation and maintenance of our plant including conducting our operations and maintenance
functions on a station-by-station rather than fleet-wide basis.

(British Energy Group, 2004 p. 49)

The prospectus also listed equipment and plant problems that were not simply a
result of under-investment and poor maintenance, but arose from the original
AGR designs. One was the failure in 2003 of a cast iron pipe carrying sea water
at Heysham 1, which resulted in unplanned losses of some 3.2 TWh. Hunterston
B, Hartlepool and Hinkley Point B and to a much lesser extent Dungeness B,
Heysham 2 and Torness nuclear power stations also use cast iron pipework for
carrying sea water and there remained a risk that other stations would suffer
similar problems (British Energy Group, 2004 p. 102).

A second problem was the finding of corrosion in steel tendons at Hartlepool
power station. The tendons are used to maintain the integrity of the pre-stressed
concrete pressure vessel. Although at Hartlepool inspection access was straight-
forward, similar wires in the boiler closure unit might also be subject to corrosion but this unit is housed inside the concrete pressure vessel and access is
much more difficult (British Energy Group, 2004 p. 103).

Third, BE research has shown that the graphite bricks in the AGR cores
suffer from degradation and can crack. Such cracking can lead to the distortion
of the core structure and the reduction of the AGRs' operational capacity. There
is no known solution to this problem (British Energy Group, 2004 p. 104).

Fourth, the design of the boiler tubes at Hartlepool and Heysham 1 stations is
such that some of the welds are susceptible to high temperature re-heat cracking.
Failure of these welds could cause the collapse of the boiler and damage to the
reactor and pressure vessel. Access is very difficult and the problem could limit
the life of the stations (British Energy Group, 2004 pp. 104–105).

Apportioning blame

The poor reliability of the AGR stations is a result partly of their inherent design
and construction and partly of poor plant maintenance. The investment
programme undertaken by British Energy Group was intended to resolve the
majority of the problems by 2008. But the AGRs have a record of unpleasant surprises. "Accordingly, there can be no assurance that the improvement in reliability achieved in other nuclear power station improvement programmes, upon
which PIP is based and which have been undertaken on newer fleets of nuclear
power stations based on non-AGR technology, will be capable of being achieved
in respect of our AGR power stations" (British Energy Group, 2004 pp. 33–34).
In October 2006 only one of the seven AGRs was running at normal capacity,
after further problems with boiler cracks and pipe leaks (*Financial Times*, 2006a)

It seems reasonably clear that BE did a poor job of maintaining its fixed
assets for the first few years after privatisation. The levels of capital spending in

1997–2000 of around £100 million a year now appear to have been too low, by the order of £50 million–£75 million a year. Operating costs were too low too. This means that the strong cash generation that supported the company's share price in 1998–1999 was not soundly based; the company was, in effect, running down its assets and storing up a bill for the future.

There is no evidence of deliberate under-investment. The fault surely lies with the lack of experienced nuclear engineering skills at the top of the company, and to some degree with ignorance by investors. The only board member with such skills was, until the appointment of David Gilchrist in late 2001, Robin Jeffrey, who had been spending most of his time building the North American business (with Gilchrist as his key lieutenant). The restructured British Energy board in 2006 had four members with nuclear experience, includ-ing the chief executive (a former president of the US electric company Duke Power), the chief nuclear officer (a former chief nuclear officer of Florida Power Corporation) and two non-executive directors (a former chairman of the French Commissariat à l'Energie Atomique and a former head of the Royal Navy's nuclear submarines).

The under-investment can be gauged by the rise in annual capital spending from around £100 million in the first five years after privatisation to a projected £250 million–£300 million in 2006–2008 (British Energy Group, 2006 p. 10) – see Figure 14.1. The human factors are a combination of too few people and the wrong management structure, both of which are being addressed. In the two years to 2005/2006, BE hired an additional 300 people and has set up a new asset planning and investment function to identify, prioritise and schedule investment. As Figure 14.4 shows, the headcount cuts in the period from 1998–2002 now look as if they were unsustainable.

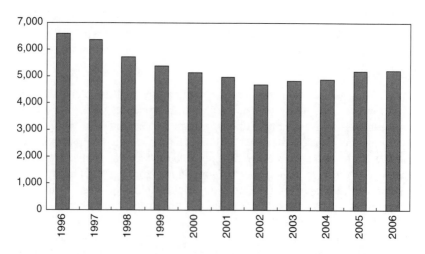

Figure 14.4 British Energy average employment, UK Nuclear, financial years 1996–2006 (source: British Energy annual reports; British Energy Group Prospectus; author's calculations).

Conclusion

BE inherited a problematic set of assets which had been made to perform reasonably well by a team of engineers who were not motivated primarily by profit. But after privatisation, the emphasis on profits and on returning cash to shareholders led to inadequate capital spending and excessive cuts in skilled labour. Station breakdowns began to rise again after 1999, exacerbating the company's financial problems. The continuing poor AGR performance after the 2002 financial crisis suggests a combination of fundamental operating weakness in the AGR design and a legacy of under-investment. Even if BE had somehow managed to survive the financial crisis of 2002, it would have faced years of higher capital spending and lower output, as its successor has.

15 The BNFL contracts

Introduction

The proximate cause of the BE board's decision to ask for government help was the failure of negotiations with BNFL over fuel reprocessing. This chapter explains how previous decades of British government policy led to BE being in this situation. It investigates the extent to which the BNFL contracts and BNFL's position on them contributed to the financial crisis and suggests that BE had good reason to expect more commercial flexibility from BNFL.

The history of nuclear fuel reprocessing in the UK

Nuclear fuel consists either of natural uranium (Magnoxes) or enriched uranium oxide. Enrichment means increasing the percentage of the fissile U-235 isotope uranium by around three times (AGRs) or five times (PWRs) from its natural level of 0.7 per cent. After the fuel has been used in the reactor it still contains a lot of potentially useful U-235, as well as plutonium and the non-fissile U-238. Reprocessing of this spent nuclear fuel means the extraction of fissile material that can be used as new fuel. The process involves dissolving the spent fuel in hot nitric acid before use of solvent extraction of the fissile material (Hewitt and Collier, 2000 pp. 248–252). It is a complicated process requiring expensive equipment capable of operating safely and securely with very dangerous substances. The material left after extraction of uranium and plutonium is largely made of highly radioactive fission products, which need to be stored carefully for decades.

The UK's long history of reprocessing arose from a combination of the military need for plutonium and the expected economic benefits of saving on fuel costs. The plant at Windscale in Cumbria, which started operating in February 1952, was built to separate both plutonium (for weapons) and uranium (for re-use in the reactor to make more plutonium) (Simpson, 1986 p. 66).

The spent fuel from the Magnox reactors that were developed from Calder Hall was intended to be reprocessed because the fuel casing could not be stored safely for long in air or water. As the Magnox reactors came on stream in the late 1950s and early 1960s, plutonium production increased. But with growing military demand for plutonium in the late 1950s, the existing reprocessing facility at Windscale was too small to cope. Work therefore began in 1957 on the unit known as B205, which was completed in 1964 and was designed to process 2,400 tonnes of spent fuel a year (Simpson, 1986 p. 110).

After the 1958 US–UK Mutual Defence Agreement opened the way for transatlantic exchange of nuclear weapon designs, equipment and testing services, the UK exported plutonium in exchange for highly enriched uranium (for use in atomic bombs) and tritium (an isotope of hydrogen used in thermonuclear bombs). Windscale's reprocessed plutonium supplied both the domestic atomic programme and the currency for trade with Americans. By the mid-1960s the military need waned because stocks were high enough. From then it was the civil need which motivated reprocessing.

The Magnox programme having turned out to be smaller than expected, the B205 reprocessing plant had spare capacity. It was widely assumed in the nuclear industry that eventually the UK would use fast breeder nuclear reactors, which would need plutonium fuel. This led to the reprocessing of AGR fuel in B205, using an additional piece of equipment called the Head End Unit (completed in 1969), to accommodate the AGR's mixed oxide fuel. Unlike the Magnox fuel, the AGR fuel was contained in stainless steel canisters which were believed capable of safe storage in air for 50 years or more (Simpson, 1986 p. 63). Reprocessing was therefore optional for the AGR fuel. But the alternative, dry storage, would have required additional capital spending at the AGR stations. Once it was decided not to do this, the AGRs were dependent on BNFL for handling their fuel. BNFL's terms for access to their storage ponds were that contacts would include reprocessing (Simpson, 1986 p. 35).

The Head End Unit was shut in 1973 following a leak, so BNFL faced a growing pile of AGR fuel with nowhere to reprocess it. On top of this, the UK had signed the Euratom treaty in 1972, which meant that the B205 plant, which had previously operated outside international (IAEA) safeguards, faced increasingly onerous technical standards, at considerable cost.

BNFL therefore decided in 1974 to build a major new reprocessing plant, called the Thermal Oxide Reprocessing Plant (THORP). The THORP investment decision was dominated by economies of scale; a larger plant would have lower unit costs. The British government supported BNFL's argument that reprocessing spent fuel from other countries, chiefly Germany and Japan, would be very profitable. And by justifying a larger plant, foreign reprocessing would reduce the costs of reprocessing the British AGR fuel.

Foreign demand for reprocessing arose from operators of the US-designed PWRs who had originally expected their spent fuel to be reprocessed in the US. But President Carter in 1977 rejected reprocessing of nuclear fuel on the grounds that the plutonium produced increased the risk of nuclear proliferation. This left the UK and France as the only countries offering a reprocessing service. Electricity companies in Japan, Germany, Switzerland and Sweden signed contracts for BNFL which would finance the building of THORP, requiring little money from the British government. The UK having missed out on the export market for the design and construction of nuclear reactors, the government was keen to get a big share of the fuel reprocessing market instead (W. Walker and Lönnroth, 1983).

In the 1977 public inquiry into building Thorp, BNFL's arguments were: i) that uranium would be in short supply globally; ii) that the fast breeder reactor programme would be successful and so there would be a need for plutonium fuel; and iii) that fossil fuel prices would remain high. Justice Parker accepted BNFL's arguments in his report and in 1978 the government approved outline planning permission for THORP.

During 1977–1981 BNFL signed "base load" contracts with foreign utilities which underpinned the costs of THORP for the first ten years. The domestic customer, the CEGB, signed cost-plus contracts in 1986. THORP was completed in 1991. But it didn't start commissioning until 1994, following another controversy and a judicial review of the government's granting of permission.

BNFL's arguments had all largely collapsed by 1994. Uranium was plentiful because the end of the USSR had freed up large stocks for the world market. Oil prices had fallen sharply from their mid-1970s highs. The fast breeder reactor programme was cancelled in 1994. Even foreign demand was in jeopardy because the German government changed the Atomic Law in 1994 that had previously banned the storing of spent nuclear fuel, thus removing the need for reprocessing.

BE and the legacy of reprocessing

The CEGB was BNFL's main domestic customer but had minimal influence on reprocessing costs. The Monopolies and Mergers Commission (MMC) report into the CEGB in 1981 remarked on the lack of control that the CEGB had over such an important part of its operating costs. Figure 15.1 shows the actual and projected real unit costs for the reprocessing of Magnox fuel as of 1981. Most commercial organisations would be concerned, if not alarmed, if one if its key suppliers proposed an eleven-fold increase in its charges over 12 years.

The MMC also remarked that: "We find it surprising that, 16 years after the first order for an AGR, the Board has still not decided how to deal with the irradiated fuel. . . . The Board . . . has not been supplied by BNFL with reliable cost estimates for reprocessing. This must have reduced the reliability of investment appraisal, and should be remedied" (MMC, 1981 para. 7.125). In other words, the CEGB had embarked on a programme of building the AGR power stations without quantifying a key part of their operating costs.

One of the reasons the earlier privatisation of nuclear power failed was the concern of potential investors over the nuclear liabilities. The Magnoxes had been withdrawn from the privatisation in July 1989 after the expected cost of decommissioning them had doubled to £600 million each and because the cost of BNFL's reprocessing of the fuel had also doubled, to £6 billion (undiscounted). Investors (and politicians) got the impression that the back end nuclear costs were liable to increase substantially without warning, which made private ownership impossible.

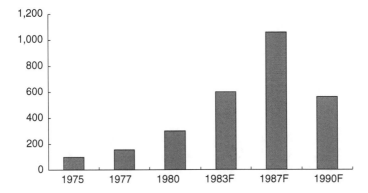

Figure 15.1 Actual and projected unit costs of Magnox fuel reprocessing (index 1975=100) (source: Monopolies and Mergers Commission, 1981 Table 7.10).

Note
F: forecast.

The very unusual fact of British Energy having very long term nuclear liabilities meant that it carried risks not normally faced by private investors. The only way such risks could be made manageable was through contracts that offered a degree of insurance against cost increases. No private company could credibly insure such long term risks so it fell to the government. But the government had insisted that the liabilities would follow the assets at privatisation. The circle was squared by BNFL. Although it was 100 per cent owned by the government, it was technically an independent company running a commercial business. BNFL provided the de facto government insurance for the nuclear liabilities which made it feasible to privatise BE.

The contracts signed between Nuclear Electric and Scottish Nuclear and BNFL in 1995 were therefore essential for the privatisation of British Energy in 1996. These contracts had two important features from an investor's point of view: i) they covered a majority of the future back end nuclear costs for the two companies; and ii) they were at fixed prices. They were also indexed to the retail price index, a point which didn't seem too important in 1996 but which meant that relative to a falling power price the contracts became increasingly costly.

The relationship between BNFL and BE was an odd one. BNFL was a monopoly supplier of reprocessing and near monopoly supplier of waste treatment and storage. "The generators, and particularly Nuclear Electric, had significant countervailing monopsony power but, in practice, had found this difficult to bring to bear on BNFL" (DTI with the Scottish Office, 1995 para. 8.14).

The renegotiation of the BNFL contracts after privatisation, in 1997, offered only good news. The percentage of future back end fuel costs covered by contracts rose to 82 per cent from 62 per cent and the net present value of the total payments fell by £400 million (British Energy, 1998a pp. 4, 20). The BE board chose to take the contract benefit in lower immediate costs, rather than spreading it out into the future (Chapter 8). This was, with hindsight, a poor decision.

As BE's UK generating profits plummeted with falling electricity prices from 2000 onwards, the board looked to cut costs in all directions. The single largest cost was the contracts with BNFL, which became more onerous with every fall in the real price of electricity. In November 2001, in its half year results statement, BE argued that it was paying the equivalent of $6/MWh for back end fuel costs, compared with only $1/MWh for its nuclear utility peers in the US. It argued that "reprocessing is no longer the most cost effective option for spent fuel and that … shareholders should no longer be required to shoulder this burden" (British Energy, 2001b p. 4). At only $1/MWh the company's UK generation business would be profitable. BE was, in its eyes, paying an excess cost of around £200m (Table 15.1).

On this account, BE shareholders were shouldering the cost of decades of bad decisions by British governments in favour of reprocessing of nuclear fuel, culminating in the burden of paying BNFL to keep its THORP plant running. There are two problems with this argument though.

First, the comparison with the US is arbitrary. It is not clear what the US costs are based on but they form part of a quite different system for dealing with nuclear waste, in which the government takes all responsibility and the electric utilities pay a fixed levy. At privatisation the UK government required BE shareholders to take responsibility; they then contracted much of this to BNFL (owned by the government). If the UK had at some point stopped reprocessing and opted for dry storage instead (the only realistic alternative) then THORP might not have been built and there would have been some reduction in back end fuel costs. But not the $5/MWh that is implied by a comparison with the US. The drystore alternative investigated in the early 1990s by Scottish Nuclear initially offered some significant cost savings largely disappeared once the project was more fully investigated (Chapter 5). It is not clear how much BE (and the UK) might theoretically have saved by abandoning reprocessing but it would probably have been much less than the £200 million estimated above.

Second, the BE shareholders (represented by the board) entered into the BNFL contracts knowingly and willingly. Their advantages – fixing a large part of the future costs with a creditworthy supplier (in effect the British government) – seemed to outweigh by far their main disadvantage, their inflexible indexation to general price inflation. Although the details were opaque to outsiders, there was no concern expressed about the contracts at the time of privatisation.

Table 15.1 British energy implied estimate of "excess" cost of reprocessing (£m)

Nuclear output 2001–2002 (TWh)	67
"Excess cost" $ per MWh	5
Total excess cost ($m)	335
Total excess cost (£m)	197

Source: British Energy 2001; author's estimates.

The failure to renegotiate in time

The argument that BE was unfairly disadvantaged by the legacy of the BNFL contracts is not convincing because they were freely entered into and broadly understood by investors. But more persuasive is the view that BE was damaged by BNFL's apparent unwillingness to renegotiate the contracts in 2002. It was reasonable for BE to expect that its principal supplier, seeing that it faced serious and possibly terminal financial difficulties, would provide some flexibility in payments.

There are precedents for contract renegotiations in the natural gas industry, which has been characterised historically by long term fixed price "take-or-pay" contracts between upstream suppliers and downstream purchasers. The trend towards market liberalisation in Europe and the UK has sometimes made these contracts unviable for the buyer, because market prices after liberalisation have fallen below the contract price. The contracted buyer then faces a loss making "out-of-the-money" contract.

The deregulation of the US long distance gas market in the early 1980s led to many take-or-pay contracts becoming onerous. The US courts would not accept that this was a good enough reason for the companies to be allowed to escape the contracts, but voluntary contract renegotiations were allowed. The deregulation of the British gas industry in the 1990s led to a number of similar cases. Two are of relevance here. The first is the case of Enron and the owners of the North Sea J-Block. Enron, having signed contracts before gas liberalisation, found that the market price of the gas was below what it was contracted to pay. Enron tried to get the contract changed but lost in court in 1997. The J-Block partners then reached a voluntary settlement with Enron in which it paid $440 million to them in exchange for a lower gas price (Pipeline and Gas Journal, 1996; World Oil, 1997).

The second case is of Centrica, part of British Gas which was spun off as a separate company in the de-merger of 1997. British Gas, a former state owned monopoly provider of gas services in the UK, had historically bought gas from upstream producers in the North Sea on long term contracts. The company would then pass this gas onto the retail market, without risk because of its monopoly. When this monopoly ended in the mid-1990s British Gas was left with a portfolio of long term contracts, some of which were at prices well above the new, lower market price. These contracts, estimated to be of the order of $61 billion (about £40 billion) were passed on to the new company, Centrica, which started trading in February 1997. Without changes to the contracts, Centrica was, in effect, bankrupt (Surrey, 1999).

But it was in the interests of the gas sellers to do deals; a bankrupt Centrica would not be able to buy any gas from anyone. During 1997 there was a series of successful renegotiations with Centrica's main suppliers: BP, Mobil, Amerada Hess, Enterprise Oil, Conoco, Elf and Total. Centrica and its predecessor British Gas paid a total of £1.1 billion compensation to these suppliers, in exchange for cancelling or amending a total of 48 billion therms of contracts.

By December 1997 the contracts had been reduced to a manageable level (Centrica, 1998 p. 3).

Both Enron and Centrica reached voluntary accommodations with their suppliers. The cost of the out-of-the-money contracts was shared in some degree between both sides. While Enron's commercial existence wasn't threatened by its J-Block contract, Centrica's viability certainly was. Understanding this, the gas suppliers could see the benefit of a deal.

BE and BNFL

The relationship between BE and BNFL in 2002 was similar to that of Centrica and its gas suppliers; the terms of the contracts signed in good faith in 1995 and 1997 proving to be difficult or impossible for BE to pay because of the unexpectedly severe fall in electricity prices. But there were two reasons why it should have been *easier* to renegotiate the contracts in this case.

First, the importance of BNFL to BE commercially was symmetrical; BE was BNFL's largest customer and the prospect of a financially distressed BE would have been alarming for BNFL. By contrast, a bankrupt Centrica would have been costly but not disastrous for large oil companies like BP and Mobil.

Second, the very long time scale of the contract meant there was never any need for BNFL to take a loss (in present value terms) on the contract. BE was seeking temporary relief, albeit that nobody knew for how long power prices would remain low. It should have been possible to devise a scheme in which BNFL accepted lower revenues in the short term for higher revenues in the longer term, while preserving BE's financial viability.

This sort of risk-sharing arrangement was what BE was hoping for. BNFL apparently accepted the principle, having decided quite reasonably that it could not accept any transfer of value to BE. So why was no deal done? There are two possible reasons. First, although BE's chairman Robin Jeffrey gave detailed financial information to BNFL and believed he had done enough to emphasise the seriousness of the situation, the BNFL team appear not to have believed that BE was truly on the brink of insolvency. In other words, there was a grave misunderstanding. It seems astonishing to an outsider that this might have happened. But this is a reasonable interpretation of the events described in Chapter 10.

The second possible reason why BE and BNFL failed to reach a deal is that BNFL was in the happy position of knowing that it would never face a loss of income even if BE did get into trouble. It could be sure that if BE failed financially that the government would be forced to protect it from shutting down and that one way or another, BNFL would continue to be paid for its services. Put bluntly, a state owned company would be bailed out by the state. If this is true then BNFL, in acting as if it were a truly independent commercial company, actually helped to bring about enormous financial costs to BE, its shareholders and creditors – and the taxpayers who were BNFL's ultimate owners. The British government, understandably wary of being seen to provide illegal state aid to a private company, stood back and allowed the negotiations to fail, even though it was the government that then had to pick up the pieces.

Conclusion

If BE had been negotiating with a "normal" private sector company in August 2002, it seems reasonable to believe that it would have been able to cut its back end fuel payments enough to avoid the financial crisis of September 2002. But no normal private company could ever have signed the long term fuel reprocessing contracts in the first place. It was always something of a fiction to argue that BE had been completely privatised when a precondition of privatisation was long term contractual insurance with a state owned company. This fiction extended to the idea that BNFL was a purely commercial company. The fiasco casts doubt on the wisdom of the British approach to managing the nuclear liabilities.

Part V

Conclusions

The multiple causes of failure

16 The international context

British uniqueness?

Introduction

The story of the British civil nuclear industry is an unhappy one. But nuclear power has had a difficult history in many other countries too. This chapter asks whether British nuclear policy choices were distinctive, in ways that might explain the financial collapse of British Energy. It argues that the UK was unusual but not unique in combining private ownership of nuclear power with liberalised power markets; this combination exists in parts of the US. The UK opted for a non-standard reactor type, but so did Canada. Lastly the UK policy of placing responsibility for back end nuclear costs and storage on the company is unusual, although shared with France and Germany. No one policy choice appears to explain the financial crisis of British Energy but the combination did create a more risky situation.

The chapter begins with a summary of the key policy choices made by the main nuclear countries, to put the UK's position in context. It then briefly explains why different countries made different choices, examining France, the US, Japan, Germany and Canada. Each country's differing energy needs and goals and system of government influenced its nuclear choices. The chapter concludes by assessing the "uniqueness" of the UK and the role of its policies in contributing to the British Energy financial crisis.

A comparison of nuclear policies

Table 16.1 compares some key nuclear policy choices in the UK with those of other similar countries. The list excludes countries such as Italy which have withdrawn from nuclear power and others such as Sweden and Spain where there is a continuing political struggle over closure. Some of the policies were under government control and the nuclear utilities in each country had to deal with them as best they can; others were partly or wholly a matter of private sector choices, at least in some countries.

The choice of reactor was entirely a government affair in the UK, Canada and France but was largely left to the private sector in the US, Germany and Japan. The UK and France initially chose the gas-cooled type, for similar reasons

Table 16.1 National nuclear power policies compared

	Private or public decisions		Public policy decisions		
	Non-standard reactor type	*Nuclear-only generation company*	*Liberalised power market*	*Reprocessing of waste fuel*	*Company responsibility for spent fuel and waste*
UK	Yes	Yes	Yes	Yes	Yes
US	–	Yes	Yes	–	–
France	–	Yes	–	Yes	Yes
Germany	–	–	Yes	Yes – until 1990s	Yes
Canada	Yes	Yes	Yes	–	–
Japan	–	–	–	Yes	–

Source: IAEA Country Nuclear Power Profiles; World Nuclear Association; Price 1990; Burn 1978.

(see below), but France later joined the mainstream PWR option. Canada, which was unusual in having access to heavy water manufacturing, opted for a distinctive deuterium-based reactor (CANDU).

British government policy created a wholly nuclear generation company in the UK but this emerged by choice in some parts of the US, as a result of the concentration of nuclear ownership from the early 1990s onwards (see below). In Germany, private utilities opted for a mixture of nuclear and non-nuclear generation, as in Japan. French policy was entirely government driven until the partial privatisation of Electricité de France (EDF) in 2005 and EDF became a predominantly nuclear generator as a result of the French government's decision in the 1970s to invest heavily in nuclear power.

Government policy was more decisive on the question of liberalising the power market. The UK was one of the first countries to choose full liberalisation, at the time of electricity sector privatisation in 1990–1991. By the time of nuclear privatisation in 1996 the generation industry was still some way from being fully competitive but new entry barriers had been scrapped and by 2000 the power of the incumbent duopolists National Power and PowerGen had largely disappeared. In the US, with its federal energy market, the degree of liberalisation has varied markedly by state, with some areas of the country resembling the UK and others still regulated on the traditional cost of service model.

Germany chose to deregulate its electricity industry in the late 1990s ahead of the slow European Union timetable on liberalisation, though it has not (yet) separated transmission from generation in the way that the UK chose when it broke up the CEGB. France has generally opposed energy liberalisation in Europe and EDF remains the most unreconstructed vertically integrated energy company in Europe. Ironically EDF has enthusiastically exploited the liberalisation of the European markets, both as exporter of power (mainly to Italy and the UK) and as acquirer of foreign electricity assets (including the UK, Germany and Italy).

The British decision to reprocess nuclear fuel was uncontroversial when it was first taken in the 1950s but reprocessing later fell out of favour in several other countries. The US dropped reprocessing in 1977 on fears of nuclear weapon proliferation. German law, which originally banned direct disposal of unprocessed waste, was modified in 1994 and the country stopped reprocessing in 2005. Canada, with abundant reserves of uranium, has never reprocessed its spent fuel. Japan remains committed to an indigenous reprocessing industry on the grounds of fuel scarcity and a possible future fast breeder reactor programme that would use the recycled fissile materials. The UK and France, having invested heavily in reprocessing infrastructure, are locked into fuel reprocessing for the foreseeable future.

The governments of the UK, France and Germany treat the back end costs of nuclear power – waste treatment and storage and decommissioning – as business costs for which the nuclear generator is responsible. British Energy in 1995 signed contracts with BNFL, a government owned company, to cover a majority of its nuclear back end costs. But it remained liable both for the costs of the contracts and for the uncontracted liabilities that cannot be resolved until the British government settles on a long term waste management policy. EDF in France has similar arrangements with the French reprocessing company Cogema (which was merged into Areva in 2001). EDF was partially privatised in 2005. The German utilities also retain financial liability and until the mid-1990s contracted with BNFL and Cogema for reprocessing and interim storage. By contrast, the US government takes ultimate responsibility for back end fuel costs and charges US nuclear operators a fixed levy per unit of power generated. So US operators have a known, current operating cost, rather than the more uncertain and complex long term liabilities faced by British Energy.

In sum, there is no single policy choice that the UK has made which makes it unique. It is in the combination of choices that the UK is somewhat unusual, namely the creation of a wholly nuclear generator privatised into an increasingly competitive generation market, with a largely non-standard fleet of power stations and with a direct obligation to fund long term reprocessing of the spent fuel (Chesshire, 1992 p. 752). Even when other countries made similar choices to the UK, they were typically characterised by more private-public sector cooperation. In France, EDF has been a major fixture of the public sector for decades. In Germany most of the ostensibly private utilities were owned and de facto controlled by state or city governments until the late 1990s (Bayernwerk by the Bavarian government until 2000, RWE by the city of Essen until 1998, EnBW by the city of Karlshuhe and other municipalities until 2001).

France

The country which the UK most resembles in its early nuclear history is France. The two countries faced similar goals and constraints in the 20 years after the Second World War and differed mainly in the association between the US and the UK, from which France was excluded. What is then most striking is the divergence in national policy choices from the late 1960s, when France adopted the American PWR reactor type.

France, like Britain, had a proud scientific heritage in the field of atomic physics. But the French were excluded from the Hyde Park agreement of 1944 between Roosevelt and Churchill. They therefore faced the reality early on that they would have to go it alone in nuclear research. The CEA (Commissariat à l'Energie Atomique, or Atomic Energy Commission) was set up in October 1945 with its main priority being basic reactor research, rather than any military goal. In 1952 the minister in charge of atomic projects, Félix Gaillard, piloted through the first five year plan, with the intention of providing France, which was poor in energy resources, with a complete nuclear industry. Deposits of uranium were discovered near Limoges in the late 1940s which allowed the CEA to develop three natural uranium fuelled, graphite-moderated reactors. They produced plutonium but also had heat exchangers to give useful amounts of electrical power. In all of this France was following a similar industrial and economic logic to the British.

Joint studies on atomic power began in 1955 between CEA and the state electricity company, Electricité de France (EDF). Together they formed an influential advisory committee, PEON (Production d'électricité d'origine nucléaire). Pierre Ailleret of EDF commented that "one cannot do other than follow the line taken by the British", meaning a combination of gas cooling and graphite moderation with natural uranium (Price, 1990 p. 49). PEON developed a first 70 MW prototype then a 200 MW station at Chinon on the Loire, which entered service in 1965.

The European Atomic Energy Community (Euratom) was formed in January 1958 to coordinate members' research into atomic energy. Britain chose not to join, leaving the French as leaders. Unfortunately US sales pressure for light water reactors in the 1960s effectively killed off French hopes of interesting the rest of Europe in the gas-cooled type; Britain's decision to remain outside Euratom, by dividing the two proponents of this technology, made American success inevitable. In 1962 West Germany awarded its first order for a commercial-size reactor to GE, for a BWR, turning down a British graphite-moderated proposal.

The French were still using graphite and gas-cooling, like Britain, because of a lack of enriched uranium. PEON proposed in 1964 that between 2.5 GW and 4 GW of gas-cooled reactors be built. But low oil prices and higher interest rates made them economically unattractive. The programme was scaled back but De Gaulle decided on a large twin reactor at Fessenheim on the Rhine. France also sold one gas-cooled reactor to Spain.

Meanwhile France's submarine programme led to research into water-cooled reactors, following a similar path to the American one. In 1967 EDF opened a 70 MW heavy water reactor at Brennelis in Brittany. EDF also collaborated with Belgium on a 240 MW PWR at Chooz in the French Ardennes. The view was gradually strengthening that France should go down the PWR route. In April 1968 PEON agreed, after assurances that France could supply enriched uranium, using technology developed for the military programme. De Gaulle, the biggest supporter of the CEA and its gas-cooled reactor technology, retired in 1969.

The largest gas-cooled reactor, 480 MW, was opened at St Laurent-des-Eaux, in 1969 and marked the end of the gas era. EDF admitted to the press on its opening day that it could not compete with oil at the current price. The same night an operator error led to a fuel element melting and the reactor was out of service for a year (Price, 1990 ch. 3).

President Pompidou decided to switch from the gas-cooled reactor to the PWR "as a response to circumstances and without great enthusiasm" (Price, 1990 p. 51). The French decision was not based on any general belief that the PWR was safer. Nor did they see any great difference on economics; the 10 per cent margin that the PWR held was within the range of possible future developments by gas cooling. But the decision was driven by the realisation that France would otherwise be cut off from the benefit of operating experience that was accumulating around the world, and probably from exports.

The French, in other words, abandoned their indigenous technology because they saw grave disadvantages from pursuing a separate technological route. They believed this would ultimately damage their economic prospects. Britain chose to back its own reactors, first in 1965 and then repeatedly through the 1970s, despite growing evidence that the world reactor market was becoming dominated by water-cooled reactors and that the British design was severely flawed.

French pragmatism paid off. A new company, Framatome, was set up at Le Cruesot, and designated monopoly nuclear constructor. France signed a licence with the US PWR manufacturer Westinghouse, which took 48 per cent of the equity in Framatome, and directed a 900 MW reactor ordered in the first year to be built at Fessenheim (instead of the gas reactor previously planned). The French sixth economic plan targeted 8,000 MW of capacity for 1971–1975. The pace increased sharply after the Yom Kippur War in 1973. Oil then accounted for 66 per cent of France's primary energy and the quadrupling of prices was therefore very costly. The French government announced in March 1974 a sharply increased rate of ordering to 5–6 stations a year, each of 900 MW. EDF stated it would be ordering no more non-nuclear power stations. It set a target of 60 per cent of French electricity to be nuclear by 1985; the actual result was 65 per cent (IAEA, 2004 table 6). Framatome, after working closely with Westinghouse on common technology, bought out the US stake and the company became an independent contractor for nuclear power stations globally, winning much of the growing business in Asia.

Forty reactors were ordered over the eight years 1974–1981, with France getting a third of its primary energy from nuclear power in 1990. While sometimes criticised for over investment, EDF had the advantage that it could export surplus power to the rest of Europe, much of it to Italy, which faced an electricity shortage following its decision to shut down its nuclear power stations after a referendum in November 1987, triggered by the Chernobyl disaster.

In November 2005 30 per cent of the equity in EDF was sold to private investors. A 2004 law requires the remaining 70 per cent to remain with the French state. EDF describes itself as "the European energy market leader and the leading electricity company in the world … beyond any doubt, *the leading company for the post oil era*" (EDF, 2006 p. 9, emphasis in original).

The remainder of the French nuclear industry – construction company Framatome and waste treatment and reprocessing company Cogema – was consolidated in 2001 into the company AREVA. AREVA is technically a private corporation but 83 per cent of the voting rights are held by the CEA and a further 5 per cent directly by the French government, which appoints four directors (out of a total of 15) to the supervisory board.

AREVA's nuclear construction subsidiary AREVA NP (formerly Framatome ANP) is 34 per cent owned by the German engineering company Siemens. AREVA NP is one of the world's leading nuclear power engineering companies, competing against Westinghouse and AECL (Atomic Energy of Canada Limited). Its European Pressurised Water Reactor (EPR) is an evolutionary development of existing French N4 and German Konvoi PWR designs, offering superior safety and a design life of 60 years, compared with the 40 years of previous European PWRs (Nuttall, 2005 pp. 145–146). The first EPR is under construction in Finland and a second is scheduled for construction for EDF at Flamanville in France. AREVA formed a joint venture with Baltimore-based utility Constellation Energy in 2005 and announced their intention to apply in 2008 for permission from the Nuclear Regulatory Commission to build and operate an EPR in the US.

US

Unlike the UK, France or Japan, the US faced no need for additional energy sources at the end of the Second World War. Development of nuclear power was initially confined mainly to the US navy's interest in submarine propulsion. This technology, which required great compactness, combined with the US having the infrastructure to enrich uranium, meant that light water reactors (LWRs) using enriched uranium soon became the dominant reactor research type, in contrast to the gas-cooled natural uranium route followed in the UK and France.

President Eisenhower's 1953 "Atoms for Peace" programme provided federal research support for nuclear power. The two engineering companies General Electric Corporation (GE) and Westinghouse Electric each built commercial nuclear power stations and began selling them round the world in the 1960s (see Chapter 3). US utilities offered a large domestic customer base, driven by concerns over the US's growing need for imported oil, and attracted by the fixed price contracts available from GE and Westinghouse. The number of water-cooled reactors in the world outstripped any other type by the early 1970s. By 1974 6 per cent of total US electricity came from nuclear power, rising to around 20 per cent from the early 1990s (World Nuclear Association, 2006b).

The industry ran into severe problems in the 1970s, as construction cost overruns became common and public opposition led to costly delays in approval and commissioning. Construction costs rose from $623 per kW of capacity in 1966–1967 to $2,132 per kW in 1976–1977 (Energy Information Administration, 1986 p. 18). The reasons included over-confident increases in plant size and a failure of economies of scale to materialise. Gains from standardisation were limited because most stations were custom built (Gielecki and Hewlett, 1994 p. 7). Problems began to emerge in the first generation of nuclear stations because damage from corrosion and stress fracturing in the harsh nuclear plant environment exceeded expectations. Repairing this damage also required units to be taken out of service temporarily (Gielecki and Hewlett, 1994 p. 3). All of these problems are reminiscent of those suffered by the British AGR programme.

The 1979 Three Mile Island incident led to even greater costs because of additional equipment required by the Nuclear Regulatory Commission. No new stations have been ordered in the US since 1979 (though a total of 27,000 MW of new nuclear capacity has registered for planning consent since the 2003

Department of Energy Nuclear Power 2010 initiative (World Nuclear Association, 2006b table 2).

The US has its own "Dungeness B" disaster story, in the form of the Shoreham station on Long Island, which is probably the most expensive power station in history. Owing to a series of management faults, lawsuits and political fighting, the Shoreham station "was built, fuelled, tested, closed and decommissioned without a single kWh of electricity ever being sold" (Nuttall, 2005 p. 8). A power station that in 1966 was expected by the local utility Long Island Lighting Company (LILCO) to cost $65 million, ended up costing one hundred times as much – $6 billion.

Performance improvement

The average load factor (capacity usage) of US nuclear power stations was mediocre until the 1990s when a sustained improvement began. By the turn of the century US load factors were touching 90 per cent, compared with less than 60 per cent in the 1980s (Figure 16.1). In 2001, the 17 reactors owned by the company Exelon (formerly Peco Energy, British Energy's partner in AmerGen) achieved a load factor of 94 per cent.

The operating improvements in US nuclear plants have been driven by a growing concentration of ownership. In the 1960s and 1970s many utilities wanted

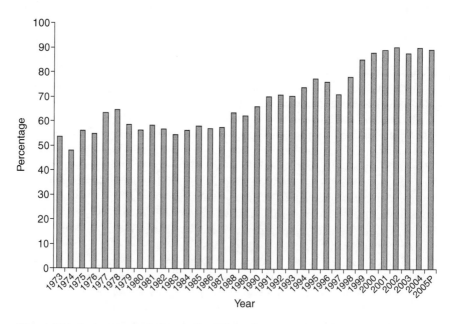

Figure 16.1 Aggregate load factor for US nuclear power stations, 1973–2005 (%) (source: Energy Information Administration, 2006 Table 9.2).

Note
P: preliminary.

to invest in nuclear power but the large scale of the power stations led to fragmented ownership, with many electric companies owning a half or third of a station. Without full ownership, many utilities lacked the incentive to manage the stations properly. The growing consolidation of the industry (which British Energy's AmerGen joint venture helped to bring about) has improved those incentives and led to companies with considerable expertise in nuclear generation.

As of the end of 1991, a total of 101 individual utilities (including minority owners) had some ownership interest in operable nuclear power plants. At the end of 1999, the number of such utilities had dropped to 87, and the largest 12 of them owned 54 per cent of the capacity, slightly up on 1991. By late 2005 only 27 companies were involved in nuclear ownership (World Nuclear Association, 2006b). The US nuclear generation industry now resembles more closely those of Germany and Japan, where ownership of nuclear plant is concentrated in a small number of major companies.

US policy on back end fuel costs

Nuclear waste, including spent fuel (given that reprocessing is banned), has always been the responsibility of the federal government. Utilities pay a 0.1c/kWh levy, which by 2006 had built up a fund of over $24 billion and is growing by $800 million a year (World Nuclear Association, 2006b). The spent fuel is stored at power stations until the Department of Energy takes delivery. The original 1998 deadline for this was missed owing to continuing opposition to the plan for a storage facility at Yucca Mountain in Nevada. Utilities in some cases have had to build additional storage space to avoid having to shut down and have successfully sued for compensation from the government.

Having stopped fuel reprocessing in 1977, the US began to revisit the subject in 2005 when the Senate allocated funds for research into proliferation-resistant reprocessing techniques. In February 2006 the US launched a Global Nuclear Energy Partnership, part of which involved research into new technologies for recycling spent fuel but without separating out the plutonium (Department of Energy, 2006). Instead, the radioactive elements would be separated out as a whole, and then burned in a new generation of advanced burner reactors, thus combating weapons proliferation and reusing the nuclear fuel.

Japan

Japan started to research into atomic power in 1954 and passed a law in 1955 prohibiting nuclear applications in the military field. The Atomic Energy Commission was set up in 1956 and the following year Japan ordered a British Magnox power station from GEC to be built at Tokai Mura. This station came on line in 1966 but, although it operated until 1998, the station was not regarded as successful and no further gas-cooled stations were built.

Instead, Japan ordered its first BWR, which began operation in 1970. The Japanese electric manufacturing companies and utilities had close links with

GE and Westinghouse. They continued to order US reactors of both the BWR and PWR types. The utilities bought the reactor designs and built them with Japanese companies, which acquired licence rights to build more. By the late 1970s Japanese manufacturers such as Hitachi, Mitsubishi Heavy Industries and Toshiba were dealing directly with utilities and establishing their own export industry in other parts of Asia.

The early reactors suffered reliability problems that required long outages; average load factors in the mid-1970s averaged only 46 per cent. But a programme of standardisation and shared best practice driven by the Ministry of International Trade and Industry (MITI) drove load factors up to around 79 per cent by 2001.

The emphasis in Japanese energy policy on fuel security led to the reprocessing of fuel, to recycle uranium and plutonium. This was done for many years by contracts with BNFL in the UK and Cogema in France, with vitrified high level waste being returned for final storage in Japan. Japan began constructing its own reprocessing plant at Rokkasho-mura, which is due to be commissioned in 2007. A government study in 2004 concluded that reprocessing would be more expensive than direct disposal but the Atomic Energy Commission advisory group nonetheless decided to proceed with the final commissioning of the $20 billion reprocessing plant (World Nuclear Association, 2006a).

Japan remains committed to fast breeder technology, albeit on a time scale of several decades ahead, which would use the four tonnes of plutonium annually recycled from the PWR fuel at the Rokkasho plant.

High level waste from reprocessing in Europe began to arrive back in Japan from 1995. It is stored in an interim storage facility at Rokkasho-mura. A permanent storage facility is supposed to be built by 2035. Funding for this is being built up by a levy on the utilities (in effect charged to their customers) of 0.2yen/kWh, targeted to reach three trillion yen ($28 billion) (World Nuclear Association, 2006a).

Germany

West Germany was one of the earliest countries to adopt atomic energy. By 2006 Germany generated about of a third of its power from nuclear, despite having shut down the Soviet designed reactors in the former East Germany after unification in 1990. The main contrast with the UK experience is the decentralised approach to decisions, reflecting the relatively weak federal government. Key decisions on reactor orders were taken by private utilities, with private manufacturers responding under a supportive government policy.

West Germany appointed a small Ministry of Atomic Energy in 1955 with very few staff, in contrast to the UKAEA. The Ministry supported research, but under federal principles the work was decentralised, leading to a number of research reactors around the country, rather than at a single national site like Harwell. As early as 1956 the major utility RWE began to favour light water reactor technology. German engineering companies AEG and Siemens had close links with GE and Westinghouse respectively. In 1958 RWE and the Bavarian utility Bayernwerk jointly ordered a 15 MW experimental reactor from AEG and GE. It began operation in June 1961 and its success led to order for 240 MW BWR in 1962 at Gundremmingen. In 1964 RWE ordered a second BWR and then a PWR from Siemens.

The German electric utilities had autonomy subject only to safety regulation. In contrast with the UK and France, the federal government didn't choose manufacturers or create consortia. The utilities faced their own choices and had big incentives not to make mistakes (Burn, 1978 pp. 101–102). As in France the utilities licensed US PWR technology and then amended it, mainly in respect of safety standards. By the 1980s German PWRs were a distinct type and Siemens was competing against Westinghouse for foreign orders.

In 1976 the Atomic Energy Act made long term storage of high level waste the responsibility of the Federal Government, but as in most countries there is no operating disposal site yet. Reprocessing of spent fuel was policy until 1994. The 1998 coalition government decided that from 2005 reprocessing would stop to be replaced by direct disposal underground. But pending the selection of a site and construction of a repository the utilities must provide interim storage of the spent fuel, currently at the power station sites (World Nuclear Association, 2005).

Canada

The Canadian nuclear research programme began with the move of British atomic scientists to Montreal and later Chalk River in Ontario during the Second World War. Atomic Energy of Canada Limited (AECL), created in 1952 as a federal government owned enterprise, developed the distinctive CANDU (CANadian Deuterium Uranium) reactor in partnership with provincial utility Ontario Hydro and the Canadian subsidiary of General Electric.

The CANDU is a pressurised water reactor but uses "heavy water" (water which contains the deuterium isotope of hydrogen and is 10 per cent denser than ordinary or "light" water) as a moderator. Heavy water, which absorbs far fewer neutrons during fission than light water, allows the use of natural uranium fuel. The US standard light water reactors require enriched uranium. Heavy water, which occurs naturally but in very low concentrations in ordinary water, is separated out using electrolysis, which uses a great deal of electricity. The first major supply of heavy water first emerged at Norsk Hydro in Norway in the mid-1930s as a by-product of the creation of ammonia-based fertiliser. The first heavy water used in the wartime atomic research in Canada originated in France. But Canada was well placed to manufacture more because it had a large electrolysis plant at Trail, British Columbia, which (like the Norsk Hydro one) was used for making fertiliser. With abundant cheap hydro electricity, the cost of producing heavy water was high but manageable (Waltham, 2002). The CANDU is more efficient in its use of uranium fuel and requires no enrichment or reprocessing infrastructure.

CANDU reactors have been sold to South Korea, China, India, Argentina, Romania and Pakistan, in most cases along with the expertise to build additional units. The advanced CANDU reactor (ACR) is being promoted by AECL as a candidate for new nuclear stations in Europe (see below). In Canada itself the CANDU is used in the province of Ontario, where it generates about half the electricity. Ontario Hydro, the provincial electric utility, privatised some of its nuclear stations in 2001 with the creation of Bruce Power, which was majority owned by British Energy until 2003 when BE was forced to sell its stake as part of its financial restructuring.

Canada has no spent fuel reprocessing industry. Responsibility for high level nuclear waste (mainly spent fuel) rests with the federal government through the Nuclear Waste Management Organisation (NWMO). Plans for deep underground storage have been discussed but no facility will be built for many years yet. Low and intermediate level waste is the responsibility of the nuclear power companies, which have built dry storage sites at their power station sites.

The perspective from 2007

The six countries considered here – the UK, US, France, Japan Germany and Canada – illustrate a wide range of policy approaches to nuclear power. The US has had the most decentralised and free market-based approach to nuclear power, with energy policy being limited until recently to the restriction on reprocessing. In France and to a slightly lesser extent in the UK, the state and its agencies has dominated decision making. In Japan and Germany, the government has supported private utilities in their decisions, though in Japan the government's policy of energy security has meant that economics have been less decisive than in Germany, where the utilities have had relatively commercial objectives.

At the time of the British Energy privatisation in 1996, there seemed little prospect of new nuclear build. But a decade later there was much talk of a "nuclear renaissance" (Nuttall 2005). US energy policy has become far more accommodating to nuclear power since 2000, although no new station has yet been commissioned. A new nuclear power station began construction in Finland in 2003 and there is a substantial programme of nuclear expansion in China, Taiwan and South Korea (IAEA, 2006).

In the event of any nuclear renaissance (including in the UK), the US, Canadian and Franco-German nuclear industries are ready to supply new reactors. The leading contenders for the next generation of reactors are: the Westinghouse AP1000; the Aveva EPR; the AECL advanced Candu or ACR; and the advanced boiling water reactor (ABWR), developed by GE and built in Japan with Toshiba and Hitachi. Of these four types, two are either operating or under construction (the EPR is being built in Finland, one ABRW is operating in Japan, another is under construction in Taiwan) and the others are advanced extensions of existing station types.

The only country with practically no indigenous capacity for designing and constructing nuclear power stations is the nation which built the first one, the UK. All of the others – the US, France, Germany, Canada and Japan – have some direct stake in the nuclear future. By a rather bizarre turn of events, the British government, through its ownership of the nuclear reprocessing company

BNFL, had a financial stake in a major contender in the new nuclear build market, namely Westinghouse. BNFL bought Westinghouse in 1999 and agreed to sell it in February 2006 to Japanese company Toshiba for $5.4 billion. The sale was undertaken "to realise its value and enable it to prosper in the private sector" (BNFL, 2006 p. 5).

The restructured and re-floated British Energy is a potential partner in any future new nuclear build in the UK, but mainly because it owns the best sites. Long-shelved plans for additional PWRs at Sizewell, Hinckley Point and Wylfa could be revisited if necessary. But BE's role would be a junior one at best. It is not clear that BE would be financially in a position to invest in new stations, nor it is obvious that the most likely investors (the French utility EDF and the German utility E.ON, both of which own large chunks of the British electricity industry) would want them involved.

Conclusion

British nuclear policy was not unique. It followed a similar logic to that of France and diverged only when the French judged the gains from following a non-standard reactor path to be less than the costs. France, Germany and Japan have all successfully taken light water reactor power station designs from the US and then commercialised them into competing types. French policy was very centralised; German decisions were largely taken by private sector utilities. Both countries retain substantial nuclear power generation and have a stake in the design and manufacture of new reactors. Canada, with a very different endowment of cheap hydro electricity and natural uranium, successfully commercialised a different reactor type, the CANDU. The advanced CANDU is a serious competitor to the Westinghouse and Franco-German new designs.

Of the main nuclear power states, only the UK has emerged with no nuclear industry to speak of and with a nuclear generator weakly placed to take part in any new nuclear power stations in the UK. It is hard to imagine the British Energy financial crisis having happened in any other country except the US, where the fragmentation of nuclear ownership (until recently) made it impossible for any single corporate collapse to have great importance. Nuclear ownership in Germany was dispersed among a number of large, regionally dominant utilities. When power prices temporarily collapsed in Germany in the late 1990s, the companies were strong enough to ride out the storm and consolidate their new oligopoly. In France the continued integration of all aspects of the electricity industry meant that EDF could always pass on to its customers any cost problems. The French power market has only recently come close to the level of liberalisation introduced in the UK in 1990. Japan's emphasis on energy security has meant that policy would never put the same premium as the British government did on the pursuit of economic efficiency through free markets. US utilities have responded to the somewhat patchy deregulation of the electricity industry by cutting costs, reorganising ownership and improving efficiency. But they have not been burdened by the legacy of fuel reprocessing contracts that constrained British Energy's ability to cut its costs.

17 Conclusion

Introduction

This chapter brings together the findings of Part IV and tries to draw some conclusions about the causes of British Energy's crisis. It briefly brings the story up to date to the end of 2006 and comments on the outlook for nuclear power in the UK and British Energy's role in it.

The multiple causes of failure

British Energy's failure had many separate causes, which intersected to drive the company to the edge of insolvency. This section reviews the arguments of the earlier chapters and tries to put the causes into some sort of ranking of importance.

Chapter 11 argued that the company's most important error was to pay back £471 million of cash to shareholders in the financial year 2000. If BE had retained that cash then its directors would probably have felt justified in drawing down its credit lines of up to £615 million, for a total of over £1 billion of financial resources. This is far more than the £650 million of government financing needed to keep it trading through to the re-flotation of the shares in 2005. But the return of value was a response to shareholder pressure and a high share price. It would have taken exceptional independence on the part of the board to have rejected that pressure completely.

Equivalently, the company could have avoided buying the Eggborough power station in late 1999 for £615 million (plus more for the coal stocks). There was some strategic merit in owning flexible generation but not at that price (Chapter 12). BE wrote off £300 million of the value two years later, though the damage to its finances was limited by the fact that the station had been re-financed through a project loan that technically wasn't owed by BE itself.

The company's exposure to the falling power price would have been reduced if it had achieved vertical integration through the purchase of a regional electricity company. The failure to merge with Southern Electric in 1997 on favourable terms seems inexcusable, not least for missing the chance to bring some first class management talent in. But Southern/BE would still have been heavily weighted towards generation profits. And it is likely that the combined company would still have succumbed to City pressure to gear up the balance sheet.

BE's asset base turned out to be riskier than at first appreciated. The ageing British AGR stations, after a run of near miraculous improvements, became unreliable just when the power market placed a premium on stability. But the deterioration in performance from 2000 probably owed something to under-investment in the previous few years. The continuing poor output record of the AGRs through to 2006 suggests that the medium term business plans of the period 1999–2002 were not credible in respect of their cost and output targets and the company would have had to dramatically increase investment at the expense of shareholder returns, even if it had avoided the financial crisis.

The company's financial position was made worse by the structurally high costs imposed by the BNFL reprocessing contracts. But given that BE was tied in to reprocessing by previous government decisions, the contracts were essen-tial to making privatisation feasible, by providing reassurance to investors over future cost escalation. But the contracts equally prevented cost cutting. BNFL's unwillingness to do a deal large enough to save BE in 2002 seems unreasonable and probably resulted from the curious status of BNFL as a purportedly com-mercial concern with monopoly power, owned by the state.

BE, having perhaps been lucky in the early years after privatisation because power prices stayed surprisingly high, was unlucky that its difficulties were pre-ceded by the Enron bankruptcy in 2001. That event alone made it impossible for BE to float a new bond in early 2002 that would have given it enough financial flexibility to survive into 2003 and perhaps until the growing North American profits were large enough to cover the UK losses. Enron also changed the whole context of corporate governance by emphasising the personal liability of non-executive directors. That might have tipped the balance of the BE board when they decided not to draw down bank credit lines in September 2002.

Lastly there is the ultimate external cause of the failure, the collapse in wholesale power prices. BE was never going to be able do much to change the path of prices. But it did too little to prepare for the risks. While its two main generation competitors were fast reducing their exposure to the power market, BE increased its own, buying a coal station at the top of the market instead of setting aside financial reserves. The combination of falling industry concentra-tion, growing new entry and a hostile regulator intent on driving down prices was fairly clear by 1999. BE's directors, having emphasised the company's unique sensitivity to lower power prices at the time of privatisation, seem to have become complacent just a few years later.

The final observation about BE's failure then brings us to the board itself. A consistent theme through many interviews with former directors and other senior managers is the fractious and antagonistic nature of board meetings from 1996 until 2001, when the growing crisis brought a belated unity under chairman Robin Jeffrey. Some of the conflict was rooted in the simmering hostility of the English-Scottish divisions arising from the shotgun wedding from which British Energy was created. That the board could be so "dysfunctional" is perplexing but it is not at all clear that the lack of harmony directly contributed to the company's failure, though it must have diverted effort and attention from more important matters.

The greater failure of the board seems to have been in its failure to recognise the company's true nature. The board was rich with talent but was under-weight in two kinds of experience. The first was nuclear engineering; for too much of the period covered by this narrative there was only one person with substantial nuclear experience on the board – Robin Jeffrey – and he was absent in North America. By the time Jeffrey brought in additional board level engineering experience in the form of David Gilchrist in 2001, it was too late. It is striking that the post-restructuring new British Energy Group has so much more senior nuclear expertise at board level. One former BE director even believed that the DTI, when setting up the original BE board, deliberately excluded former nuclear industry personnel because civil servants believed the industry's record was one of deceit and incompetence (private interview). If true, this would be ruefully ironic, that the privatised nuclear company was starved of expertise because of the admittedly manifold faults of the public sector nuclear industry.

The second deficit in board experience was that needed to recognise the enormous commercial risks the company faced. One reason that National Power and PowerGen started selling their power stations in 1999 was that both employed people from the oil industry, who had been seared by the collapse of oil prices in the mid-1980s. They knew that if the power price fell it might really plummet (private interviews). BE's board seem to have shared the views of their shareholders and of financial analysts, that it was essentially another utility. This was a gravely mistaken perception. Had the board realised they were presiding over a commodity manufacturing company they might have adopted a very different financial strategy. It was a minority view but it is worth noting that some analysts did point out the risks from an early stage: "Electricity prices should increasingly be seen as just another commodity price" (BZW Research, 1996b p. 7).

Some conclusions from the BE failure

Privatisation was right

Nothing in the analysis of this book suggests that it was wrong to privatise nuclear power in the UK. The combination of liberalised power markets with a purely nuclear company that retained full financial responsibility for its liabilities was unique to the UK. But BE was not doomed to fail and might well have survived if only it had retained greater financial flexibility. Nuclear power is run successfully in the private sector in many countries and there is no reason to believe the UK is different.

Ironically the period when nuclear was managed best in the UK *was* in the public sector, in the five years when Nuclear Electric and Scottish Nuclear provided the focus on efficiency that had been lacking in the days of the CEGB. Those companies' achievements in productivity suggest that private ownership is not necessary for good management. But the more general record of public enterprise in the UK suggests a presumption in favour of private ownership, so long as any public/private conflicts are dealt with appropriately (see below).

Nuclear power is compatible with liberalised power markets

Nuclear power stations have inherently high fixed costs and inflexible operations compared with fossil generators. When combined with a liberalised power market this means a wholly nuclear company faces a high level of financial risk. But that risk is not significantly different from the risk of a steel or chemical company, which have long since adapted to private ownership.

The UK policy of adding the further financial risk of the nuclear liabilities makes a nuclear generator even riskier, by increasing the sensitivity of profits to changes in prices. In the US, nuclear generation has thrived in competitive power markets, but without BE's fuel reprocessing burden. The German utilities that own nuclear stations and have similar obligations to BE have a much broader portfolio of power and other assets which reduces their exposure to power prices.

This suggests that the long term future of British Energy is as part of a larger and more geographically diversified company, if politics permit.

The UK approach to nuclear liabilities was flawed

The insistence that the liabilities follow the assets made for a good political sound bite. But the idea that a private company can be relied upon to provide for costs that fall due up to 80 years hence was always rather fanciful. The government insisted that BE set up a separate fund for decommissioning costs (although the fund, by being heavily invested in equities, had the same liability mismatch of most British pension funds in the late 1990s). It should have also required a similar fund to cover other nuclear liabilities. It would then have been obvious that the company faced large, debt-like obligations that should take precedence over payments to shareholders.

BE's unusually complex finances were not properly understood by shareholders and analysts. Seeing large cashflows, well in excess of accounting profit, the financial markets believed the company should pay out "surplus" cash. But much of that cash belonged in effect to the future liabilities. A separate fund would have made this clear and reduced the risk of excessive dividend payouts. Anybody looking at the long term path of future cashflows shown in Figure 11.4 must be struck by the obvious risk that the company runs out of cash long before the decades of liabilities fall due. Deliberately paying out excessive dividends is criminal but there is no suggestion whatever that this was the case. But there was always a risk of more human commercial misjudgement, combined with what economists call moral hazard.

So why did the Treasury not force BE to set aside more of its cashflows in the early years to ensure it met its liabilities? After all, the Treasury was the de facto guarantor of those liabilities. There are two plausible reasons. The first is dogma, the over-confident belief in the ability of private financial markets to price and deal with risk. Unfortunately those markets sometimes take time to learn how to price new sorts of risk. The market did indeed learn about nuclear risk in a competitive power market but only after it was too late.

The second, less forgivable reason must be that a separate fund for the non-decommissioning liabilities would have reduced the value of BE at privatisation. The short term interest of the taxpayer was in maximising the value of BE as a saleable assets. But this conflicted with the long term interest of taxpayers in ensuring that the liabilities were kept in the private sector.

British Energy's crisis tells us little about the case for new nuclear power

BE's story illustrates some of the challenges for nuclear power in the private sector, such as the high fixed costs and inflexibility of nuclear plant. But there is little to influence the case for or against new nuclear stations. The problem of fuel reprocessing is presumably no longer relevant but arrangements will still be needed to ensure that near term cashflows are appropriately set aside for longer term decommissioning and waste disposal. Other countries have dealt with these facts as they have with the private ownership of nuclear as part of a broader generation portfolio. British Energy tells us more about past nuclear policy than the future.

Aftermath of the crisis: the restructuring

The financial restructuring of British Energy after the September 2002 crisis is admirably covered by the National Audit Office (NAO) Report of March 1996 (National Audit Office, 2006). The NAO concludes that the government had two reasons for not simply letting the company slide into insolvency. First, there was a risk that the company would shut down power production at the risk of substantial power cuts. Second, there was a safety risk; nuclear power stations must be monitored and maintained, even if they are closed, to protect the public.

A third reason not mentioned in the NAO report but which was certainly on the minds of the civil servants involved was to minimise the financial cost to the government of taking back the nuclear liabilities that had been transferred at privatisation. Although it was inevitable that the government would have to take on part of these, the cost would be minimised if a restructured, viable British Energy could be organised (private interviews).

The key points of the restructuring were as follows. Having provided the critical funding to keep the company trading, the government assumed the position of senior creditor and led the restructuring process. The other creditors, which included banks, bond holders and those who had contracts to sell power to BE, were encouraged (though some would say forced) to take part in a deal whereby they swapped their claims on the company for equity. Existing shareholders saw their equity cut in value by 97.5 per cent. In effect, the company's equity was given to the creditors. Administration was always a possibility if the creditor deal failed (which it could if any creditor refused to sign up). But it was obvious that there was no likely buyer of BE as a going concern and the value of individual second-hand nuclear power stations was even more questionable. A financially restructured BE offered more potential value, while keeping the UK's lights on. The government took on the nuclear liabilities in exchange for a contingent cash payment (the "cash sweep") that varied according to the company's annual financial performance. The company's non-UK assets were sold. The government ended up with 65 per cent of the equity.

The new British Energy Group plc had its shares re-listed in January 2005. By this time wholesale power prices had risen dramatically because older coal power stations had been shut down and the price of gas had tripled on the back of the worldwide rise in oil prices. Most British electricity is now generated by gas so the price of gas forces up the price of power. Since nuclear costs are independent of hydrocarbon prices nuclear power becomes far more profitable when gas prices rise.

The NAO report summarises the financial outcome of the restructuring for the various groups involved (Table 17.1) as of February 2006. The dramatic rise in electricity prices since the financial collapse of 2002 meant that the taxpayer and creditors were substantially better off as a result of the restructuring. The creditors' claims summed to £834 million before BE asked for government help in September 2002. Having agreed to convert these claims to equity, the creditors found their new shares were worth a total of £1,871 million when the company re-listed on the stock market in January 2005. With a sharp rise in the shares since then the creditors' shares were worth £3.87 billion by February 2006. British Energy Group's share price was then £6.19.

The value to the taxpayer was even more striking. When the new BE shares were re-listed the taxpayer (through the Department of Trade and Industry) had incurred a net £233 million liability, since the estimated cash contribution from the company fell short of the new (£1,165 million higher) nuclear liabilities estimate derived from the Nuclear Decommissioning Authority. But by February of 2006 the company's hugely improved cashflows had made the taxpayer a net beneficiary, to the tune of £2.5 *billion*. The cash sweep is a form of equity interest in the company (but without voting rights) and the taxpayer, having been forced into this arrangement, has been amply compensated for the risk. In July

Table 17.1 Summary of financial impact of restructuring (£m)

	Before approach to government (3 September 2002)	*At re-listing of shares (17 January 2005)*	*NAO valuation (28 February 2006)*
Shareholders	307	66	107
Creditors	834	1,871	3,867
Taxpayer	–	(233)	2,466

Source: National Audit Office 2006, Table 3.

2006 the government announced its intention to sell part of the 65 per cent stake it acquired through the restructuring (*Financial Times*, 2006c).

Even the original shareholders have benefited from the rise in power prices. Their diluted shareholding was worth only £66 million at the time of the re-listing but had risen to £107 million by February 2006. This was still a long way below the £307 million value of the old shares before the crisis but much better than seemed likely when BE was on the brink of insolvency in December 2002.

These happy numbers need to be revised down sharply because by November 2006 the share price had fallen back to £4.70, because of cracks in the boilers of some AGRs and cooling pipe leaks at another. These reminders of the company's troubled engineering heritage led to a sharp reduction in expected output for the year and uncertainty over the future of the AGRs. Only one out of seven AGRs was operating normally in October 2006 (*Financial Times*, 2006a).

The outlook for nuclear power in the UK

The government's latest energy review, published in July 2006, focused on climate change and concluded that "new nuclear power stations would make a significant contribution to meeting our energy policy goals" (DTI, 2006 p. 17). But "it will be for the private sector to take decisions on proposing new power stations, based on commercial considerations" (DTI, 2006 p. 161) A consultation process on new nuclear build was launched after the review, ahead of a White Paper in 2007. An important part of new policy would be to streamline and accelerate the planning process to avoid repeated Sizewell B length inquiries.

There are at least three companies with the expertise and financial strength to build a nuclear station in the UK (EDF, RWE and E.ON), either separately or in consortium. All are non-British companies with major British electricity subsidiaries. Whether British Energy itself invests in new stations is unclear given the company's operating difficulties and its financial relationship with the British government. Its ownership of some of the most likely sites for new stations gives it a potential interest. British companies would probably have only a limited role in construction, since the expertise built up around the construction of Sizewell B in 1996 has now largely dissipated. The choice of design is probably limited to the French-German European Pressurised Reactor (EPR), currently under construction in Finland and France, and the Westinghouse AP1000 PWR, both forms of pressurised water reactor.

The result of 50 years of British nuclear policy is that the future of new nuclear power stations in the UK is largely a matter of non-British companies using non-British technology. The country with the most to gain from any nuclear renaissance is France, which started with a similar policy to that of the UK but abandoned its own reactor technology for the proven US PWR design. The French dominate the European nuclear industry and have the world's largest nuclear operator. This is not the same as concluding that British electricity policy more generally has been a failure but it is difficult not to conclude that the French government has played the better long game in nuclear power.

Conclusion

The long story of British nuclear power is a discouraging one, especially because it has no villains, only engineers, civil servants, politicians and financiers trying honestly to do the best they could. The focus of this book has been on the period when nuclear power was organised into specialised companies and the main job was to optimise the operations (1990–1996) and then value (1996–2002) of assets that were inherited from long before. The period of greatest success was in the public sector, when a combination of inspired leadership and motivated workers overcame years of difficulties with the AGR technology and briefly made it the world's most successful. The same team oversaw the successful completion of Britain's only PWR.

The privatised period has the air of tragedy about it, because the financial crisis that ruined reputations (including that of nuclear power itself for a while) and cost millions, need not have happened. The faults of the company's decision makers and of those analysing the company were mostly those of misunderstanding the nature of the beast. Both directors and analysts mistook a temperamental racehorse for a steady, reliable carthorse and placed too great a burden on its back. If there was one explanation for the company's collapse and the ignominious failure of privatisation it was the use of inappropriate concepts and tools for the job.

Timeline of key events 1945–2006

October 1945	Chiefs of Staff call for British atomic bomb
May 1947	Decision to build two reactors at Sellafield (re-named Windscale)
October 1950	First Windscale pile goes critical; second in June 1951
October 1952	Successful atomic bomb test at Monte Bello, Australia
January 1953	Churchill authorises construction of Calder Hall gas-cooled reactor
July 1954	Creation of the UK Atomic Energy Authority
February 1955	White Paper "A Programme of Nuclear Power" proposes 1,500–2,000 MW of nuclear plant
October 1956	Calder Hall first reactor opened by the Queen; Suez crisis
March 1957	Government increases nuclear programme to 5,000–6,000 MW
October 1957	Fire at Windscale pile no. 1 causes level 5 nuclear incident
December 1957	Creation of the Central Electricity Generating Board (CEGB)
June 1960	White Paper "The Nuclear Power Programme" slows pace of build
April 1964	White Paper "The Second Nuclear Programme" sees 5,000 MW more plant
May 1965	Government approves AGR for new Dungeness B station
October 1965	White Paper "Fuel Policy" proposes nuclear programme rises to 8,000 MW
July 1974	Government approves building of two SGHWRs; HTR is cancelled
August 1976	Energy Minister Benn announces SGHWR is being deferred
March 1977	President Carter stops fuel reprocessing in the US
June–September 1977	Windscale Inquiry under Justice Parker; recommends THORP go ahead

January 1978	SGHRW is cancelled; two new AGRs to be built; option for PWR to be kept open
July 1979	Last AGR is ordered for Heysham, Lancashire
December 1979	Energy Secretary David Howell announces ten new PWRs to be built
February 1982	Government scales back PWR programme
January 1983	Sizewell B inquiry begins; runs till March 1985; recommends go-ahead
March 1984	Miners strike first in Yorkshire and Scotland then nationally
March 1985	Miners return to work after CEGB manages to avoid power cuts
May 1987	Conservative election manifesto promises privatisation of electricity
February 1988	White Paper on electricity privatisation including nuclear power
July 1989	Magnox reactors withdrawn from privatisation
November 1989	AGRs and Sizewell B excluded from privatisation; further nuclear build halted
December 1989	Nuclear Electric and Scottish Nuclear created to own nuclear stations
February 1991	Electricity generators National Power and PowerGen privatised
February 1992	Robin Jeffrey appointed as chief executive of Scottish Nuclear
June 1992	Robert Hawley appointed as chief executive of Nuclear Electric
May 1994	Government nuclear review launched
March 1995	New reprocessing contracts signed between NE, SNL and BNFL
May 1995	Government decides to privatise a merged NE and SNL; John Robb made chairman of new holding company, later named British Energy
June 1996	British Energy prospectus published, warning of risk to dividend from lower power prices
July 1996	Announcement of closures at Hinckley Point B and Hunterston stations create controversy
July 1996	Shares privatised at £2.03; close down 5 per cent on first day of trading
November 1996	First interim results show large jump in operating profit; shares reach £2.33
June 1997	First full year results well received; Robert Hawley receives CBE; then resigns
August 1977	Board of BE rejects merger with Southern Electric

September 1997	BE announces new BNFL contracts worth £400 million; AmerGen joint venture with PECO Energy begins
November 1997	New chief executive, Peter Hollins, announced
June 1998	NE and SNL to be fully merged into single company
July 1998	AmerGen first investment: Three Mile Island unit 1
November 1998	BE makes bid for London Electricity but loses to EDF
January 1999	BE shares reach all time high of £7.33
May 1999	BE announces 56 per cent increase in profits and return of £432 million to shareholders
June 1999	BE buys SWALEC supply business for £107 million
November 1999	"Temporary" output shortfall leads to share price fall; BE buys Eggborough coal station for £615 million
December 1999	BE referred to Competition Commission after dispute with regulator
January 2000	Nuclear Installations Inspectorate halts cost cutting pending inquiry into safety
May 2000	BE announces 18 per cent profit fall; 50 per cent dividend cut; risk of loss next year; Standard & Poor's cuts credit rating to BBB+
July 2000	BE takes 17 year lease on 8 Ontario nuclear reactors
August 2000	BE sells SWALEC supply for £210 million
October 2000	John Robb announces intention to quit as chairman July 2001
December 2000	Management Today readers vote BE "least admired" company
March 2001	NETA (New Electricity Trading Arrangements) starts operation
May 2001	BE makes small profit; power prices down 16 per cent over previous year
June 2001	Peter Hollins resigns from company; Mike Kirwan announces to cease being finance director; government announces energy review
July 2001	Robin Jeffrey takes over as chairman and chief executive
November 2001	Interim results show output up again, profits growing in North America and cost cutting continuing; BE expects profit for full year 2001/2002
December 2001	Enron declares bankruptcy
January 2002	TXU mothballs British coal stations owing to low power prices; Jeffrey writes to Brian Wilson, Energy minister
February 2002	BE and BNFL pledge cooperation on new nuclear stations; government energy review recommends keeping nuclear option open but no support

February 2002	BE makes £300 million write down on Eggborough power station; £209 million write down on power contracts owing to lower power prices
March 2002	AES mothballs coal power station
May 2002	Full year results show balance sheet has 137 per cent gearing; dividend is maintained at previous year's level; one unit of Torness station shut down
June 2002	BE $400 million bond issue fails in US
July 2002	BE commissions Accenture power price forecast
August 2002	Wholesale power price reaches all-time low of £10.39/MWh; Dungeness B shut down; then Torness unit 2 closed; investor conference call, Jeffrey pledges "we do not face a financial crisis"
3 September	BNLF term sheet delivered to Jeffrey; falls far short of expectations
5 September	BE board decides cannot draw down credit lines and asks for government help; shares suspended
9 September	Government grants £410 million credit facility; shares resume trading and fall to 28p
26 September	Government increases credit facility to £650 million
27 November	European Commission approves temporary government financial support
December 2002	Shares fall to 5p
February 2003	BE agrees standstill with creditors; Bruce Power sold and proceeds used to repay £275 million of government credit
January 2005	High court in Scotland approves restructuring; shares re-listed
August 2006	Shares reach £7.60 on back of high electricity prices
October 2006	Shares fall to £4 following discovery of serious cracks and leaks in AGRs; only one AGR working normally
November 2006	Chief nuclear officer quits company following warning that reactor cracks will hit output for rest of financial year

Glossary

AES   International power company based in the US which invested in UK generation in the 1990s, including Drax power station.

AGR   Advanced Gas-cooled Reactor. Higher performance development of the Magnox reactor.

Base load   That part of electricity demand which is continuous over time and which is largely met by nuclear supply.

BEA   British Electricity Authority. Organisation set up to run the nationalised electricity industry in 1948. Replaced by CEA in 1957.

BNFL   British Nuclear Fuels Limited. Government owned holding company for various activities including THORP reprocessing plant.

Breeder reactor   A reactor which "breeds" its own fuel by converting otherwise useless material such as U-238 into plutonium.

BWR   Less common form of light water reactor, using water as coolant and moderator. Differs from PWR in that the steam driving the turbines is generated in the reactor core rather than by separate heat exchangers, meaning there is a single circuit rather than two.

CANDU   CANadian Deuterium Uranium reactor. Heavy water-moderated reactor developed in Canada that uses natural uranium fuel.

CCGT   Combined cycle gas turbine. Turbine that optimises thermal efficiency by using waste heat from the gas burning cycle to make steam that drives a second and possibly third turbine. Used in most modern gas-fired power stations. Capable of reaching thermal efficiency of up to 60 per cent.

CEA   Central Electricity Authority. Replaced BEA as organisation running the electricity industry from 1957 until the creation of the CEGB in 1957.

CEGB   Central Electricity Generating Board, owned and managed power stations and the national grid in England and Wales from 1957–1990.

Coolant   Material used to cool nuclear reaction and transfer heat for the generation of steam to turn a turbine. Water (both light and heavy) is most common coolant. The UK reactors mostly use gas. Sodium is also used in some experimental reactors.

DCF   Discounted cashflows, a technique for valuing financial assets.

Drax   Location of UK's largest coal power station, 4,000 MW, in Yorkshire. Owned by Drax Group plc.

Dividend yield   Dividend expressed as percentage of current share price.

Dividend cover   Ratio of net profit to dividends. Reciprocal of payout ratio.

Drystore   Form of storage of spent nuclear fuel in air.

DTI   Department of Trade and Industry.

EBITDA   Earnings before interest, tax, depreciation and amortisation. A measure of gross profit that adjusts for the main non-cash expenses. Typically compared with enterprise value as a valuation ratio.

EDF   Eléctricité de France; partially privatised electric utility that owns most of the French electricity industry plus several companies abroad, including in the UK.

Eggborough   Large 2,000 MW coal power station in Yorkshire, sold by National Power to British Energy in 2000.

Enrichment   Process of increasing the proportion of U-235 in uranium above its naturally occurring level of 0.7 per cent using gaseous diffusion or centrifuge.

Enterprise value   Value of a company's gross assets, equivalently the market value of its equity, debt and any other liabilities.

E.ON   Large international utility company based in Düsseldorf, Germany.

Fissile   Having capability of sustaining a chain reaction of nuclear fission. Examples are U-235 and plutonium.

Fission   Process whereby a neutron causes a uranium atom to split into other lighter atoms, releasing energy.

FPL   Florida Power and Light. Florida-based utility company.

Gearing   Ratio of debt to shareholder equity in a company's capital structure.

Half-life   Period over which radioactivity decays to half its original amount. A measure of the time over which material remains radioactive and potentially dangerous.

Heavy water   Water containing the heavier isotope of hydrogen, deuterium, which has a neutron, whereas ordinary hydrogen has none. Like ordinary ("light") water, heavy water is a good moderator. But heavy water absorbs far fewer neutrons and so allows the use of natural uranium, unlike light water which needs enriched uranium.

HTR   High temperature (gas) reactor. Prototype of advanced gas-cooled reactor developed by UKAEA with European support and cancelled in 1994.

IAEA   International Atomic Energy Authority.

INPO   Institute of Nuclear Power Operators. US industry body set up after Three Mile Island accident in 1979.

Interest cover   Ratio of earnings before interest and tax to net interest expense, a measure of a company's financial strength.

Isotopes   Forms of the same element differing only in the number of neutrons. Isotopes are chemically similar and can only be separated with difficulty, as in the enrichment of uranium to separate out the isotope of fissile U-235 from the non-fissile U-238.

kWh   One thousandth of a MWh. Amount of energy consumed by a domestic one bar electric fire over one hour.

Leverage   Ratio of debt to shareholder equity in a company's capital structure (US).

Light water   Ordinary water, as opposed to heavy water.

Load factor   Percentage capacity usage over a year, theoretically up to 100 per cent but good performance would be 80–90 per cent.

LWR   Light water reactor; reactor using ordinary water as coolant. There are two forms, the PWR and BWR.

Magnox   First generation British reactor type, named after the magnesium oxide fuel casing.

Man-Sievert   A unit of measure of the collective radiation does received by a given group of people.

Moderator   Material used to reduce the speed of electrons in order to increase the probability of fission. Water is most commonly used but UK reactors use graphite.

mSv   Measure of 1/1000th of a sievert. The average adult receives one to two millisieverts a year from natural sources which is referred to as background radiation.

MWh   Megawatt hour. Unit of energy calculated from power rating in Megawatts, multiplied by number of hours the power rate is sustained.

National Grid   High voltage transmission network in England and Wales, owned by the company National Grid plc.

National Power   Larger of the two privatised generation companies created out of the CEGB in 1989. Separated in 2000 into International Power and Innogy (now owned by German utility RWE).

NE   Nuclear Electric plc. Government owned company that owned nuclear power stations in England and Wales until the creation of British Energy and Magnox Electric in 1995.

NETA   New Electricity Trading Arrangements; system of bilateral trading and balancing market which replaced the Pool in 2001.

NNN   National Power Nuclear. Subsidiary of National Power plc created to hold the nuclear power stations ahead of privatisation. Became Nuclear Electric plc in 1989.

OFFER   Office of Electricity Regulation, set up to regulate the electricity industry until replaced by OFGEM.

OFGEM   Office of Gas and Electricity Markets, created in 1999 by combining OFFER and the gas regulator.

Payout ratio   Proportion of net profits that is paid out to shareholders in the form of dividends.

P/E ratio   Price to earnings ratio; the ratio of a company's share price to its earnings per share, a commonly used valuation measure.

PIP   Performance Improvement Programme. Management scheme to raise performance. British Energy Group implemented a major PIP in 2004.

Plutonium   Metallic radioactive element used in nuclear weapons and reactors, normally the isotope Pu-239 which has a half-life of about 24,000 years.

Pool Name of the electricity trading and pricing system used in UK from 1990 to 2001, when it was replaced by NETA.

PowerGen Smaller of the two privatised generation companies created out of the CEGB in 1989. Bought by German utility E.ON in 2001.

PWR Pressurised water reactor. The most common form of light water reactor, using ordinary water as coolant and moderator, in combination with slightly enriched uranium.

Reprocessing Chemical treatment of spent nuclear fuel to isolate re-useable fissile material such as U-235 and plutonium from the nuclear waste products.

Revalorisation Annual charge in the profit and loss account for the increase in value of the nuclear liabilities arising from price inflation and the unwinding of one year's discount factor.

RWE Large international utility company based in Essen, Germany.

Sellafield Site of BNFL reprocessing operation in Cumbria, northern England.

SGHWR Steam generating heavy water reactor. Prototype reactor developed by UKAEA but cancelled in 1978.

SNL Scottish Nuclear Limited. Government owned company that owned nuclear power stations in Scotland from 1989 until merger into British Energy in 1995.

SSEB South of Scotland Electricity Board. Public sector entity which owned the electricity industry in lowland Scotland, including Hunterston A and B nuclear stations. Privatised (without nuclear stations) as Scottish Power in 1991.

Take-or-pay Contract in which the customer is obliged to pay for a volume of commodity used, whether or not they actually consume it.

Terminal value Used in DCF valuation to estimate the future value of an asset or company beyond a period of explicit forecasts (typically ten years), using a perpetual growth formula.

Thermal efficiency Rate at which energy is converted from fuel (such as coal, gas or uranium) to electricity in power stations.

THORP Thermal Oxide Reprocessing Plant. Factory owned by BNFL at Sellafield, northern England, which reprocesses spent nuclear fuel.

TOP Target Outstanding Performance. Management programme set up by Scottish Nuclear Limited to boost productivity.

TWh Terawatt hour. One million MWh.

UKAEA UK Atomic Energy Authority, set up in 1954.

Uranium Naturally occurring metallic element that is radioactive. Mostly made of non-fissile U-238 isotope, with 0.7 per cent fissile isotope U-235.

WANO World Organisation of Nuclear Operators. Set up in wake of Chernobyl disaster to foster improved operations and safety in nuclear power.

Windscale Former name of the Sellafield BNFL site and location of air-cooled nuclear reactors used for first military supplies of plutonium in the 1950s.

Bibliography

ABN Amro Hoare Govett (1996) British Energy: A Short Introduction to the Business. 7 March.

Accountancy Age (2001) FRS 17 forces BOC share price fall. 17 December.

Accounting Standards Board (2006) Accounting standards [Electronic Version]. Retrieved 2006/12/02 from www.frc.org.uk/asb/technical/standards/accounting.cfm.

AES Corp. (2003) Annual report for 2003.

Arnold, L. (1992) *Windscale, 1957: Anatomy of a Nuclear Accident.* Dublin: Gill and Macmillan.

Bader, L. N. (2003) Treatment of pension plans in a corporate valuation. *Financial Analysts Journal*, 59 (3), 19–24.

Barker, R. (2001) *Determining Value: Valuation Models and Financial Statements.* Harlow: Pearson.

Benn, T. (1989) *Against the Tide: Diaries 1973–1977.* London: Hutchinson.

Benn, T. (1990) *Conflicts of Interest: Diaries 1977–1980.* London: Hutchinson.

BNFL (2006) Annual report and accounts 2006. www.britishnucleargroup.com/content.php?pageID=318

Bolter, H. (1996) *Inside Sellafield.* London: Quartet.

Brealey, R. A., Myers, S. C. and Allen, F. (2006) *Corporate Finance* (8th edn). New York: McGraw-Hill Irwin.

British Energy (1992) Chief Executive's Notebook. *Nuclear Times.* September.

British Energy (1993) Chief Executive's Notebook. *Nuclear Times.* December.

British Energy (1995) Press release. 11 December.

British Energy (1996) Interim results for 1996–1997. 21 November.

British Energy (1997a) Interim results for 1997–1998. 20 November.

British Energy (1997b) Press release. 16 June.

British Energy (1997c) Updated information on recently-signed contracts for fuel services. 5 September.

British Energy (1998a) Annual report for 1997–1998. June.

British Energy (1998b) Press release – British Energy integration. 23 June.

British Energy (1999a) The Art of Energy – Annual report and accounts 1998–1999. June.

British Energy (1999b) Interim results statement for 1999–2000. 10 November.

British Energy (1999c) Output statement. 29 November.

British Energy (1999d) Preliminary results for 1998–1999. 12 May.

British Energy (2000a) News statement – Government clearance of Eggborough acquisition. 17 January.

British Energy (2000b) Preliminary results for 1999–2000. 10 May.

British Energy (2000c) Press release. 25 May.

British Energy (2000d) Statement. 30 September.

British Energy (2001a) Chairman's statement at annual general meeting. 17 July.

British Energy (2001b) Interim results statement for 2001–2002. 10 November.

British Energy (2001c) Preliminary results for 2000–2001. 16 May.

British Energy (2001d) Replace nuclear with nuclear. September. www.strategy.gov.uk/downloads/work_areas/energy/submissions/BritishEnergy.pdf

British Energy (2002a) Annual report for the year 2001–2002. June.

British Energy (2002b) Press release. 24 July.

British Energy Group. (2004) Prospectus [Electronic Version]. Retrieved 2006/12/05 from http://www.british-energy.co.uk/pagetemplate.php?pid=226.

British Energy Group (2005) British Energy News, Dungeness B special supplement. Autumn.

British Energy Group (2006) Annual report for 2005–2006. June.

British Government (1955) *A Programme of Nuclear Power*. Cmnd 9389 London: HMSO.

British Government (1957a) *Accident at Windscale No. 2 Pile on 10 October 1957*. Cmnd 302 London: HMSO.

British Government (1957b) *Capital Investment in the Coal, Gas and Electricity Industries*. Cmnd 132 London: HMSO.

British Government (1960) *The Nuclear Power Programme*. Cmnd 1083 London: HMSO.

British Government (1964) *The Second Nuclear Programme*. Cmnd 2335 London: HMSO.

British Government (1965a) *Fuel Policy*. Cmnd 2798 London: HMSO.

British Government (1965b) *Fuel Policy*. Cmnd 2738 London: HMSO.

British Government (1967) *Fuel Policy* Cmnd 3438 London: HMSO.

Burn, D. (1978) *Nuclear Power and the Energy Crisis: Politics and the Atomic Industry*. London: Macmillan for the Trade Policy Research Centre.

BZW Research (1995) Introducing British Energy. October.

BZW Research (1996a) The cash generator. 5 March.

BZW Research (1996b) The price of power: a view of the generating market in England and Wales. 21 May.

BZW Research (1997) British Energy. July.

Cabinet Office (2002) *The Energy Review*. London: HMSO.

Caves, R. E. (1968) *Britain's Economic Prospects*. Washington, DC: The Brooking's Institution.

CEA (1957) Annual report 1956–1957.

CEGB (1965) An appraisal of the technical and economic aspects of Dungeness B nuclear power station. July.

Centrica (1998) Annual report and accounts 1997. March.

Chesshire, J. (1992) Why Nuclear Power Failed the Market Test in the UK. *Energy Policy*, 20 (8), 744–754.

Chew Jr., D. (ed.) (2001) *The New Corporate Finance: Where Theory Meets Practice* (3rd edn). New York: McGraw Hill.

Citrine, L. (1956) In Twenty Years' Time: Meeting the Growing Need for Electricity. *The Times*. 17 October.

Citrine, L. (1967) *Two Careers*. London: Hutchinson.

248   *Bibliography*

Competition Commission (2001) *AES and British Energy: A Report Made under Section 12 of the Electricity Act 1989* (No. CC 453).

Daily Mail (1996) Salomon sounds warning over British Energy float. 14 July.

Daily Mail (2000) Bid talk gives a powerful glow. 18 May.

Daily Telegraph (1994) City diary. 26 April.

Daily Telegraph (1995a) Major urged to agree £2 billion nuclear sale. 17 March.

Daily Telegraph (1995b) Nuclear digs in over break-up prospect. 31 March.

Daily Telegraph (1996) US group denies nuclear bid move. 22 February.

Department of Energy (1987) *Sizewell B Public Inquiry: Report by Sir Frank Layfield.* London: HMSO.

Department of Energy (2006) Global nuclear energy partnership. Retrieved 2006/12/06, from www.gnep.energy.gov/.

Department of Justice (1997) DoJ and FTC horizontal merger guidelines revised April 8 1997 [Electronic Version]. Retrieved 2006/12/06 from www.usdoj.gov/atr/public/guidelines/horiz_book/15.html.

Dow Jones International News (1998) British Energy jumps 8.1% on bullish trading statement. 9 March.

DTI (1993) *Prospects for Coal: Conclusions of the Government's Coal Review, March 1993.* Cmnd 2235 London: HMSO.

DTI (1995) Press release: John Robb appointed as chairman designate of nuclear holding company. May 17.

DTI (2006) *The Energy Challenge: Energy Review Report 2006.* Cm 6887.

DTI with the Scottish Office (1995) *The Prospects for Nuclear Power in the United Kingdom: Conclusions of the Government's Nuclear Review May 1995.* Cmnd 2860 HMSO.

Easterbrook, F. H. (1984) Two agency–cost explanations of dividends. *American Economic Review*, 74, 650–659.

EDF (2006) Annual report for 2005. www.edf.fr/html/ra_2005/uk/index.html.

Energy Information Administration (1986) *An Analysis of Nuclear Power Plant Construction Costs* (No. DOE/EIA-0485): Department of Energy, Washington D.C.

Evans, J. E. and Green, R. J. (2005) *Why Did British Electricity Prices Fall After 1998?* Working Paper 05–13. University of Birmingham Department of Economics.

Ferguson, N. (2001) *The Cash Nexus: Money and Power in the Modern World 1700–2000.* London: Penguin.

Financial Services Authority (2003) Press release FSA/PN/114/2003. Letter to British Energy 29 October. www.fsa.gov.uk/Pages/Library/Communication/PR/2003/114.shtml.

Financial Times (1992) Nuclear evangelist in the hottest seat. 28 July.

Financial Times (1993a) Energy minister attacks Nuclear Electric. 26 November.

Financial Times (1993b) Minister eases threat to more than 3,000 Nuclear Electric jobs. 10 February.

Financial Times (1993c) Sizewell C go-ahead sought amid safety fears. 14 October.

Financial Times (1993d) Sparks fly over nuclear costs. 1 November.

Financial Times (1994a) Littlechild favours sell-off of nuclear power industry 10 July.

Financial Times (1994b) N-plant risks "can be priced". 4 October.

Financial Times (1994c) Nuclear Electric outline £1 billion subsidy plan. 28 June.

Financial Times (1994d) Nuclear Electric sale hope recedes. 30 November.

Financial Times (1994e) Treasury urges prompt sale of nuclear power industry. 12 March.

Financial Times (1994f) Fund urged for closing reactors. 3 May.

Financial Times (1995a) Construction of N-plants axed. 12 December.

Financial Times (1995b) Robb takes the nuclear hot seat. 29 May.

Financial Times (1996a) British Energy plots a cautious way forward. 17 June.

Financial Times (1996b) Lex. 10 October.

Financial Times (1996c) Management – Marketing and Advertising – Final burst of privatisation. 30 May.

Financial Times (1996d) Minister throws nuclear sell-off into confusion. 22 January.

Financial Times (1996e) Row over nuclear closure costs threatens £2.6 billion sell-off. 20 January.

Financial Times (1997a) Comment on British Energy results. 5 June.

Financial Times (1997b) Fast breeder among a pool of utilities. 16 September.

Financial Times (1997c) Lex. 17 June.

Financial Times (1999a) British Energy plans to return £432 million of cash. 13 May.

Financial Times (1999b) British Energy readies itself for spending spree. 11 November.

Financial Times (1999c) US groups dig deep to win the right to get switched on. 27 April.

Financial Times (2000a) British Energy sells SWALEC after one year.

Financial Times (2000b) British Energy sinks on profit warning. 11 May.

Financial Times (2000c) British Energy to take lease on Canadian site – Nuclear power complex to cost more than £1 billion. 12 July.

Financial Times (2000d) Lex. 12 July.

Financial Times (2001a) BNFL sell-off unlikely in this parliament; Nuclear industry chairman admits company would struggle to attract investors as it announces heavy losses. 21 June.

Financial Times (2001b) Hollins quits British Energy. 8 June.

Financial Times (2001c) Nuclear power back on agenda: Environmentalists fear energy review will lead to revival. 26 June.

Financial Times (2002a) Energy price cuts start to bite: Overcapacity and the "Enron effect" mean mothballing has begun. 15 March.

Financial Times (2002b) Excerpts from British Energy's analysts' conference [Electronic Version]. Retrieved 2006/12/06 from FT.com.

Financial Times (2006a) Fall-out from past hits British Energy. 23 October.

Financial Times (2006b) Gordon Horsfield, Drax chairman, sells £12 million-worth of shares. 19 June.

Financial Times (2006c) UK government to cut stake in British Energy.

Ford Foundation (1977) *Nuclear Power Issues and Choices*. Cambridge, Mass.: Ballinger.

Gielecki, M. and Hewlett, J. (1994) Commercial Nuclear Electric Power in the United States: Problems and Prospects [Electronic Version]. *Energy Information Administration/Monthly Energy Review* Retrieved 2006/12/06 from tonto.eia.doe.gov/FTPROOT/features/hewlett1.pdf.

Gowing, M. (1974a) *Independence and Deterrence: Britain and Atomic Energy, 1945–1952. Vol.1, Policy making*. London: Macmillan.

Gowing, M. (1974b) *Independence and Deterrence: Britain and Atomic Energy, 1945–1952. Vol.2, Policy execution*. London: Macmillan.

Green, R. J. (1999) Draining the Pool: The Reform of Electricity Trading in England and Wales. *Energy Policy*, 27 (9), 515–525.

Guardian (1995) Scottish Nuclear chief forced out in management shake-up. 20 July.

Guardian (1999) News in brief. 14 April.

Hannah, L. (1982) *Engineers, Managers and Politicians: The First Fifteen Years of Nationalised Electricity Supply in Britain*. London: Macmillan.

Health and Safety Executive. (2000) An audit by the HSE on British Energy Generation Limited and British Energy Generation (UK) Limited 1999.

Helm, D. (2003) *Energy, the State, and the Market: British Energy Policy since 1979.* Oxford: Oxford University Press.

Henderson, P. D. (1977) Two British Errors: Their Probable Size and Some Possible Lessons. *Oxford Economic Papers*, 29 (2), 159–205.

Hennessy, P. (2002) *The Secret State: Whitehall and the Cold War*. London: Allen Lane.

Henney, A. (1994) *A Study of the Privatisation of the Electricity Supply Industry in England and Wales*. London: Energy Economic Engineering.

Herald (1995) Political panic that led to nuclear sell-off. 28 April.

Hewitt, G. F. and Collier, J. G. (2000) *Introduction to Nuclear Power* (2nd edn). London: Taylor and Francis.

Hinton, C. (1961) Nuclear Power. *Three Banks Review* (December 1961), 3–18.

Horne, A. (1989) *Macmillan: The Official Biography. Vol. 2*. London: Macmillan.

House of Commons (1963) *Select Committee on Nationalised Industries Report. The Electricity Supply Industry. Vol. 1, Report and Proceedings.* HC236–1 London: HMSO.

House of Commons (1965) *Select Committee on Science and Technology – United Kingdom Nuclear Reactor Programme Evidence*. London: HMSO.

House of Commons (1973) *Select Committee on Science and Technology "Nuclear Power Policy". Second report 1972–1973*. HC350. London: HMSO.

House of Commons (1981) *Select Committee on Energy "The Government's Statement on the New Nuclear Power Programme". Session 1980–1981, vol.1: Report and Minutes of Proceedings.* HC Paper 114–1. London: HMSO.

House of Commons (1992) *Trade and Industry Committee, Minutes of Evidence, 24 November 1992*. HC 237-ix. London: HMSO.

House of Commons (1993) *Trade and Industry Select Committee, "British Energy Policy and the Market for Coal" 26 January 1993*. London: HMSO.

House of Commons (1995) *Trade and Industry Committee Nuclear Privatisation Minutes of Evidence 1994–1995 22/10/1995*. 795-I. London: HMSO.

House of Commons (1996) *Trade and Industry Committee 2nd Report on Nuclear Privatisation February 1996*. HC43–1 London: HMSO.

HSBC James Capel (1996) British Energy. 24 May.

HSBC James Capel (1997) British Energy. 5 June.

IAEA (2004) Country nuclear power profiles: France [Electronic Version]. Retrieved 2006/11/20 from www.pub.iaea.org/MTCD/publications/PDF/cnpp2004/CNPP_Webpage/countryprofiles/France/France2004.htm.

IAEA (2006) Power reactor information system [Electronic Version]. Retrieved 2006/11/20 from www.iaea.org/programmes/a2/index.html.

Independent (1995a) Aiming to win a nuclear bet. 1 May.

Independent (1995b) Obituaries. 23 November.

Independent (1996a) Energy share proceeds fall far short. 12 July.

Independent (1996b) Red faces as Sids lose out in British Energy float flop. 16 July.

Independent (2000) British Energy asks for £2.6 billion discount on BNFL contracts. 11 May.

Independent (2002) British Energy gets £500 million rescue. 9 September.

Independent on Sunday (2002) Ministers in secret plan to bail out nuclear giant. 25 August.

Jensen, M. and Meckling, W. H. (1976) Theory of the Firm: Managerial Behavior, Agency Costs, and Ownership Structure. *Journal of Financial Economics*, 3, 305–360.

Jensen, M. C. (1986) Agency Costs of Free Cash Flow, Corporate Finance, and Takeovers. *American Economic Review*, 76, 323–329.

Lawson, N. (1992) *The View from No. 11: Memoirs of a Tory Radical*. London: Bantam Press.

Ledger, F. and Sallis, H. (1995) *Crisis Management in the Power Industry*. London: Routledge.

Lloyd, G. (1955) Speech to press conference. 15 February 1955.

Marshall, L. (1989) Speech to the British Nuclear Energy Society. 30 November.

McKerron, G. (1984) Is Sizewell a Good Investment? *Public Money*, December, 15–19.

MMC (1981) *CEGB: A Report on the Operation by the Board of its System for the Generation and Supply of Electricity in Bulk*. HC 315. Monopolies and Mergers Commission. London: HMSO.

MMC (1996) *National Power plc and Southern Electric plc: A Report on the Proposed Merger*. Cm 3230. Monopolies and Mergers Commission. London: HMSO.

Morgan Stanley Dean Witter (1997) British Energy: Rewards outweigh risks. 27 August.

National Audit Office (2006) The restructuring of British Energy [Electronic Version]. Retrieved 2006/03/17 from www.nao.org.uk/publications/nao_reports/05–06/0506943. pdf.

National Grid (2003) Seven year statement March 2003 [Electronic Version]. Retrieved March 2003 from www.nationalgrid.com/uk/Electricity/SYS/archive/.

Newbery, D. M. (1998) The Regulator's Review of the English Electricity Pool. *Utilities Policy*, 7 (3), 129–142.

Newbery, D. M. (2005) Electricity Liberalisation in Britain: The Quest for a Satisfactory Wholesale Market Design. *Energy Journal* (Special Issue on European Electricity Liberalisation), 43–70.

Nuclear Electric (1989) Annual report 1988–1989.

Nuclear Electric (1991) Annual report 1990–1991.

Nuclear Electric (1992) Press release – Nuclear chief backs partnership with coal. 19 October.

Nuclear Electric (1993a) Chief Executive's notebook October 1993. *Nuclear Times*. January.

Nuclear Electric (1993b) Interim results presentation, 1993–1994. 2 December.

Nuclear Electric (1993c) Press release. 27 July.

Nuclear Electric (1994a) Annual report 1993–1994.

Nuclear Electric (1994b) Chief Executive's notebook. *Nuclear Times*. February.

Nuclear Electric (1994c) City update No. 8. February 1994.

Nuclear Electric (1994d) Submission to Nuclear Review. 20 June.

Nuclear Electric (1995a) Annual report 1994–1995.

Nuclear Electric (1995b) Chief Executive's notebook. *Nuclear Times*. March.

Nuttall, W. J. (2005) *Nuclear Renaissance – Technologies and Policies for the Future of Nuclear Power*. London: Institute of Physics.

Observer (1996) Sizewell B leak adds fuel to sell-off crisis. 14 July.

OFGEM (2002) The review of the first year of NETA – A review document. Volume 1 [Electronic Version]. Retrieved 2006/12/06 from www.ofgem.gov.uk/temp/ofgem/ cache/cmsattach/1984_48neta_year_review.pdf.

OFGEM (2004) Domestic competitive market review 2004 [Electronic Version]. Retrieved 2006/12/06 from www.ofgem.gov.uk/temp/ofgem/cache/cmsattach/6740_ DCMR_publication_Ch_4_to_7__2_.pdf?wtfrom=/ofgem/whats-new/archive.jsp.

Parker, M. (2000) *Thatcherism and the Fall of Coal*. Oxford: Oxford University Press.

Parkinson, C. (1992) *Right at the Centre: An Autobiography*. London: Weidenfeld and Nicolson.

Patterson, W. C. (1985) *Going Critical*. London: Paladin.

Pipeline and Gas Journal (1996) Enron challenges North Sea Gas agreement. 223 (5).

Plowden, E. (1956) The second industrial revolution – nuclear power the basis. *The Times*. 17 October.

Plowden, E. (1976) *Report of a Committee of Inquiry*. Cmnd 6388. London: HMSO.

Pocock, R. F. (1977) *Nuclear Power: Its Development in the United Kingdom*. Old Woking: Unwin Brothers.

Powell, D. (1993) *The Power Game: The Struggle for Coal*. London: Duckworth.

Price, T. (1990) *Political Electricity: What Future for Nuclear Energy?* Oxford: Oxford University Press.

Pryke, R. (1981) *The Nationalised Industries: Policies and Performance since 1968*. Oxford: Robertson.

Reuters (1995) UK to privatise nuclear power generators together. 5 September.

Reuters (1996) Interview – Debut disappoints British Energy. 15 July.

Reuters (1997) British Energy jumps after Offer proposal. 21 August.

Reuters (1999) British Energy to go non-nuclear in the U.S. 27 July.

Reuters (2000) Merrill ups British Energy rating. 5 June.

Reuters (2002a) British Energy drained by low prices – minister. 28 August.

Reuters (2002b) Research alert – Deutsche Bank ups British Energy to "buy". 29 August.

Scotsman, The (1995a) Business view – Bold experiment in nuclear fusion behind a brass plate in Edinburgh. 14 June.

Scotsman, The (1995b) Spirit of Scotland damaged by Hann's farewell to East Kilbride. 20 July.

Scotsman, The (1997) Business view – Hawley caught in crossfire two years after shotgun wedding. 17 June.

Scottish and Southern Energy (2006) Annual report and accounts for 2005–2006.

Scottish Nuclear Limited (1991) Annual report 1990–191991.

Scottish Nuclear Limited (1993) Annual report 1992–1993.

Scottish Nuclear Limited (1995a) Annual report 1994–1995.

Scottish Nuclear Limited (1995b) Press release. 19 July.

Scottish Nuclear Limited (1995c) Press release – What's in a name? 9 April.

Scottish Office (1995) News release. 9 May.

Simpson, J. (1986) *The Independent Nuclear State: The United States, Britain and the Military Atom* (2nd edn). London: Macmillan.

Soter, D., Brigham, E. and Evanson, P. (2001) The Dividend Cut "Heard Round the World": The Case of FPL, in Chew Jr., D. (ed.) (2001) *The New Corporate Finance: Where Theory Meets Practice* (3rd edn) New York: McGraw Hill.

Standard & Poor's. (1999) Press release. 19 November.

Sunday Times (1996) Pressure grows on nuclear chief. 25 February.

Sunday Times (1998) British Energy plots Yorkshire bid. 27 September.

Sunday Times (2002) Ministers plan rescue for ailing nuclear firm. 25 August.

Surrey, J. (1999) Stranded gas contracts: The British experience. *Energy and Environment*, 10 (1), 79–85.

The Times (1956a) Faith and decision. 17 October.

The Times (1956b) The Queen opens the first nuclear power plant. 18 October.

The Times (1965) Economic gas-cooled reactor for Dungeness. 30 July.

The Times (1967) Electricity chief defends AGR on cost basis. 2 June.

The Times (1971) Fresh snags likely to push Dungeness B costs still higher. 11 March.

The Times (1972) Dungeness B power plant encounters fresh difficulties. 4 April.

The Times (1978a) The man in the seat of power. 19 June.

The Times (1978b) New nuclear power stations to use advanced gas cooled reactors. 26 January.

The Times (1978c) Saga of delays at nuclear power station. 26 May.

The Times (1989) Thatcher calls for global green crusade. 9 November.

The Times (1992) BP to shed 350 jobs in Scotland. 6 June.

The Times (1994a) Actors and reactors in the power game. 22 October.

The Times (1994b) AEA commercial arm to be sold off. 18 February.

The Times (1994c) Nuclear sell-off ruled out before the next election. 20 May.

The Times (1995a) Cabinet approves two-in-one sale of nuclear power. 5 May.

The Times (1995b) Ministers in power struggle over nuclear privatisation. 1 April.

The Times (1995c) Obituaries – John Collier. 21 November.

The Times (1996a) British Energy dividend warning. 11 June.

The Times (1996b) British Energy to shed 1,460 jobs. 10 October.

The Times (1996c) BZW acts to stem Energy shares slump. 16 July.

The Times (2000a) Bid hopes give a boost to Salvesen – stock market. 29 September.

The Times (2000b) Corporate Britain chooses its favourites. 1 December.

The Times (2002) Regulator rejects power price complaints. 27 August.

The Times (2004) Sir James Hann. 20 February.

Varley, J. (2004) Good is not good enough [Electronic Version]. *Nuclear Engineering International*. Retrieved 2004/09/01 from www.neimagazine.com/storyprint. asp?sc=2024453).

Walker, P. (1991) *Staying Power*. London: Bloomsbury.

Walker, W. and Lönnroth, M. (1983) *Nuclear Power Struggles: Industrial Competition and Proliferation Control*. London: George Allen and Unwin.

Waltham, C. (2002) An early history of heavy water [Electronic Version]. Retrieved 2006/12/02 from www.cns-snc.ca/branches/manitoba/history.html.

Williams, R. (1980) *The Nuclear Power Decisions: British Policies, 1953–1978*. London: Croom Helm.

World Nuclear Association (2005) Nuclear power in Germany [Electronic Version]. Retrieved 2006/12/02 from www.world-nuclear.org/info/inf43.htm.

World Nuclear Association (2006a) Nuclear power in Japan [Electronic Version]. Retrieved 2006/12/02 from www.world-nuclear.org/info/inf79.htm.

World Nuclear Association (2006b) US nuclear power industry [Electronic Version]. Retrieved 2006/12/02 from www.world-nuclear.org/info/printable_information_papers/ inf41print.htm#table2).

World Oil (1997) J-Block settlement is reached. 218 (7), 9.

Index